WinterCLIMBING+

The positive approach to improve your climbing

Neil Gresham
Ian Parnell

CW00740694

Uncredited photos by Ian Parnell
Other photos as credited
Illustrations by Ray Eckermann
Printed by John Browns Printers
Distributed by Cordee (**www.cordee.co.uk**)

Published by ROCKFAX Ltd. January 2009
© ROCKFAX Ltd. 2009

ISBN   978 1 873341 96 4
www.rockfax.com

Cover: Sue Knott climbing a WI6 pillar in the Route 41 Area of Pont Rouge, Quebec, Canada.

This page: Climbers high on the classic Tower Ridge IV Ben Nevis, Scotland.

Gareth Lewis on the *North East Face of Pen y Fan* in the Brecon Beacons of South Wales. The mountain on the right is Cribin on which there are also some easier grade routes (around II to III).
Photo by Mark Salter.

Starting Out

Equipment

Mountain Safety

Ice : Style-Ethics

Ice : Techniques

Mixed : Style-Ethics

Mixed : Techniques

The Mind

Training

Destinations

About this book

This book is for any climber who fancies trying their hand at the awe-inspiring activity of winter climbing. Whether you are a rock climber who has considered transferring your skills to the frozen stuff, or an experienced winter hillwalker who has toyed with the idea of tackling something a little steeper, Winter Climbing+ is bursting with tips and ideas to help you steer a straight course on your journey.

Winter climbing and mountaineering

The novice may ask how winter climbing differs from mountaineering and the answer to this should be kept simple. With mountaineering, the objective is usually to reach the summit, whereas the winter climber is often more interested in the chosen route and its associated technicalities. Of course there is plenty of overlap between the two and it is sometimes hard to tell them apart. Most winter climbers who have the mountains in their blood may chose to bag a nearby summit after a climb, if time and weather permit. Similarly, mountaineers often need to rely on winter climbing skills if their chosen route turns out to be a little more than a mere 'snow plod'. There is a broad church here so let's not get too bogged down.

Winter climbing styles

Within winter climbing itself there are also sub-categories that have developed as the activity has diversified. From waterfall ice, to snow-ice, to sport mixed and trad mixed, it is quite possible that one 'winter climber' may be playing a completely different game to the next.

There are some who gravitate towards the safe but technically demanding challenges at accessible crags, and others who prefer the seriousness and commitment of a remote mountain setting, and of course, there are many who simply can't get enough of the full spectrum. Whatever your taste, it is surely the thrill of pushing your limits in such a raw and potentially severe environment that explains the lure.

Why winter climb?

The beauty of winter climbing lies in the fact that even the most experienced climbers can't always predict exactly how things are going to turn out. Some days, when you thought you heading for a pleasant excursion, you may inadvertently be signing up for a major ordeal. Any winter climbing experience will involve a certain amount of pushing yourself when you are scared, cold, tired and thirsty. The nice thing is that you will never know exactly how much until you get home! The secret for success is to turn the negative into a positive. Within difficulties there are hidden possibilities. Within suffering lies potential for learning and ultimate satisfaction of the experience . Your aim should always be to get yourself up and off the hill with the least amount of fuss, using every trick in this book. But you must also accept that a battle may break out from time to time and be prepared to see it through. The stakes are high with winter climbing - massive amounts of effort are required but the rewards are always in proportion.

What is Winter Climbing+ all about?

An enormous variety of skills must be embraced in order to become a competent winter climber. Your entire winter climbing performance can be regarded as a system whose weak links inhibit progress far more than the strong links assist. More seriously, the weak links or gaps in your knowledge are far more likely to put you in danger. There will be new skills to master according to your level and your chosen style of climbing. Whether you are attempting to climb your first snow gully, or redpoint your first M10, this book will cover the all the relevant ground to help you become a better and safer climber.

What the '+' stands for

There has been a tendency for some 'How To' texts on this subject to focus so much on safety skills that they can send out a subconscious message that makes the reader overly fearful. While we recommend that you absorb every safety skill in this book, we also acknowledge that you will need to take risks in a controlled and strategic way in order to achieve some of your goals. Of course it is important to know when and how to back-off, but it is also essential to have the relevant climbing skills to be able to go for it when the moment is right. This book will arm you, not just with the tips for staying out of trouble, but with the positive skills to lead you safely to the top, such as technique, strategy and mental preparation. Every journey into the mountains has the potential to be exciting and memorable and we hope this book will make a difference to your enjoyment as well as your performance.

About the authors

Neil Gresham

Neil Gresham started climbing on the sandstone outcrops of Kent. He battled his way through a trad climbing apprenticeship in South West England. He then moved to Sheffield where he got into sport climbing while attempting to study. Neil discovered winter climbing in Scotland in the early 1990s with a group of seriously misguided sport climbers and reckons he was lucky to survive. Though well known for his rock-climbing achievements, Neil has also climbed WI 7 on ice, flashed M9 and made rapid ascents of M10s. Neil has also competed for Britain in the Ice World Cup in 2000 and 2001. These days he is perhaps best known for his training articles and masterclasses.

www.climbingmasterclass.com

Ian Parnell

Ian Parnell is a professional photographer who admits to an addiction to winter climbing. Whether it is putting up new routes at his favourite haunts in Scotland, or heading in mid summer to the chalk cliffs of South England, Ian is happiest when swinging ice axes. Ian enjoys all aspects of the winter game having climbed up to Scottish IX, WI7 and M9 as well as numerous new routes in the Himalaya. His favourite part of winter climbing is travelling to new areas and the 'warm rush' when the circulation returns to pumped arms after a challenging lead.

www.ianparnell.com

Starting Out Equipment Mountain Safety Ice : Style-Ethics Ice : Techniques Mixed : Style-Ethics Mixed : Techniques The Mind Training Destinations

Starting Out

Equipment

Mountain Safety

Ice · Style · Ethics

Ice · Techniques

Mixed · Style · Ethics

Mixed · Techniques

The Mind

Training

Destinations

End of another day on the summit plateau of Ben Nevis, Scotland.

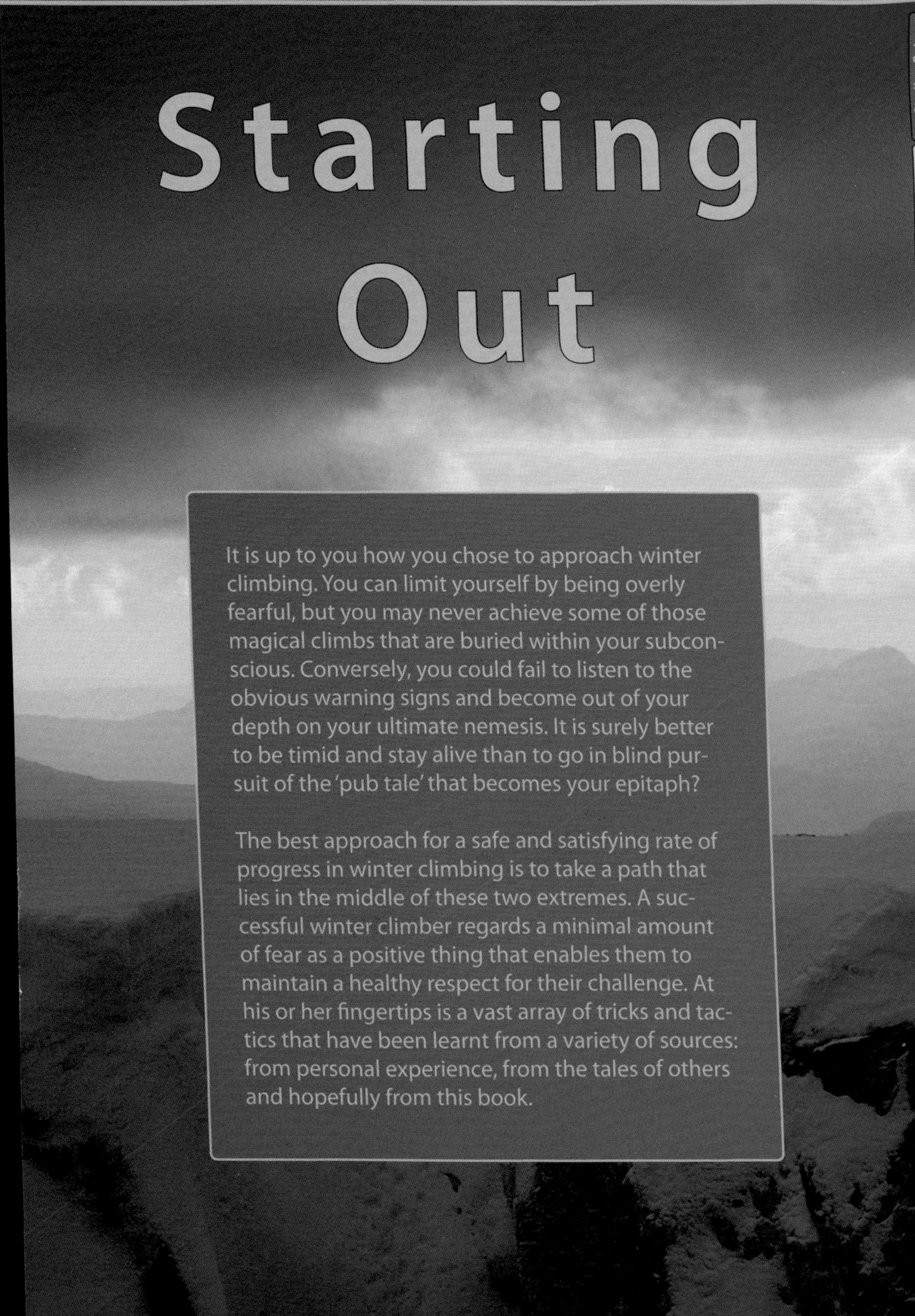

Starting Out

It is up to you how you chose to approach winter climbing. You can limit yourself by being overly fearful, but you may never achieve some of those magical climbs that are buried within your subconscious. Conversely, you could fail to listen to the obvious warning signs and become out of your depth on your ultimate nemesis. It is surely better to be timid and stay alive than to go in blind pursuit of the 'pub tale' that becomes your epitaph?

The best approach for a safe and satisfying rate of progress in winter climbing is to take a path that lies in the middle of these two extremes. A successful winter climber regards a minimal amount of fear as a positive thing that enables them to maintain a healthy respect for their challenge. At his or her fingertips is a vast array of tricks and tactics that have been learnt from a variety of sources: from personal experience, from the tales of others and hopefully from this book.

Starting Out

Equipment

Mountain Safety

Ice : Style-Ethics

Ice : Techniques

Mixed : Style-Ethics

Mixed : Techniques

The Mind

Training

Destinations

Early days

Unless you are a true deviant, it is likely that the most enjoyable part of your first winter climbing experience will be getting back to the car in one piece! The feelings of exhilaration are usually well and truly tempered by fear, the rushing pain of 'hotaches' and the sheer effort of your first 'big day out on the hill'.

Your first few experiences on ice will determine whether or not you will get hooked and come back for more punishment, and in this sense, your fate will rest in the hands of others. Many are put-off for life by over-zealous mentors and it is well worth establishing the motives of your first winter climbing partner. People who come disguised as keen tutors are often simply keen to get a belay on something hard and deliver a baptism of fire. Even if you do find the perfect mentor, who takes you to the

ideal beginner's route, it is still likely that you will experience an epic or two when you are first let off the leash, especially if you climb in Scotland!

The advice is to remember that ice climbs are deceptive. A grade II can be grade V if it is out of condition. Even if you have good mountain skills, you should also never forget that the approach and descent are invariably the most dangerous parts of the climb. Every ice climber has their share of epic tales and an uncanny number of these are associated with their apprenticeship. Most will describe a love-hate relationship with winter climbing during the early days. The effect of experience combined with reading this book will be to straighten out the roller-coaster ride. And the more you get into it, the more you realise that it is actually impossible to enjoy ice climbing while actually climbing!

Joe Williams on *Cascade Falls*, WI3, Canada.

Getting into winter climbing from rock climbing

Winter climbing shares many similarities with rock climbing in terms of the basic movement patterns and rope-work procedures, and yet is has some fundamental differences.

With axes and crampons as mechanical extensions to hands and feet, the first thing that hits you is the loss of touch which often creates a sensation of insecurity. In rock climbing you can 'feel' when a hand or foot is slipping, but with winter climbing the only time you will know that a pick or crampon point is unstable is when it rips.

Next is the loss of dexterity when it comes to performing the simplest of operations, such as placing protection. Even if you have perfected your glove systems, things will always feel slightly clumsier. Similarly, you will always feel 'trussed up', even if you opt for the least restrictive clothing. You must accept that you're never going to be as free to move as you are when rock climbing.

Next is the issue of risk. Mixed climbing, whether it is protected by bolts or trad gear, is generally comparable to rock climbing, except that you have the additional risk of colliding with picks or crampon points during a tumble.

Ice, however lends itself to a slightly bolder approach. People rarely fall when leading on water ice. The quality of ice screw protection varies dramatically from totally 'bomber' in solid blue water ice, to totally useless in snow ice or chandelier ice. When you consider the very high chance of catching a crampon and twisting or breaking an ankle and somersaulting, it's best not to test your protection out.

Add to this, the possibility that on fragile columns, you may bring the whole thing down with you if you attempt to place, or worse still, fall onto a screw, this tends to paint a picture that ice climbing is about being steady and competent and climbing well within your grade. Heroics are for the guys in lycra with the competition tools.

Remember that one of the biggest mistakes is to convince yourself that your rock climbing experience gives you a fast-track ticket to harder ice grades. Some of the worst ice climbing epics have been encountered by cavalier rock climbers who have become grotesquely out of their depth. You may have the fitness to climb grade VI, but if your skill level equates to grade II, then it is grade II that you should attempt to climb.

Short single pitch venues such as Krokan at Rjukan in Norway are good starting places where top-roping can help develop a feel for climbing on ice.

Winter climbing styles

Throughout this book we use specific terms to describe particular styles of winter climbing. Most winter climbers will opt to dabble in all aspects of winter climbing, but there are those who choose to specialise in these sub genres.

Ice

Ice climbs are the 'classic' interpretation of winter climbing. Most pure ice routes will involve every move and each crampon and axe placement on ice. The thinnest and hardest climbs can force you to make use of rock features either side of the ice flow, although this style of climbing is heading towards mixed. Typically ice forms when watercourses such as steep riverbeds to free-dropping waterfalls freeze during the winter months. Ice can also build up on slabby rock walls as snow alternately melts and re-freezes, this snow-ice is common in Scottish climbing areas such as Ben Nevis.

Striding Edge on Helvellyn. Photo Mick Ryan.

Mixed

Mixed climbs refer to any winter routes that aren't climbed 100% on ice. Some mixed routes require moves combining placements on both rock and ice whilst on others the two techniques are rarely truly mixed; such as a rock wall leading to hanging icicle. In the UK, and areas such as Poland, frozen turf is seen as another important possibility for axe placements.

Within the broad umbrella of mixed climbing there are several further demarcations.

Trad mixed

This refers to mixed climbs which are protected by removable protection such as nuts and cams, perhaps with the occasional peg runner. Most trad mixed climbs tend to follow lines of weakness in the rock which might offer the best protection possibilities such as cracks, chimneys or grooves. Due to the difficulty in hanging on long enough to place protection, trad mixed routes usually follow terrain that is slabby-to-vertical with only the occasional overhanging section.

Sport mixed

Sport mixed

Winter sport climbs protected by bolts are almost always mixed routes. They were initially developed as means to access ice features that didn't reach the ground, such as hanging icicles. As skills have developed the rock sections have got more important in their own right to the extent that there are even climbs with no ice at all. These are known as 'dry-tooling' routes and, although still climbed with ice axes and crampons, they can be climbed all year round.

Starting Out

Equipment

Mountain Safety

Ice : Style-Ethics

Ice : Techniques

Mixed : Style-Ethics

Mixed : Techniques

The Mind

Training

Destinations

SCOTLAND'S NATIONAL OUTDOOR TRAINING CENTRE

COURSES FOR BEGINNERS TO ADVANCED TRAINING & ASSESSMENT FOR INSTRUCTORS AND LEADERS

Winter
Mountain

inspiring adventure since 1948
www.glenmorelodge.org.uk
Glenmore Lodge Tel: 01479 861256 Email: enquiries@glenmorelodge.org.uk

Starting Out

Equipment

Mountain Safety

Ice : Style-Ethics

Ice : Techniques

Mixed : Style-Ethics

Mixed : Techniques

The Mind

Training

Destinations

Learning the basics

With both ice and mixed climbing, it is preferable to climb lots of routes to learn and practice your tool skills with the security of a top rope, or following a more experienced leader. Also, removing ice screws will help you develop an understanding of how ice screws work and to develop a system for placing them. It simply is not advisable to start leading straight away on ice unless you have an extensive background of leading on rock. Beware that some rock climbers can be their own worst enemy, thinking that they have the skills and fitness to jump in at the deep-end. If your first experience of climbing ice or mixed is on the sharp end then pick something as easy as possible and make sure you take some advice about conditions on the day. Practise by bouldering around at the base of the route to get a feeling for tool mechanics and make sure you practise placing protection (ice screws in particular) before you leave the ground.

Ice

On your initial lead, you should be able to stand comfortably on your front points and place as many screws as you need. A good option is to place two screws next to each other (at least 1 metre apart) and to clip one rope in each. Although this would be considered overkill by a competent ice climber, you cannot afford to take chances. Many ice falls form with several different lines of different difficulty and a great option in this case is to lead the very easiest line and then to rig a solid top-rope on the more difficult lines, but you should only do this if you are entirely confident in your top-rope belay.

If at any point you start to feel out of your depth, then you should be prepared to retreat since you are unlikely to have the ability to push on into the unknown when you are dangerously pumped. Clip an axe, but try not to weight it, place some solid screws and reverse safely, adding extra gear and abseiling if necessary. Remember that getting safely off the crag is far more important than the cost of the pieces of gear you might have to leave behind. See page 167 for more on 'getting out of trouble'.

Mixed

It is nearly always best to learn your tool skills on ice before attempting to mixed climb. It is also highly advisable to have some rock climbing experience under your belt too.

The basic movement skills, ropework and protection systems are best learnt in a warmer, less extreme environment, without clumsy gloves and with ice tools in your hands. Above all else, don't presume that a pedigree of rock climbing experience will enable you to take to mixed climbing automatically. Make sure you allow plenty of time to translate your skills on easy routes first.

Breaking trail into Stob Coire nan Lochan, Glen Coe, Scotland.

A deep stance kicked out of the snow allows safe gearing up without the risk of your kit rolling back down the hill.

Starting Out
Equipment
Mountain Safety
Ice · Style-Ethics
Ice · Techniques
Mixed · Style-Ethics
Mixed · Techniques
The Mind
Training
Destinations

The walk-in

Many believe that a winter climb is won or lost on the approach. Make sure you are fit enough and that you are only carrying the things you need. Start early and allow extra time if there has been fresh snowfall. Take poles for difficult terrain and pay careful attention to your clothing systems. It is vital not to over-heat or to allow your clothing to wet-out excessively, either from sweat or precipitation - see page 53 for ideas and tips. Plan your route the night before by verifying the advice on the approach in the guidebook against a map. Your primary consideration should always be the threat of objective dangers such as avalanche or deteriorating weather.

Gearing up

Find a spot that's safe from ice debris, especially if there are already people on the route above you. It must also be somewhere you can find if it's dark on the descent. Your first priority is to keep your hands warm so use 'thinny' dextrous gloves for putting on your technical gear. This is key to avoiding hotaches. If your thermal top is wet from the approach then change it straight away before you cool down. Be aware that, if you are leaving a pack at the base of the route, it could get buried if it snows so consider using walking poles to mark the spot or stand your packs up on end rather than lying them flat. This is also the final chance to go through a list of essential things that you may have left in your pack such as your headtorch, snacks and fluids.

Reading the conditions

Winter climbing in Scotland can be a particular challenge largely due to the rapidly changing and fickle conditions. Predicting when the right conditions might occur is one of the most sought after secrets to successful Scottish winter climbing. The real masters will call on their experience built up over many seasons but a few guidelines to look out for are as follows:

Freezing level

Most mountain forecasts show the altitude at which the temperature drops below freezing also modern guidebooks show the altitude at the base of the cliff, otherwise check the map contours. For turf to be well frozen a sustained period of freezing over several days will be required however be aware that, if it snows before the freezing level drops, the snow will act as an insulating blanket preventing the turf properly cooling.

Wind

Hoar frost grows towards the wind on faces exposed to medium or higher winds. Wind direction is also important to identify as it will move snow around, scraping exposed slopes of excess snow and dumping it on lee slopes.

Snow

Surprising amounts of snow can build up within a day or two high on the hills. Also if the cliffs have been damp, a drop in temperatures can allow snow to stick to even the steepest of faces. High winds, and in particular storms, will increase this process.

Freeze-thaw cycles

Freeze-thaw is a crucial process for all ice routes but particularly Scottish snow-ice routes. Early in the season, despite some snow and cold, many routes will still be in poor condition as there have not been enough freezes and alternative minor thaws to build up ice and consolidate and harden the snow layers into climbable neve. This is why areas such as the high walls on Ben Nevis i.e. *Indicator Wall*, are best at the end of the season.

As a general guideline, good early season options include ridges and rocky buttresses that aren't reliant on turf. In mid season ice routes should begin to form and turfy mixed routes will be the main targets. In the late season, high level ice routes can remain in condition well into March and April.

You're not sport climbing now. Andy Benson taking in the challenge of full Scottish conditions in Glen Coe, Scotland.

'The sport climber hits the ice'
- Neil Gresham

On my first winter climbing trip to Scotland, we were greeted with disbelief when we were asked by our new mentors in Fort William what grade we climbed on rock.

'French 8b! There's no one up here climbing that sort of level. You don't need us to show you anything, you may as well get straight on a grade V.'

My sport climbing pal, Ian Harrison had at least done one ice route before, although he confessed that he'd aided it, clipping into his axes to place screws. So inspired by their confidence in our ability, the next morning we trudged up to attempt a grade IV ice route called the *Screen in Glencoe*.

Ian set off in the lead, armed only with the knowledge that our friends considered placing screws on aid to be unacceptable. It all seemed a bit arbitrary to me but Ian made every attempt not to clip into his axes on the ascent. The result was that he ran out a full 50m of rope without placing any protection. He had also climbed past the only worthwhile belay point and was attempting to complete a two pitch climb in a single rope length.

'I can see a tree up there,' he shouted, 'think I'll just go for it. If the rope pulls tight, start climbing!'

And sure enough it did, and Ian still had another fifteen metres to go. So I set off, bludgeoning and shattering the ice, tensing every muscle in my body and squeezing the shafts of my

axes like a vice. My main concern was my feet - there must be a problem with these stupid crampons because my front-points aren't going in. With my heels high in the sky, every kick just glanced off and I was forced to do a series of pull-ups and one-arm lock-offs with my body dragging uselessly against the slab!

After ten moves I was done-for and screamed to Ian fifty metres above me that I was about to come off. I watched uselessly as my anaesthetised fingers uncurled from the axes but could do nothing to stop them. And at the exact second my wrists slid through my leashes I heard a shout from above:

'OK mate, you're on belay!'

I was still there, and so was he.

Lessons learned:

1) Practise at ground level or on something easy before you get committed.

2) Never start on anything harder than grade II or III if you are leading.

3) Beware of sandbaggers!

Axe basics

Plunging

The default technique for moderate-angled snowy slopes or gullies is to use the shaft of the axe like a walking stick 'plunging' it deep into the snow. On moderate ground it is typical to use just one axe in the uphill hand as you zig zag up a slope. As the terrain steepens you'll need to plunge both axes and may opt to take a more direct line.

When the ascending axe is plunged in at waist height, similar to a rock climbing mantleshelf manoeuvre.

The head of axe gripped in the palm of your hand.

Daggering

On harder snow such as neve it might not be possible to plunge your axe shaft in, similarly as the angle of slope increases plunging will prove awkward. In these cases it is time to switch to 'daggering' the blade in.

Head of axe gripped in the palm of your hand.

Blade daggered down and towards you into the slope.

The blade should be buried deep in snow and in at least several inches in hard neve/ice.

Tip of shaft also engaged digging into slope.

Body pulling and pushing down like a rock climbing mantelshelf manoeuvre.

Starting Out

Equipment

Mountain Safety

Ice : Style-Ethics

Ice : Techniques

Mixed : Style-Ethics

Mixed : Techniques

The Mind

Training

Destinations

Technical tool placements

The classic ice axe grip is the most versatile in winter climbing. Essential for steeper ground or any terrain with hard snow and ice, you can swing to get a stick in ice, hook rock features or twist the axe into cracks. These placement possibilities are covered in detail in the ice chapter (page 134) and mixed chapter (page 188).

Unknown climber picking his way up *Pernile*, Scottish III, on Aonach Mor, Scotland.

Crampon basics

Crampon placement on soft snow

Kicking steps is the key to safe efficient movement through the fluffy white stuff. You may have to kick several times to create a secure step. If ascending a slope lean in and lead with your toes to create an incut slot, when descending punch in with your heels or sidestep down for greater security. When traversing a slope either face in or use the inside edge of your crampons to kick in. You can reuse your kicked slots for your trailing leg however it is worth re-kicking in case the snow platform has crumbled under the leading foot. If the snow is hard, you should try to roll your ankles to angle your feet, meaning the whole of the crampon base is in contact with the snow. This is called French Technique.

Steep or deep snow will require more involved techniques, perhaps clearing the top layer to get at firmer load-bearing snow beneath, or using your hands and knees to build up foot platforms.

Balling

Certain types of soft snow can often build up in clumps stuck to your crampons. This potentially serious hazard is referred to as 'balling up' and can quickly (within a few steps) build up so much snow that your crampon points no longer bite into snow or ice. Anti-balling plates, which should be fitted to all crampons, help alleviate build-up but you will still need to stop occasionally to knock off snow build up with a tap from the side of your ice axe against your boot edge.

Andy Nisbet kicking solid steps on *Easy Gully*, Scottish I, Aonach Mor, Scotland.

Guy Robertson on the first winter ascent of *Sundance*, VIII, 8 on Beinn Eighe.

Starting Out

Equipment

Mountain Safety

Ice : Style-Ethics

Ice : Techniques

Mixed : Style-Ethics

Mixed : Techniques

The Mind

Training

Destinations

Starting Out

Equipment

Mountain Safety

Ice : Style · Ethics

Ice : Techniques

Mixed : Style · Ethics

Mixed : Techniques

The Mind

Training

Destinations

Crampon placement on hard snow/ice

Low angle

On very low angle ice the most secure approach is to flex your ankle so that all the bottom points of your crampon are engaged with the snow. Options include splaying your feet out 'duck-like' to climb directly up moderate-angled slopes, or as the ground steepens turn side ways and either take a zig-zag line, or side-step directly upwards. Either way you will need to have your feet facing sideways across the slope, or even slightly downward pointing, to maximise the bite of your crampons. Sharp crampons will greatly add to your security and you may wish to stomp your feet to drive all the points into the ice.

Low-angled ice or hard snow

Moderate angle

Once the slope angle rears above 40° or so you will find it awkward to keep the soles of both feet flat against the ice and so a combination of front pointing with your lead foot and bracing the other foot sideways with all the bottom points engaged is used.

Moderately-angled ice or hard snow

High angle

The default position for higher angle ice, or rock, is 'front pointing', using the large main points at the toe of your crampons backed up by the shorter subsidiary points. Precise and delicate placements can be made on the smallest of holds.

More on crampons on page 66.
More on crampon placement on pages 132 and 187.

High-angled ice or rock

Learn to look forward to the weather forecast.

Let's face it, these days the weatherman rarely brings good news. That can mean another winter languishing on the sofa, waiting for spring to arrive. Unless of course, you learn to embrace winter conditions.

At Plas y Brenin we run a full programme of winter hillwalking, winter mountaineering and winter climbing courses designed to give you the confidence to overcome the unexpected challenges that the mountains throw up in the depths of winter. What's more we offer you the choice of enjoying our high standards of instruction, accommodation and facilities in Wales or Scotland at our base near Glencoe.

For the summer hillwalker our five-day Welsh Winter Hillwalking course will give you a perfect grounding in how to navigate safely in fading light and poor conditions, how to respond to prevailing weather conditions and how to keep yourself and your party safe in a hostile environment. If you don't have that much time to spare, our Welsh Winter Skills programme runs over two days, condensing all of the above into an intense confidence-building weekend. Or you may choose to focus solely on clocking up some 'mountain miles' on a week-long tour of Snowdonia's Fourteen highest peaks - a uniquely challenging and rewarding experience in winter conditions.

For the more experienced there's the variety and scale of the Scottish Mountains. We also run a full programme from our base in Scotland with everything from Scottish Winter Hillwalking and Mountaineering weeks right up to technical Scottish snow and ice climbing courses.

Whether you decide to join us in Scotland or Wales this year, you'll find yourself looking forward to your next course at Plas y Brenin.

For your free 72-page colour brochure telephone Plas y Brenin on 01690 720214 or simply send an e-mail to brochure@pyb.co.uk.

> The **Professional's** Choice

www.pyb.co.uk

Plas y Brenin The National Mountain Centre Capel Curig Conwy LL24 OET Tel: 01690 720214 Email: info@pyb.co.uk

Introductory climbs - ridges

What to expect

Ridges are typically the most dominating feature of any mountain and were often the first routes tackled by winter pioneers. By their nature ridges are usually free of the avalanche hazards found on more open slopes, finding your route is straight forward and the compelling line and situations make ridge climbs attractive propositions. On the other hand, ridges are open to the worst the weather has to offer and can be terrifying in very high winds, route finding can be more challenging than expected and, due to the often low angle of ascent, any falls are likely to be bruising affairs.

Almost all ridges are protected by traditional gear with many of the most coveted found in the winter trad climbing meccas of Scotland. In terms of grade, many ridges are likely to be low in terms of technicality, but due to their length shouldn't be under-estimated in terms of commitment.

Tactics

The key decision for moderate and intermediate ridge climbs is assessing which sections to belay and pitch on, and which parts you might consider moving together. This of course will depend on the competency of both members of your party. For example, for most Scottish grade I ridges, which are an extension of winter hill walking, you would expect to move together up the whole climb. Moving up to Scottish grade II, with routes such as *Fiacaill Ridge* in the Cairngorms, you will probably choose to take a quick belay either side of the steepest short steps. By the time you get Scottish grade IV most

climbers will be belaying the majority of the route, however on longer ridges, such as *Tower Ridge* on Ben Nevis, it is vital to take advantage of any opportunity to move together when easier sections appear. Each year many parties spend cold nights out benighted on *Tower Ridge* after moving too slowly on the easier sections of this huge 600m route.

The other important tactic on ridges is 'micro-route finding'. While it might seem unlikely that you can get lost on a huge soaring ridge, you will often be faced with decisions on which way to negotiate the many obstacles typical of most ridges. Pinnacles or gendarmes offer some of the toughest challenges, not just in climbing their steep faces, but often the equally steep descent required on their other side. In extreme cases this can require time consuming and potentially risky abseils. Often it may be more prudent to try to outflank these obstacles and traverse around, so make sure you've done your research with the guidebook before you start. A similar challenge in reverse can be presented by sudden cuts or chasms into the ridge - *Tower Gap* on *Tower Ridge* is one such obstacle. When descending these features it is vital to remember to place protection to safeguard your second even if you as leader don't need it since your rope is above you.

Moving together

The most efficient way to move together is to shorten the ropes. This is done by both climbers taking quarter to a third of the rope up in coils, re-tied off and secured to your harness with the spare loops carried over your shoulder. You will then have less rope between you to get snagged and caught and will be closer together for more efficient communication. If you approach a longer difficult section then either climber can drop their coils giving them more rope between belays.

Technique

Most technical ridges are very mixed in nature and so expect to encounter sections of snow, the odd step, or slab of ice, as well as lots of rock. One of the most rewarding challenges of ridge climbing is swapping between the most appropriate techniques as the terrain changes. The individual techniques for snow, ice and mixed climbing are covered in detail elsewhere in this book but you would expect to both plunge and dagger with your axes on snow, front point on ice as well as use both hands and axes on the rocky sections. You will often find it useful to be able to stow one of your axes and use a hand and an axe as an efficient combination.

Protection

The variety of terrain found on a ridge usually presents lots of possibilities for protection. The bulk of your protection is likely to be on rock, sometimes in the form of spike runners, so aim to take at least 6 slings or more as well as a set of rocks and hexes (see page 78 for more on rock gear). Depending on the route and conditions, it may well be worth taking a couple of ice screws for the occasional ice patch. A very

useful form of protection is the rope itself which can be woven either side of large protruding rock features such as pinnacles - just beware of rope drag. On sharp protectionless ridges such as flat snow crests if one of you slips the fall can be stopped by the other climber jumping or running down the opposite face. Although this alarming manoeuvre is very much a last resort, it does work!

Left: *Tower Gap* on *Tower Ridge*, Ben Nevis, Scotland. Photo by John Trudgill.
Above: A long wait to cross *Tower Gap* as the sun sets. Photo by Dale Bloomer.

Starting Out
Equipment
Mountain · Safety
Ice · Style · Ethics
Ice · Techniques
Mixed · Style · Ethics
Mixed · Techniques
The Mind
Training
Destinations

Starting Out
Equipment
Mountain Safety
Ice : Style-Ethics
Ice : Techniques
Mixed : Style-Ethics
Mixed : Techniques
The Mind
Training
Destinations

Introductory climbs - gullies

What to expect

Snow and ice gullies are the lines of weakness cutting through steep buttresses and often offer good introductory climbs at many crags. On the Continent, and in the Americas, these gully lines can start as low as WI1 while in Scotland there is a wealth of gullies from grade I through to grade VI.

Route finding on gullies is usually straight forward; just follow the line of snow and ice upwards and don't stray onto the skirting steep walls. There are a few hazards to be wary of however. Foremost is that gully lines are often notorious funnels for snow swept down the face and spindrift channelled down a gully can, in extreme cases, be strong enough to knock a climber from their stance. This snow can also build up in the gully itself burying useful ice and, at worst, become an avalanche threat. Most disconcerting of all can be the huge waves of overhanging snow known as cornices that often build up at the top of gully lines. In stable temperatures many cornices will stay solid but in a state of thaw, or after a sudden drop in temperature, they can collapse which is extremely dangerous for anyone in the vicinity. If in doubt avoid any gully line with an unstable looking cornice.

Belays

One way to minimise the danger presented by cornices is to do your best to find sheltered belays tucked into corners, caves or protected spots in the side rock walls of the gully. Digging a pit in the snow gives you a solid stance and also enables you to check the layers of snow, giving a small snapshot of potential avalanche risk. See page 88 for more on mountain safety.

Protection

Belays and runners will prove to be a mixture of ice screws and rock protection with the occasional bollard or axe belay in the snow. For gullies up to Scottish grade III, three or four ice screws should prove sufficient as you are likely to find as much snow as ice. Keep an eye out for any cracks or spikes in the surrounding rock walls as these can provide the most secure protection and belays; 3 to 4 slings, a set of wires complemented by larger hexs would make up a typical rack for moderate to intermediate gullies.
See pages 72 and 78 for more on protection.

John Trudgill climbing *Black Spout Gully (Left Hand Branch)*, Lochnagar, Scotland. This gully is frequently used to approach other routes.
Photo by Brian Duthie.

Movement

Most of your climbing will be using a mixture of traditional snow and ice techniques, from plunging and daggering up snow, through to front pointing up ice as the angle steepens. Techniques differ when you are forced to negotiate those dreaded cornices at the top of gullies in order to top out. If at all possible try to traverse around any cornices or at least until under the smallest section. Place protection if possible before tackling any cornice as the overhanging snow they are made up of is highly unlikely to offer any protection possibilities. Any cornice less than a metre or so in size should allow you to chop through its lip, be careful however as you dig away at it as sudden collapse is possible. Chopping through the lip of cornices is a time consuming process that shouldn't be rushed. Be methodical making sure you kick in big solid steps into the back of any channel you can excavate.

In order to top out you may well have to chop well back from the lip to find stable snow and then still need to plunge your tools and even your arms fully into the snow.

If a cornice is much bigger than a metre overhanging you may be forced to chop an enclosed tunnel inside the overhanging snow. However this is a very draining and serious exercise that can take many hours and it might be a better option to consider a lengthy traverse to find another option to top out, or even abandon the summit and descend the route. Particularly late in the season in Scotland cornices can grow to huge proportions and it is not unusual for even modestly graded climbs to become un-climbable. Remember that it's better mountaineering to turn round rather than head straight into danger.

Below left: Surmounting the cornice at the top of *Number Four Gully*, Ben Nevis, Scotland.
Below right: Ian Parnell topping out through a cornice 'chop' on Ben Nevis, Scotland.

Arresting slips

The ice axe self arrest is an essential skill that should be acquired by all winter climbers before heading out on the hill. Once perfected it can quickly stop slips and slides in many situations, although it is worth noting that on steep slopes or ice the self arrest may not work.

The following techniques aim to orientate you so that you are sliding feet-first in a front-on position. If you are already in this position then you need only apply the technique shown in the shared final stage.

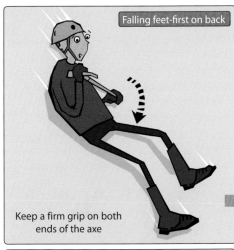

Falling feet-first on back

Keep a firm grip on both ends of the axe

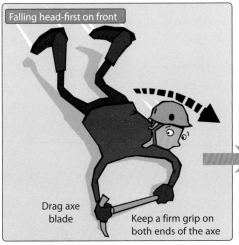

Falling head-first on front

Drag axe blade

Keep a firm grip on both ends of the axe

Let your body pivot until your legs are facing down-slope

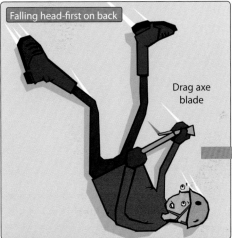

Falling head-first on back

Drag axe blade

As your body pivots around roll onto your front

Starting Out | Equipment | Mountain Safety | Ice : Style-Ethics | Ice : Techniques | Mixed : Style-Ethics | Mixed : Techniques | The Mind | Training | Destinations

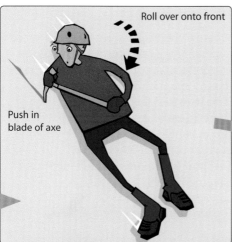

Roll over onto front

Push in blade of axe

Practice makes perfect

Ice axe arrest is not as easy as it looks and it is well worth spending an afternoon sliding down a snow slope with a safe run out and practice all the techniques shown in these diagrams. The force required to dig in an axe into a slope is surprisingly large once you gather speed!

Legs are facing down-slope

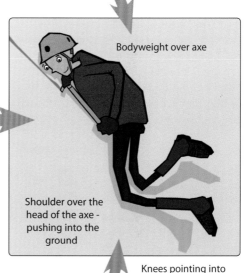

Bodyweight over axe

Shoulder over the head of the axe - pushing into the ground

Knees pointing into the slope, feet up to avoid snagging crampons

As you roll onto your front try to get your shoulder over your axe head

Legs are facing down-slope

Walking poles

If you are using walking poles then make sure you put them away and get your axes out early since this arrest technique does not work with walking poles.

Starting Out

Equipment

Mountain Safety

Ice : Style-Ethics

Ice : Techniques

Mixed : Style-Ethics

Mixed : Techniques

The Mind

Training

Destinations

Starting Out

Equipment

Mountain Safety

Ice : Style-Ethics

Ice : Techniques

Mixed : Style-Ethics

Mixed : Techniques

The Mind

Training

Destinations

Belays

When winter climbing, though the principles of ropework are the same as in trad rock climbing, there are a number of hazards that are far more significant than they are in the rock climbing game.

Choosing a belay site

Ice and snow are much less secure than solid rock, and dodging sizeable blocks of falling ice is a frequent hazard - beware belaying below hanging icicles, cornices or any features that are prone to collapse. Consider where the next pitch goes and try to belay out of the fall line. An alternative is to look for shelter in caves or below bulges or ice mushrooms.

Try to select a belay site that corresponds to an appropriate place to stand, but never let this take preference over the quality of the anchors. It is better to take a hanging or 'semi-hanging' belay on good anchors than stand on a comfortable ledge which has poor anchors, or is a dangerous place to stand (in the fall-line). Only take hanging belays if anchors are good and be aware that your weight on the ice screws can cause 'pressure melting' of the ice!

Constructing a belay

Your priority in arranging belay anchors should be to obtain solid rock protection first, but if this isn't available then go for ice screws, and finally a snow belay if nothing else is on offer (page 30). However remember that a good ice screw will almost certainly be better than a poor piece of protection in loose rock. Pegs are useful for belaying on loose or heavily iced-up rock.

Equalising a belay

When anchors appear bomb-proof, place a minimum of two. The less sure you are about the quality of the ice, rock, or snow, the more you will need to place. There is no hard-and-fast rule for this so you must use careful judgement. Equalise the protection making up your belay so that each component is loaded equally. See **Trad Climbing+** for an in-depth treatment of building belays.

Adding yourself to the belay

With hanging or semi-hanging belays on ice, use your axe to chop out a small foot-ledge to make it more comfortable to stand and reduce the loading on the anchors. Kick out a ledge, or better still, a bucket-seat (page 30) if you are on a snow slope.

Always brace yourself when the belay is anything other than perfect, and be prepared to take as much of the strain as possible yourself, rather than letting it go through to the belay anchors.

Backing up the belay with your axes

If you have no other gear available and you need to back up your belay, you can do it with your axes. (Note this is not as strong as placing another ice-screw) Do this by placing the picks deep in the ice and clipping the eye on the head or shaft and then equalising it into the system. Beware clipping parts of the axe such as leash-less grips that are not strength rated. With snow, plunge the shafts and clove-hitch the rope around the axe head or build an axe belay (page 33).

Mountain Technology Warthog   Camp Lost Arrow Peg

Special notes for ice screw belays

✓ Inspect the ice very carefully for air pockets and fracture lines.

✓ Place a minimum of two screws in bombproof, bullet-hard ice and make sure they are equalised using a sling or the rope.

✗ Do not place screws too close to each other - a minimum of one metre apart is a good rule of thumb.

❗ Listen very carefully for excessive cracking when placing the screws and, if in doubt, replace them.

✓ Place as many as you can if the ice is soft, fragile, or shallow.

✓ Save long ice screws for belays.

Two screws in bullet-hard ice equalised with a sling. The fact that the belay is under tension means that screwgate karabiners are not strictly necessary.

Belaying off Abalakovs

Some climbers will build an Abalakov (page 34) for a belay because it may be stronger than individual screws and will make things quicker for the abseil descent. However, only do so if you can do it quickly as your second will already be shivering! A better tactic is to build it while you are belaying your second, but only do so if you have an auto locking plate, keeping control of the rope at all times. Make sure you practise this first.

Staying warm on belays

The best way to stay warm on a belay is to ask your leader to speed up! Ice routes are bad enough on cold days but trad mixed routes will always be the worst for long belaying stints. If possible, try to pick a belay ledge that enables you to move around, but never put this before the priority of safety. Avoid stomping, especially when the rope is nearby and instead do sets of squats. One-armed shoulder circles are also good providing you always keep the rope locked off with the spare arm.

A tempting technique to keep your fingers warm is to take them out of the finger holes in your belay gloves and to curl them across your palm (only do this with the hand that isn't holding the breaking end of the rope). With hand warmers this is particularly effective. However, this is only advisable if you have a toasty pair of climbing gloves stashed in your thermal top ready to go for the next pitch. If your belay gloves are all you've got then avoid this technique because you will only make the finger holes colder and you will suffer even more when you start climbing. A better option is to keep clenching your fingers in and out to keep the blood circulating.

Starting Out · Equipment · Mountain Safety · Ice : Style·Ethics · Ice : Techniques · Mixed : Style·Ethics · Mixed : Techniques · The Mind · Training · Destinations

Snow belays

Creating a decent belay in snow is one of the more challenging skills that need to be learnt in winter climbing, however it is an essential skill. Whether on a grade I gully route, or topping out *Orion Face* up onto the summit plateau of Ben Nevis, every level of winter climber will need to be able construct a solid belay in soft snow.

Bucket seat

At the centre of all snow belays is a solid secure stance. Typically this will be a pit for you to sit in, scooped out of the snow, known as a 'bucket seat'. The depth you will need to dig will depend on the consistency of the snow with say 30cm depth in typically supportive neve but deeper in loose light powder snow. Excavate a good pit for your bum and then thrust you heels down in front of you for further support.

You should now have a good wall of snow at your feet building up between your legs. Bear in mind the direction of pull any fall will take. Typically a bucket seat is designed to withstand a downslope force.

Above: testing a bucket seat belay.
Below: bringing up two seconds using a waist belay on steep ground above Coire an Lochain, Cairngorms, Scotland. The climber is attached to snow belay (buried axe) and sitting in a bucket seat. Photo by George McEwan.

Body belay

Since snow is inherently more fragile than ice and rock, you have to adopt particular belaying tactics when handling the rope in order to lessen the force. One of the most effective ways is to wrap the rope around your waist in a 'body belay'.

A body belay won't hold the rope as securely as a belay device but, used correctly, a body belay can work surprisingly well. The key advantage is that there is always more slippage of the rope than when using a belay device - this gives a softer dynamic belay which will protect fragile snow anchors.

The disadvantages are obviously that, with this slippage, the climber will fall further. More importantly, if the belay is set up wrongly the rope can quickly become uncontrollable with the likelihood that the belayer will be injured and the climber dropped.

✔ Rope wrapped around waist above hips and harness.

✔ Rope twisted around brake arm.

✔ Grippy gloves to increase friction and avoid rope burn.

✔ Cross arms to lock belay.

✔ Live rope on same side as belay anchor.

Above: a waist belay from a bucket seat.
Below: James Woodhouse ascending steep ground near Coire Cas, Scotland. His belayer is using a waist belay while attached to a buried axe and sitting in a bucket seat. Both photos by George McEwan.

Starting Out
Equipment
Mountain Safety
Ice : Style-Ethics
Ice : Techniques
Mixed : Style-Ethics
Mixed : Techniques
The Mind
Training
Destinations

Portable snow protection

There are several forms of snow protection available on the market (see page 72 for more on gear). The two most commonly used are snow stakes and snow flukes (marketed under the name 'Deadman'). Snow stakes can work well in hard snow where they can be hammered in at an angle of about 10-15° away from the direction of pull. Deadmen need firm snow (although in hard solid snow they can be difficult to place) and crucially need to be placed correctly (see page 75 for more on placing Deadmen). If correctly placed, when weighted, the Deadman will be dragged deeper and more securely into the snow.

Simple and secure, abseiling off a snow bollard to avoid the cornices. Simon Richardson atop the *Tower Gully* on Ben Nevis, Scotland.

It is worth practising this placement before you use a Deadman since, if the placement is incorrect, the plate will be pulled quickly to the surface and fail. While these two bits of kit can provide protection where little else is available, they are slightly limited to specific snow types and require you to carry more gear.

Following are some more anchor systems that are simple to construct and none of them require any extra equipment to be carried other than your axes.

Snow bollards

One of the simplest and most effective snow anchors is to chop out a bollard from the snow and lasso with a loop of rope re-tied back to your harness. Depth and size will depend on the consistency of the snow but the bigger and deeper the

bollard the greater the security. Usually you are aiming for a minimum of one metre in diameter in firm solid snow while in soft snow the bollard could be up to three metres wide. Make sure there is a deep in-cut groove so that when you wrap the loop of rope round it won't slip.

It is possible to reinforce a bollard by packing the inside edge with your rucksack or a plunged axe shaft. A typical instance for using a snow bollard would be topping out of a route onto a snowy plateau devoid of other belay features and in similar terrain to make an abseil descent when cornices block descent gullies.

A Buried axe belay on top of Ben Nevis, Scotland. Quick to set up and a winner in the right snow.

Buried axe belay

This is a good option in firm snow and should be quicker to build than a large bollard. A T-shaped trench is dug into the snow with the down-stroke of the T facing in the line of pull down the snow slope. Attach a sling on a large screw-gate karabiner to the middle of the shaft of one of your axes and bury this in the upper horizontal slot of the T with the sling running down the lower slot. Your other axe can be plunged in vertically to reinforce the T-anchor.

Boot-axe belay a.k.a. 'stomper'

The is a very quick anchor to set up that, though inherently weak, can provide reassurance for short tricky steps on moderate ridge routes and topping out on snow routes. Plunge the axe shaft fully into firm snow (you should have to stomp down with your foot on the head) clip a screwgate karabiner through the hole in the axe head and clip the rope through that. With both feet standing on the top of the axe, the rope can then run up to shoulder belay (as shown to the right). Alternatively, you can use a waist belay, but in this standing position you will need to run the rope through a screwgate karabiner of your belay loop to avoid it slipping off your hips.

A boot-axe belay.
Photo by George McEwan.

Starting Out | Equipment | Mountain Safety | Ice · Style·Ethics | Ice · Techniques | Mixed · Style·Ethics | Mixed · Techniques | The Mind | Training | Destinations

Starting Out

Equipment

Mountain Safety

Ice : Style · Ethics

Ice : Techniques

Mixed : Style · Ethics

Mixed : Techniques

The Mind

Training

Destinations

Abalakov hooks and cord

Abalakov threads are threads drilled into solid ice, and threaded with a length of cord which is then tied into a secure loop. They often provide the only means of descent from a long ice route. On popular routes you may find them in place, but you should always plan to back these up. Also, if you do use an old Abalakov, take great care to ensure you are using the thread itself and not the long tails of the old knot which might have refrozen into the ice!

For some reason, the Abalakov hook and cord always seem to be the easiest items to forget to take with you. Ideally the cord should be 5 or 6mm in diameter and you can cut it to length using the rear side of your pick, a pocket knife, or the saw attachment that sometimes comes with purpose-made Abalakov hooks.

❶ Find a clear, flat and structurally solid piece of ice close, but not too close to your ice screw belay.

❷ Place a long screw at 60° to the ice and remove.

❸ Place a bright piece of cord or the brightly coloured handle of an Abalakov threader in the hole you have made to use as a guide for the next step.

Now place the long screw again, at 60° to the ice, but this time so it forms the other side of an equilateral triangle and the end of the screw connects with the hole from your previous placement.

A Grivel Candela - a tool designed specifically for creating Abalakov threads - the serrated edge is for cutting nylon cord. It can be stored inside an ice screw.

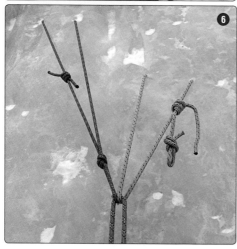

❹ Remove the screw, place the cord in one of the screw holes and use the Abalakov hook to snag it and pull it out. Now tie a double fishermans knot to create the thread.

❺ Bounce test it, staying connected to the other belay at all times.

❻ It is advisable to build another one (not too close to the first) even if the first passes the bounce test.

❼ The first person to abseil should always have a back-up anchor which is usually a connection from the original screw belay to the Abalakov (this should be done with some slack in the system). The second person removes this. It is advisable for the person below to tie both ends of the abseil rope into the belay.

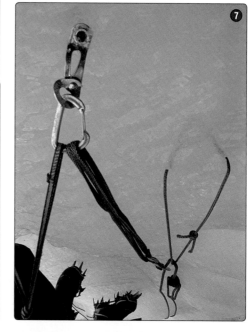

Starting Out

Equipment

Mountain Safety

Ice : Style-Ethics

Ice : Techniques

Mixed : Style-Ethics

Mixed : Techniques

The Mind

Training

Destinations

Indoor ice climbing

Indoor ice climbing walls can provide an excellent opportunity for learning the basic ice climbing skills in a less extreme environment. Although these facilities are becoming more widespread, they tend to be less popular with experienced climbers - the inherent limitation is that they soon become chopped to pieces and riddled with holes that allow placements to be gained all too easily. Nonetheless, there are some worthwhile exercises that can be performed by novice and intermediate level climbers. These are listed in chronological order, according to your skill level. Intermediates may wish to pass on some of the initial exercises and move on to the more advanced drills.

Weighting your crampons

Find an easy-angled part of the ice wall - then, at ground level, kick in with your feet, keeping them level, your heels down, and engage the secondary points. Now try leaning in, bracing your knees against the ice and taking as much weight on them as possible, using a hand on one axe for minimal support.
See page 132 for further notes on crampon placements.

Practice swings

Still at the base of the wall, try a few light and carefully aimed axe swings. Don't aim for existing holes and instead try to make your own placement. Aim for concave or flat parts of the ice rather than convex bulges. Try not to place the pick too deep - just past the first tooth is all that is required. Carefully test each placement to gain a feel for how solid they are.
See page 134 for further notes on the axe swing.

First climb

Chose an easy-angled line on the ice that will allow you to lean in and weight your feet as much as you can. Always attain a balance position between each move and avoid over-reaching, stepping wide or keeping your feet too close together. Relax your grip as much as you can and keep breathing regularly. Avoid the existing holes and try to make your own placements.
See page 140 for further notes on movement.

1-axe climbing

Try climbing with one axe on a line that is just less than vertical. This will teach you to move in balance and not to over-rely on your arms. Use some of the existing holes if you really get stuck but try to make your own placements wherever possible.

No axe climbing!

A more advanced exercise is to climb with no axes at all on an easy-angled line. You can use your gloved hands on the ice for balance. This really will get you trusting your feet!

Minimal kicks

Now go back to climbing with both axes but try kicking in as lightly as possible or, better still, not kicking at all and just balancing your mono-points on dimples in the ice. Avoid the existing holes and instead try to make your own crampon placements. This exercise will help you to use your feet more gracefully, like a rock climber.

High-tooling and swapping axes

Switch to something a little steeper and experiment with swapping hands using the high-tool bar. Be careful to maintain a downward pull so as not to lever the axe out.

Screw placements

Try placing screws inter-mittently, focusing on keeping your feet level and secure, your arms straight and swapping hands mid-operation to reduce the pump.
See page 150 for further notes on placing screws.

Laps

Having practised the above techniques, all that remains is to see if you can maintain your form under the influence of fatigue, so a good game is to pick a steep line and to lower off quickly and run a series of laps. Now you will really have to focus on keeping your arms straight, relaxing your grip, breathing, shaking out and moving fluidly. Try not to sprint up the wall and instead move at a slow steady pace, as if you were leading a real route.

No crampons!

An advanced exercise for training rather than technique is to perform laps with no crampons. This will certainly improve your body tension and get you very pumped! Beginners should not try this exercise as it may teach you bad habits and cause you to become less reliant on your feet.

Indoor ice climbing walls allow year-round training, and an accessible way to have a go at ice climbing before venturing into the mountains.
Photo by Gavin Newman of The Ice Factor - **www.ice-factor.co.uk**

Starting Out | Equipment | Mountain Safety | Ice : Style-Ethics | Ice : Techniques | Mixed : Style-Ethics | Mixed : Techniques | The Mind | Training | Destinations

Starting Out

Equipment

Mountain Safety

Ice : Style-Ethics

Ice : Techniques

Mixed : Style-Ethics

Mixed : Techniques

The Mind

Training

Destinations

Equipment and Clothing

Starting Out

Equipment

Mountain Safety

Ice · Style·Ethics

Ice · Techniques

Mixed · Style·Ethics

Mixed · Techniques

The Mind

Training

Destinations

Equipment and clothing play a central role in ice and mixed climbing strategy. It only takes one or two epics caused by bad gear to shape your attitude to this subject. An experienced winter climber strives to continually evolve their equipment and clothing systems, picking up new tips and discarding out-dated methods. The subtlest tweak should be tested when climbing well within your limits, as it is vital to get used to new gear slowly, to learn how it adapts to different climbing styles or conditions.

There are specific systems that are geared for ice and mixed or common systems that work for either discipline. Some climbers obsess over this subject but others find it a chore. Either way it pays to have a base level of knowledge because your climbing will undoubtedly benefit. This chapter will help you make sense of it all and find out what works best for you.

Hardshell clothing

When conditions are damp, or the ice is running with water, Hardshell wear provides the best means of staying dry. Laminated shell materials with a membrane, like Gore-tex Proshell or eVent, will also offer a high level of breathability.

Hardshell wear is so named because of its toughness and inability to stretch (in comparison to Softshell) although some designs also incorporate stretch panels in an attempt to make the garment move more freely. Hardshell wear tends to be the first choice for ice climbers unless conditions are particularly dry, in which case, Softshell may provide a stretchier and more breathable option.

Mixed climbers tend to prefer the improved comfort and freedom of movement offered by Softshell and may only choose to wear Hardshell when climbing longer routes in the high mountains, or when conditions are particularly unpleasant.

Shell pant features

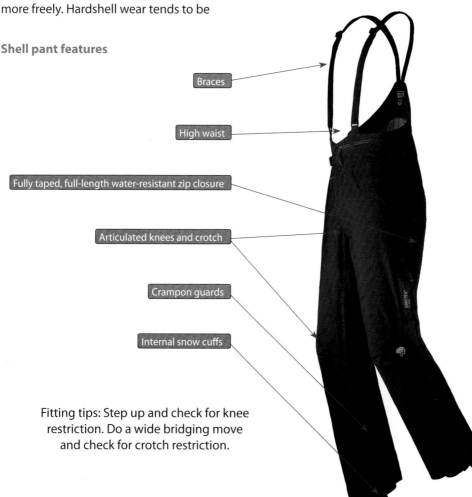

Braces

High waist

Fully taped, full-length water-resistant zip closure

Articulated knees and crotch

Crampon guards

Internal snow cuffs

Fitting tips: Step up and check for knee restriction. Do a wide bridging move and check for crotch restriction.

Starting Out
Equipment
Mountain Safety
Ice : Style-Ethics
Ice : Techniques
Mixed : Style-Ethics
Mixed : Techniques
The Mind
Training
Destinations

Shell jacket features

A good shell jacket will have the following features:

Full coverage hood, with stiffened visor, that fits over a helmet with 'single-pull' toggle closure

Re-inforced elbows and shoulders

Fully taped, pit-zips for ventilation

High pockets (which don't interfere with harness)

Articulated elbows

Water resistant zips or storm flaps over zips

Internal waist draw-cord

Stretch panels (optional)

Fitting tips:

✔ Your jacket should be flush at the front to minimise sag over your harness.

✔ Check the sleeve length when at full reach and see that the hem doesn't rise up excessively.

✔ Shoulders and elbows should be totally unrestricted.

✔ Body should not be too long so as to tangle with harness or restrict movement.

✘ All you will need underneath is a midlayer fleece so do not size-up for wearing a down jacket underneath.

✘ The drawcord closure should not restrict sight or articulated movement.

Connoisseur's tip:

Most hardshell garments look pretty similar from the outside but the very best hardshell jackets are the ones with the neatest most flexible seams and the slimmest tape, as these feel less restrictive to wear and have a lower pack size. Look on the *inside* for build quality.

Starting Out · Equipment · Mountain Safety · Ice : Style-Ethics · Ice : Techniques · Mixed : Style-Ethics · Mixed : Techniques · The Mind · Training · Destinations

Softshell clothing

Softshell is the generic term given to a wide range of garments that offer a combination of stretch properties and resistance to wind and water. The extent to which they hold out the weather varies dramatically, according to the presence or absence of a membrane and the nature of the outer material.

Membrane softshell

Softshell garments that are taped and have a membrane laminated to a nylon outer, may be almost as tough and waterproof as their Hardshell cousins; yet they usually feel slightly stretchier and more comfortable to climb in. Many of these garments have a thin microfleece laminated to boost warmth. As such they are ideal for ice climbing on moderately damp days and for most mixed climbing situations. It is only when the ice is really hosing wet that hardshell is preferable. Equally, when mixed climbing, you'll need to be on something really sporty and acrobatic to feel the need for the additional stretch properties and breathability of lighter softshell garments.

Contrary to perception, most softshell membranes don't actually breathe as well as the best hardshell materials.

Non-membrane softshells

Light softshell garments that don't have a membrane are usually made from polyester which has a surface coating that it is designed to 'shed' light moisture but not keep out heavy rain. These will breathe and stretch better than anything, but they will not keep you warm and dry on bad weather days! They will rarely be adequate for ice, or mixed climbing in the mountains, but they will suit sport-style mixed climbing like nothing else.

Fitting tips:
It is usually possible to fit Softshell apparel slightly closer than Hardshell owing to increased stretch properties.

Connoisseur's tip:
Look out for Softshell products with 'welded' seams, or welded panels and pockets, as these prove to be stretchier and more supple than sewn seams.

Karen McNeill appreciating the flexibility of movement offered by her softshell jacket.

Hardshell verses softshell

	Waterproof	Windproof	Toughness	Stretch/ Comfort	Ice	Trad Mixed	Sport Mixed
Hardshell	3	3	3	1	3	2	1
Membrane Softshell	2	3	2+	2	2+	3	2
Softshell	1	2	1	3	1	2	3

In the foulest of weather hardshell offers superior protection to softshell. Ben Bransby somewhere in a Cairngorm blizzard, Scotland.

Starting Out

Equipment

Mountain Safety

Ice : Style-Ethics

Ice : Techniques

Mixed : Style-Ethics

Mixed : Techniques

The Mind

Training

Destinations

Choosing a layering system

A thick 'winter spec' base layer top (right) with long sleeves and a high zip-neck works well in conjunction with high waist thermal pants or salopettes. Mid layer fleeces should be kept as thin and unrestrictive as possible and may not be necessary in conjunction with a softshell outer jacket that has a thin fleece lining. The 'shaggy' pilled-style mid layer fleeces (below right) often stretch better and offer more static warmth than standard fleece. They also feel less restrictive as they create less friction with the outer shell. Fleeces with windproof membranes are a bad idea as a mid layer as you will be prone to over-heating.

Layering tips:

A highly versatile clothing system is to do away with a bulky mid layer fleece and climb in just a thermal base layer with a hard or soft shell outer layer, and then to carry a down or synthetic belay jacket in a stuff bag, clipped to the back of your harness for belays. Mid layer fleeces feel restrictive and often seem to be too warm for climbing and too cold for belaying.

Headwear

The head is not only one of the major areas of potential heat loss but the key to a winter climber's temperature regulation. There are various head cover options on the market and it would be normal for a climber to take a selection with them to adapt to different conditions and act as spares for emergencies. The lightest headwear comes in the form of head-bands, or gaiters that, while not offering complete protection, can be worn over the ears or neck to eliminate drafts while still allowing lots of heat regulation - these are ideal for the walk in. The traditional 'beanie' shaped hat is still the most popular, with the thinner versions offering ideal insulation under a helmet. For the most severe weather particularly where winds are blasting spindrift down your route, a full balaclava is the headwear of choice.

Down jackets and belay jackets

A down jacket should be regarded as a piece of safety equipment for long mountain routes when it is particularly cold. They are also essential garments for easy-access sport mixed cliffs where you can afford to pack those extra luxuries to keep you warm whilst resting and belaying. A pair of insulated belay pants with full-length side zips may also make the day a lot more pleasant.

Beware using a down jacket for belaying unless it has a light waterproof coating or a membrane material to cover it for additional moisture protection. Down jackets often wet-out in damp, humid winter conditions without even having made direct contact with precipitation.

Pure quality goose down jackets will have the lowest pack-size and a 'box-wall' construction with internal baffles. They will always be warmer (though slightly bulkier) than jackets that are merely 'stitched through' to hold the insulation.

Synthetic belay Parkas made with insulators such as Primaloft may be less thermally efficient than down but are likely to keep doing their job long after the down has wetted out and given up.

Clothing care and maintenance

Dry your clothing out at first opportunity, especially if you are out on the hill again the next day. Keep it clean to avoid the dreaded 'alpine musk' and wash shell wear with 'tech-wash' from time to time to help restore the DWR (durable water repellent

Tim Emmett enjoying the warmth of a down jacket whilst on belay duty in the -20°C conditions of Quebec.

finish). Tumble drying and ironing on a moderate heat will also assist this.

Avoid washing down jackets, even with the right tech wash product, because you virtually have to get in the tumble drier with them to stop them from turning into a sodden lump. Instead, wipe the dirty areas clean with a warm damp cloth with mild soap. Most dry cleaners who say they can clean down products are usually talking about the quilt on your bed, but a few of the specialist manufacturers either have their own wash service or can recommend one.

Starting Out

Equipment

Mountain Safety

Ice : Style-Ethics

Ice : Techniques

Mixed : Style-Ethics

Mixed : Techniques

The Mind

Training

Destinations

Boots

For valley ice, mixed climbing or for any winter climbing that isn't at altitude, leather boots are nearly always the way forward as they are lighter, more comfortable and sensitive for climbing than plastics. Leather ice climbing boots are insulated to varying degrees and the warmest boots always tend to be the ones with the most support and the stiffest soles. Clearly these boots will also be the heaviest and offer the least sensitivity for climbing.

Many keen winter climbers will have two pairs of leathers with different amounts of insulation in order to match them to the conditions or style of climbing. In general, the lighter more sensitive leather boots are best suited to the higher technical demands of mixed, whereas the warmer stiffer models lend themselves more to ice. It is worth noting that modern plastic boots are so much better than their predecessors, and for front pointing on ice on very cold days they may prove to be the warmest and most supportive option.

Boot care

Always dry your boots out after use but avoid direct heat sources (i.e. close to the radiator but not on it). Spray them with re-proofing spray from time to time.

Boots and foot warmth

The key is to start with warm feet as this sets the precedent for the rest of the day. A strange thing about hill boots on very cold days is that they often feel colder on the car journey than normal shoes or trainers. The answer is not to wear them and to stash them right below the foot heater next to your feet so the hot air blasts into them. Don't put your socks on the wet floor mats, and instead wear a pair of loose fitting and comfortable shoes. Never leave your boots in the car over night, or in the car boot during the journey. Foot warmer packs are also a pretty good idea for abnormally cold conditions.

A good leather winter climbing boot will have the following features:

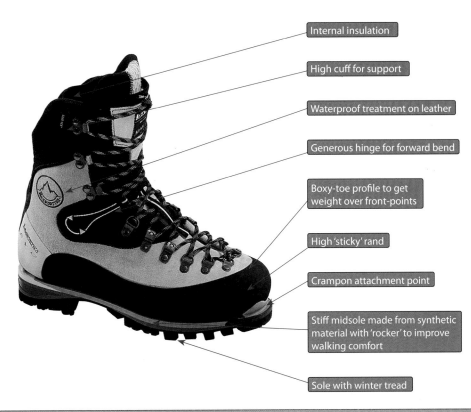

Internal insulation

High cuff for support

Waterproof treatment on leather

Generous hinge for forward bend

Boxy-toe profile to get weight over front-points

High 'sticky' rand

Crampon attachment point

Stiff midsole made from synthetic material with 'rocker' to improve walking comfort

Sole with winter tread

Fitting tips:

> Boot fit is a greater priority than owning a specific brand.

> If you're buying from scratch then choose boots first and then match crampons to them.

> Beware buying new boots if your old crampons don't fit them unless you are prepared to buy new crampons as well.

> When testing for walking, check that the top cuff bends forward and that the sole rocks and flexes in the right place to suit your foot.

> Stand up and down on your toes and watch out for heel lift and abrasion.

> Kick into the floor hard (with permission) to test for toes hitting the end when front-pointing or walking downhill.

> Try standing on a small edge to test for support in a climbing situation.

> For low-volume feet some models offer additional tongue padding or thicker foot-beds.

> For general fit improvement try customised moulded foot-beds.

> Unlike rock shoes, winter boots are usually the same size as your street shoes or half a size bigger to allow for thick socks.

Starting Out

Equipment

Mountain Safety

Ice · Style·Ethics

Ice · Techniques

Mixed · Style·Ethics

Mixed · Techniques

The Mind

Training

Destinations

Sport mixed / fruit boots

Racy mixed boots with an integral bolt-on crampon (sometimes known as fruit boots) are standard equipment for sport mixed climbing. The weight saving they offer gives a massive advantage on steep terrain, along with rockshoe-like performance and sensitivity. The only snag, is that they will shred everything in your pack unless you keep them in a special protector bag, and you will also have to walk-in wearing something more appropriate.

Most fruit-boots have light and relatively flexible midsoles so don't expect a rigid platform to stand-on and prepare for a calf-pump, should you ever be unfortunate enough to use them on slabs.

You will also notice that you have less kicking power on ice (rather like swinging an axe with no head weight) so beware using them on long ice pitches. Further weight is saved from the minimalist crampon fittings with short points, and again, don't expect the world from these on sustained ice and avoid walking on hazardous terrain.

Most fruit boots have minimal insulation, which is fine for short climbing bursts, but cold feet are to be expected if you're tempted to use them on multi-pitch routes. Ethical issues regarding the use of fruit boots mostly surround the inclusion of heel spurs that tend to make steep mixed routes significantly easier. For more on the ethics of heel spurs see page 176.

D.I.Y. fruit boots

Some manufacturers offer bolt-on crampon kits for making your own fruit boots, but you'll need to grind the soles off an appropriate pair of mid-stiffness climbing boots first. A shoe resoler should be able to help with removing the sole from a pair of shoes, but for your first effort, be prepared to set a weekend aside for this!

Taking things to extremes, some climbers have even bolted just the front half of a crampon kit to approach shoes or chunky rock shoes. The weight saving is well worth it and the absence of the rear points reduces snagging on clothing when executing figure-of-four moves (see page page 202). This should be regarded as the absolute extreme of how far the gear should be pushed and don't expect any stability or performance on ice or vertical terrain. Fruit boots will make technical rock moves easier, but can only cope with short sections of ice, preferably where that ice has been 'hooked out' by previous ascents removing the need to kick new foot placements.

Fruit boots offer lightness and precision for the most technical mixed climbs.

Starting Out

Equipment

Mountain Safety

Ice : Style-Ethics

Ice : Techniques

Mixed : Style-Ethics

Mixed : Techniques

The Mind

Training

Destinations

Neil Gresham climbing *Slaughterhouse,* M8+, Canada with a pair of D.I.Y. fruit boots.

Gloves

Cold hands are now much less of an issue in ice and mixed climbing due to the development of leash-less tools and superior gloves. Nonetheless, glove selection is still crucial.

There is the constant need to balance warmth and water resistance with feel and dexterity. Many who use leashes find keeping their hands warm to be a constant battle, even with thicker gloves, but leash-less climbing makes it possible to get the blood back into your hands more readily and hence opens up new options for thinner gloves. Keeping your hands warm is as much a result of skill and technique as the choice of gloves that you make.

Softshell gloves

These are a great all-round option for leash-less climbing on anything other than very cold or wet days owing to their improved sensitivity compared with insulated shell gloves. This style of glove may have a stretch membrane but they are unlikely to be taped. They are ideal for routes with both ice and mixed pitches where you need an optimum blend of warmth and dexterity. Some models also have knuckle padding. Expect a snugger fit than you would get with a shell glove.

Insulated hardshell gloves

These are usually the best choice for water ice (especially with leashes) or for very cold or wet days, but worst for dexterity and hard mixed climbing. It may prove difficult, or frightening, to grip your axes securely when leash-less climbing with thick gloves.

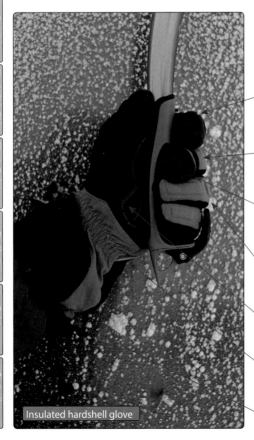

Stitching on back of fingers for durability (not on fingertips)

Loop on finger for clipping to harness

Hardshell material, fully taped, fixed synthetic lining (that doesn't pull out when you remove your hands)

Knuckle padding

Grippy palm

Ergonomic shape

Insulated hardshell glove

Full coverage cuffs with single-pull closure

Starting Out · Equipment · Mountain Safety · Ice : Style-Ethics · Ice : Techniques · Mixed : Style-Ethics · Mixed : Techniques · The Mind · Training · Destinations

Neoprene gloves

Lightweight 'neoprene' style gloves

'Thinny' neoprene gloves are ideal for general mixed climbing where maximum grip adhesion is required. They also offer high dexterity for clipping or placing trad gear. Good thinny neoprenes have snug cuffs to prevent snow entry and a grippy palm material. They are unlikely to be warm, waterproof or protective enough for ice climbing on most days, although they may work well as liners below a shell glove as part of a glove system. A good option is to use a system with neoprene gloves for leading and shell gloves (with removable insulation) to slip over the top when belaying and seconding.

Sport mixed gloves

These are the very thinnest 'cycling style' gloves that serve only one purpose, which is to provide maximum grip adhesion. The palm material should be covered in sticky 'patches' and cuff closure should be Velcro to prevent slippage. The warmth afforded by these gloves will be almost negligible but the reason to wear them is because they provide better grip than climbing with bare hands, and they will protect your skin from developing calluses.

The thinner gloves are, the snugger they should fit. But there should be no spare material at the end of the fingers or bagginess in the palms of any technical climbing gloves. You should be able to open your hand fully and watch out for excessive tightness in the palm which may cause 'thumb cramps' when climbing.

Dachsteins

Dachstein gloves are still popular for moderate level ice climbing as they are cheap, hardwearing and offer a reasonable degree of warmth when wet.

Belay gloves

A versatile system is to take heavier, warmer gloves or mitts for seconding and belaying, and to climb in lighter gloves. Whatever your glove system, it always pays to take a spare pair!

Liner gloves

Fleece gloves are good for the walk-in although Windstopper gloves (or something with a membrane) will be better if the snow is deep and you need to put your hands down for balance. Always wear thin liner gloves for gearing up. You may also decide to take a spare pair in your jacket on the climb, as they take up so little room.

Glove caution

Make every effort to keep snow out of your gloves; keep them in your jacket whenever possible. This is your best tip for avoiding hotaches. When carrying belay gloves on your harness don't clip them into their wrist draw cords as they will fill up with snow - instead use the finger loops.

Starting Out

Equipment

Mountain Safety

Ice : Style-Ethics

Ice : Techniques

Mixed : Style-Ethics

Mixed : Techniques

The Mind

Training

Destinations

Starting Out

Equipment

Mountain Safety

Ice : Style-Ethics

Ice : Techniques

Mixed : Style-Ethics

Mixed : Techniques

The Mind

Training

Destinations

Clothing systems for walking-in

Gaiters

Every effort should be made to protect your feet from snow dropping into your boots so gaiters are essential when the snow is fresh or heavy. They may also save you from a humiliating U-turn on Scottish bog trotting days, unless you don't mind ascending a grade V looking like a mud wrestler! Go for high ventilation materials (such as Gore-tex Proshell) and look out for models with side-venting systems. Velcro closure is infinitely easier to operate than zip closure.

Tim Emmett keeping his feet dry thanks to his gaiters whilst wading towards the crags at Freissinieres, France.

Light membrane leg wear

On damp or windy days, you will be prone to over-heating if you walk-in wearing full shell gear, so an alternative is to wear breathable lightweight membrane materials such as Windstropper NTS light. These work especially well on your legs which are less prone to sweating than your upper body, but more susceptible to picking up moisture from surrounding snow.

Regardless of your system, you will always get sweaty on the walk-in, especially round your back, and it is worth taking a spare thermal top to change into when gearing up at the base of the route. If you don't do this it will put you under pressure to make constant adjustments to your clothing on the approach to make sure that you don't spend the rest of the day in wet thermals.

Headwear

Ice and mixed climbing helmets should be well-fitting, lightweight, with an easy size adjustment system, and with ventilation and head-torch attachment points. Check that the brim covers your head fully, to protect from ice debris. Foam designs are lighter but polycarbonate helmets may be slightly more compact and have a tougher outer shell.

There is a tendency to overheat in helmets with a standard thick fleece hat, or get cold with no hat at all, so it's well worth taking a thin 'helmet-liner' as well as a fleece hat so that you have options. For bad weather days, a full coverage Windstopper hat with ear flaps and a drawstring that fits under your chin can be great in conjunction with a fleece neck tube for the walk-in. If it gets worse then a balaclava is a claustrophobic but necessary last resort.

Jon Bracey opts for goggles to keep out spindrift while belaying in Glen Coe, Scotland.

Eyewear

If you are short-sighted, try to wear contact lenses as glasses will constantly mist up when ice climbing, especially on wet days. In general it can be worth taking goggles, or a visor, to protect your eyes from ice splinters or a bouncing tool when mixed climbing. On high wind days goggles may prove essential particularly when topping out into a blizzard.

Starting Out · Equipment · Mountain Safety · Ice : Style-Ethics · Ice : Techniques · Mixed : Style-Ethics · Mixed : Techniques · The Mind · Training · Destinations

Tools

Axes

Your axes are your hand extensions and are perhaps the most important pieces of equipment to get right. There are characteristics which make an axe more suitable for ice or for mixed climbing, like shape and pick angle, and there are characteristics that make an axe more suitable for different individuals like weight, balance and grip diameter. An understanding of ice axe mechanics is essential to enable you to match your tools to the style of climbing and climb better on the day.

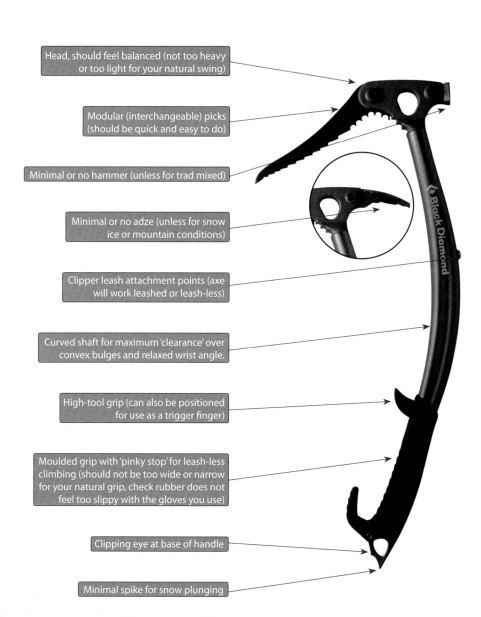

Head, should feel balanced (not too heavy or too light for your natural swing)

Modular (interchangeable) picks (should be quick and easy to do)

Minimal or no hammer (unless for trad mixed)

Minimal or no adze (unless for snow ice or mountain conditions)

Clipper leash attachment points (axe will work leashed or leash-less)

Curved shaft for maximum 'clearance' over convex bulges and relaxed wrist angle.

High-tool grip (can also be positioned for use as a trigger finger)

Moulded grip with 'pinky stop' for leash-less climbing (should not be too wide or narrow for your natural grip, check rubber does not feel too slippy with the gloves you use)

Clipping eye at base of handle

Minimal spike for snow plunging

Starting Out

Equipment

Mountain Safety

Ice : Style-Ethics

Ice : Techniques

Mixed : Style-Ethics

Mixed : Techniques

The Mind

Training

Destinations

Sandy Ogilvie making a night-time ascent of *Montmorency Falls*, WI3, Quebec, Canada.

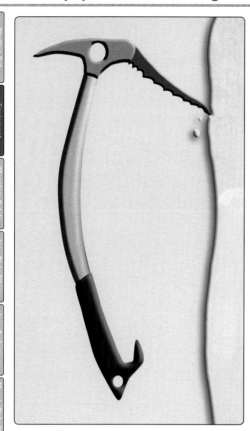

Optimum shape for ice

> Pure curve - allows a natural swing with maximum shaft clearance.
> Subtle Z-bend - less clearance but high-tool grip option.
> Shallow pick angle - easy swing and ice penetration but reduced hooking power.

Optimum weight and balance for ice

For average ice conditions, lighter tools are less fatiguing to lift and swing provided they are kept razor sharp, although larger people sometimes prefer the feel of a heavier tool. An axe with a heavier head may also prove to be an energy saver on hard brittle ice days. Bolt-on head weights are good for matching a tool to the ice conditions. Balance is also an important issue - if the weight of the head is too far forward then the tool will swing oddly but modern tools are getting better and better at eliminating this. Head weight and balance are far more noticable factors than overall tool weight.

Poor shapes for ice

❶ Straight shaft - produces a bent and fatiguing wrist angle and poor clearance over bulges.

❷ Acute Z-bend - results in a poor swing and poor clearance over convex features.

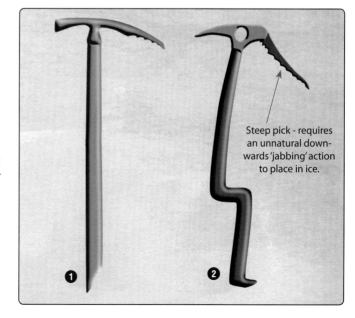

Steep pick - requires an unnatural downwards 'jabbing' action to place in ice.

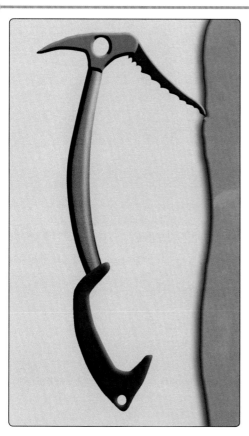

Optimum shape for sport mixed

> Acute Z-bend with high-tool - most ergonomic grip angle
> Steep pick for hooking
> As light as possible
> Minimal or no adze and hammer

Optimum for trad mixed

The modern approach is to opt for the same style of leash-less tool as used for sport mixed, although traditionalists may favour a slightly less curved or bent shaft for ease for clearance when hammering pegs or manoeuvring in confined cracks. Clipper leashes can increase options for placing gear but pick a tool that will work leashed or leash-less. It is also important to go for a system that allows larger adzes and hammers to be fitted.

Poor shapes for sport mixed:

❶ Radical looking but poorly conceived leash-less shape - shaft angle changes when you use high-tool handle, rendering it useless.

❷ Straight shaft - fatiguing wrist angle, no high-tool option.

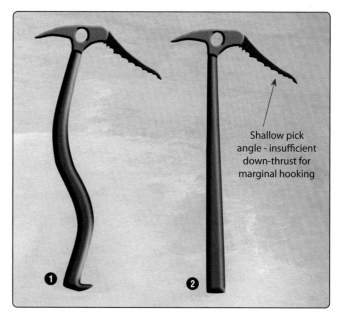

Shallow pick angle - insufficient down-thrust for marginal hooking

Starting Out
Equipment
Mountain Safety
Ice : Style-Ethics
Ice : Techniques
Mixed : Style-Ethics
Mixed : Techniques
The Mind
Training
Destinations

Starting Out

Equipment

Mountain Safety

Ice : Style - Ethics

Ice : Techniques

Mixed : Style - Ethics

Mixed : Techniques

The Mind

Training

Destinations

Axes for Alpinists

Alpine climbers, or those doing very long ice routes in the mountains, may prefer the simple curved shaft axe for its ease of swing and plungability. The high-tool design of a typical leash-less tool may prove a cumbersome obstruction.

Leash-less conversion kits

Some classic tools have bolt-on plastic components that can be used to convert them into leash-less tools. By fitting a 'pinky stop' and 'high-tool' grip stop to your current classic axe you may save yourself the spend of a new tool. Note that these are nearly always specific to each model.

Pinky stop set-up

Check that the pinky-stop is not too tight or too loose for your hands with the range of gloves that you intend to use. Note that some climbers prefer a snug jam-like fit whereas other prefer a little more space.

Trigger fingers

A trigger finger is an optional grip designed to provide additional support by allowing the user to place their index finger above the grip. Some insist that trigger-fingers dramatically increase their energy saving by improving grip adhesion, others find them awkward and clumsy, or even painful. There are two positions for setting up a trigger finger: one is to have a separate trigger finger and high-tool grip stop, the other is to have a shared trigger-finger and high-tool grip stop. The latter setup is achieved by positioning the high-tool stop as low as possible to enable it to be reached with the index finger. This option allows you to switch between a trigger-finger and a normal grip to reduce

An ice axe with an optional 'trigger finger'

the strain in your forearms by using the muscles in two different ways. It is vital to experiment with trigger fingers to see if they work for you before committing to using them on a route.

Third tools

Some climbers will carry a third tool in case they drop or break an axe but most climbers prefer to take the chance and save weight and clutter. Be sure to carry it within a rucksack if you go for this option.

Different tools

A few climbers will experiment with different types of axe in each hand - for example, a straighter axe for hammering and a curved one for superior swinging. There are endless possibilities but most prefer the simplicity of identical tools, with a hammer on one and an adze on the other.

Axe heads

Aluminium axe heads tend to be fractionally lighter than steel but they are prone to becoming scratched and burred when driven into cracks on trad mixed routes and this may make modular parts difficult to remove.

Starting Out
Equipment
Mountain · Safety
Ice : Style-Ethics
Ice · Techniques
Mixed · Style-Ethics
Mixed · Techniques
The Mind
Training
Destinations

Sue Nott using traditional curved shaft tools for a more comfortable swing on *Pinnochio*, ED, in the French Alps.

Picks

Most manufacturers supply two different specification picks for their modular ice axes: one which is thinner and sharper (sometimes coded 'B') and one that is fatter and tougher (sometimes coded 'T'). These categorisations often cause some confusion.

B-spec picks

B-spec picks are designed to give better ice penetration, but their sharpness will also lead to greater holding power for marginal hooking placements when mixed climbing. It is vital to note that B-spec picks are not approved by manufacturers for sideways 'torquing' so great care should be exercised on certain mixed routes. Note that B should be regarded as the minimum spec for a technical tool.

T-spec picks

T-spec picks are the approved choice for mixed routes where the picks are being torqued heavily and frequently - for example Scottish style. They may also be a prudent choice for longer mountain mixed routes where breaking a pick could have serious consequences.

Goulotte picks

Though less popular these days, some still swear by the properties of the 'duck-nosed' Goulotte picks for poor quality snow ice or neve climbing. These picks are likely to represent a hazard on modern mixed routes!

B-spec picks

T-spec picks

A Goulotte pick

Spare picks

The decision to carry a spare pick is always a tricky one not least because it is difficult to carry something that may stab you if you fall off. Most climbers don't bother on shorter routes and, on long routes, it is best to keep it buried in a rucksack. Never carry a pick in your pocket unless it is very well wrapped or taped up. Practise changing picks and make sure you select a brand of axe that isn't a nightmare to change on the hill.

Hammers and adzes

Modern tools come with minimal 'sized-down' adzes and hammers, and will suit the requirements of steep ice or sport mixed where the adzes and hammers are barely used at all. However, check that they are part of a modular system when you buy them as you may wish to slot in some heftier affairs for trad mixed, or snow ice routes, where you will need to place pegs and do a lot of clearing or digging with the adze.

Andy Nisbet using the traditional one hammer/one axe combo to traverse into *Easy Gully*, Grade I, on Aonach Mor in Scotland.

Starting Out

Equipment

Mountain Safety

Ice : Style-Ethics

Ice : Techniques

Mixed : Style-Ethics

Mixed : Techniques

The Mind

Training

Destinations

Pick filing

Picks should be kept razor sharp using a file, especially for mixed climbing and for cold, brittle ice days. The sharper the pick, the more energy you will save. For safety reasons, most picks are not sharp enough straight from the manufacturer so you will need to modify them.

The easiest way to stabilise the tool for filing is to rest the pick across the shaft of the other tool. This will help you avoid vibrating it excessively or doing an uneven job. Use a large flat file for the pick and top blade and, if possible, a small round file for the teeth.

See page 70 for crampon sharpening.

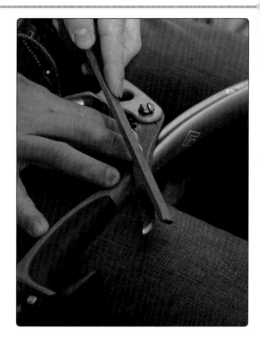

✔ Sharp point and front blade, rounded at top to minimise snagging.

✔ Steeply inclined sharks tooth for grabbing down (created by filing away first tooth).

✔ Sharp top edge to assist extraction.

✔ Teeth bevelled and slightly reduced in size.

✔ Teeth for 'can-opener' moves.

✘ Blunt end and top edge.

✘ Angular top.

✘ Front teeth blunt and too long.

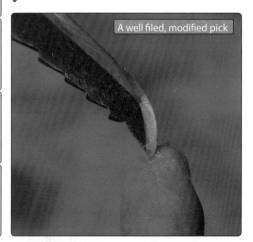

A well filed, modified pick

A blunt, poorly maintained pick

Filing notes

> The front point of the pick must always strike first so keep checking for alignment as you shape it.

> Making a 'sharks tooth' usually means losing the first tooth but far better to do this than make a flimsy 'mini first tooth'.

> Filing and re-filing shortens the pick. It's just about okay to lose the second tooth in order to make a new 'sharks tooth' but once this has blown then it's time for a new pick.

> Bevelling the teeth effectively sharpens them and will increase holding power.

> Making the teeth smaller will reduce snagging and assist removal but don't over-do this or you'll sacrifice holding power.

> Remember that modifying a pick will void the manufacturer's warranty and that the more heavily you do it, the more you will weaken it.

> Use less modified picks for big, serious or committing routes and save the 'kitchen-knifes' for when you're next to a bolt.

Well maintained tools pay dividends for Kenton Cool on *Patri Left-hand*, WI4, Cogne, Italy.

Starting Out

Equipment

Mountain Safety

Ice · Style·Ethics

Ice · Techniques

Mixed · Style·Ethics

Mixed · Techniques

The Mind

Training

Destinations

Clipper leashes

The issue of leashes becomes a personal one after all the debate has been considered. The merits of both leashed and leash-less climbing for ice are discussed in detail on page 120.

On the whole, leashes are becoming a thing of the past for shorter technical climbs owing to the array of advantages offered by going leash-less. But consensus is arising that if you must use leashes then clipper leashes are the ones to go for. Fixed leashes can be difficult to escape from to place pro, and most designs are prone to freezing although they do have advantages in certain situations.

A good clipper leash will offer a quick escape yet it will be secure enough for you to drop the tool without fear of accidental unclipping. Early designs were unsatisfactory and runaway axes were common, in particular with the ones that relied on small wire-gate karabiners. These designs were okay provided you kept a constant eye on the leash and checked that it wasn't twisted before you released the tool.

The two shop tests for clipper leashes are ease of operation with gloved hands, and accidental unclipping when dropping. For the latter test you should physically try to make it unclip itself. Regarding freezing, there will always be a chance whatever the design. So the golden tip is to use a tool that will still work leash-less if you run into trouble.

Clipper leash set-up length

The classic mistake is for the leash to be too short and this will reduce swinging performance and increase grip fatigue. Set it so your hand sits comfortably in the leash-less 'pinky stop' at the bottom of the grip, even if the leash feels fractionally slack. If the axe doesn't have a 'pinky stop' then the little finger should be half-over the bottom of the grip. Set it and re-set it for the gloves you'll be using on the day.

Leash attachment

The clipper leash attachment point is a critical thing to get right. Be wary of designs that don't give you a degree of choice over this. The key point is that the clipping mechanism sits perfectly into your thumb and index finger when you try to grasp it. If it's too long then you'll have to flick it awkwardly to latch it and if it's too short then don't even bother trying!

Usually, when the set-up is right the leash is attached approximately halfway down the shaft, or very slightly towards the head of the axe. In an ideal world, the balance point halfway down the shaft will also represent the correct length for clipping, because this will also mean that the tool will hang horizontally when you let go of it and will return easily to your hand. But if you have to sacrifice this in the interest of getting the right length for clipping then make sure you do. This may all sound a bit fussy but it actually makes the difference between cruising steep ice pitches and having a total epic.

Starting Out

Equipment

Mountain Safety

Ice · Style · Ethics

Ice Techniques

Mixed · Style · Ethics

Mixed · Techniques

The Mind

Training

Destinations

Sandy Ogilvie appreciating his clipper leashes on an unnamed steep WI5 at Kaldakinn, Iceland.

Crampons

The first priority in selecting a crampon for ice is to find the right type, and the second issue is boot-crampon compatibility. A technical climbing crampon must have step-in bindings in order to get a secure attachment. For the majority of ice and mixed situations the best choice is crampons with modular front-points that can be converted from dual to mono, as well as altering the length and spacing. These should be vertical and toothed as opposed to flat; although classic flat front-points may offer more purchase on poorly consolidated snow ice.

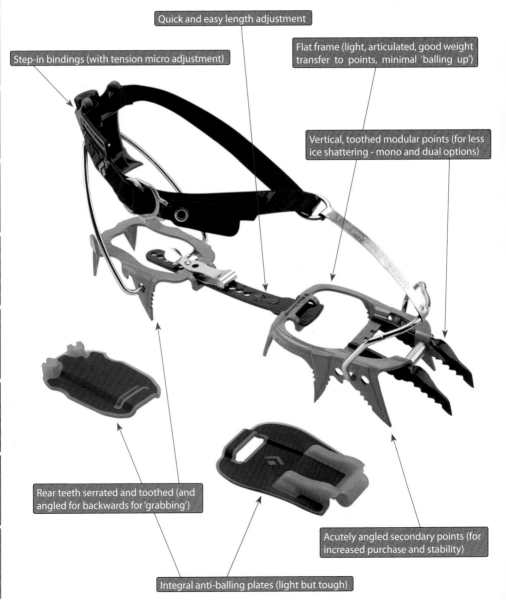

Quick and easy length adjustment

Flat frame (light, articulated, good weight transfer to points, minimal 'balling up')

Step-in bindings (with tension micro adjustment)

Vertical, toothed modular points (for less ice shattering - mono and dual options)

Rear teeth serrated and toothed (and angled for backwards for 'grabbing')

Acutely angled secondary points (for increased purchase and stability)

Integral anti-balling plates (light but tough)

Starting Out

Equipment

Mountain Safety

Ice : Style-Ethics

Ice : Techniques

Mixed : Style-Ethics

Mixed : Techniques

The Mind

Training

Destinations

Starting Out

Equipment

Mountain Safety

Ice : Style·Ethics

Ice : Techniques

Mixed : Style·Ethics

Mixed : Techniques

The Mind

Training

Destinations

Kristoffer Szilas showing well balanced footwork
on *Gargoyle Wall* VI,6, Ben Nevis, Scotland.

Starting Out

Equipment

Mountain Safety

Ice : Style-Ethics

Ice : Techniques

Mixed : Style-Ethics

Mixed : Techniques

The Mind

Training

Destinations

Lightweight variations

Some crampon systems have been designed with lighter weight step-in binding systems but these can be a little flimsy and fiddly.

Mono or dual points?

Dual points may provide more stability for long slabby pitches, and will work well on 'plasticy' ice that is flat and homogenous. Monopoints will have the upper-hand on brittle, thin or featured ice where accuracy and minimal shattering are required.

Monos also provide the option for pivoting on your feet, and for standing in pick placements on verglas to reduce shattering. Dual-points are good for beginners (though not essential) and monos for intermediate to advanced ice climbers.

Mono-point set-up

Mono-points work best if the point is offset slightly towards the inside edge of the boot. The point should effectively run underneath the ball of the big toe in order for optimum balance and power to be obtained.

Dual point width spacing

Beware setting dual points too close together as this may cause excessive shattering on brittle ice. However, if your dual points are too wide apart then they may feel clumsy and difficult to control on featured ice. The mid width spacing setting is nearly always best.

Point length

For most situations a medium length setting will work well, however on brittle ice or verglas, or on super-hard mixed routes, you may wish to set the points back in order to minimise leverage and reduce the feeling of clumsiness. When climbing softer snow ice, or for warmer ice days, you may wish to lengthen the points to increase penetration.

Crampons for trad mixed climbing

For trad mixed, many still prefer flat, stubby, filed-down dual points seeing as these line up well on ledges and keep your weight very close to the wall. The modern take is to go for mono points that are set up vertically to experience the advantages for slim cracks, pockets and for pivoting on holds. It is well worth experimenting with both options.

Mono point

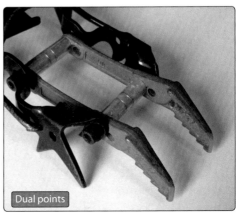

Dual points

Boot-crampon compatibility

Boot stiffness

A fitting system is sometimes used in shops to match boots to crampons, where boots are graded from 1 to 3 according to stiffness, and crampons are then matched accordingly. This can be useful but it also causes confusion when assessing the lighter weight winter climbing boots and crampons that lie in between the 2 and 3 categories.

The key issue for winter climbing is that the boot is stiff enough to take a *step-in crampon* (a modern step-in crampon is not dependent on the straps for fit, they are only present as back-up in case the crampon pops off). Traditionalists still insist on calling the preferred type of boot 'fully rigid' but the reality is that the best ice climbing boots have a moderate amount of flex in order to save weight and improve walking comfort. The main thing, when choosing a lighter more technical winter boot, is that it is not blatantly a winter walking boot in terms of shape and features as well as stiffness.

A typical lightweight mixed climbing boot and monopoint crampon combination.

Crampon fit

Good ice climbing crampons are shaped left and right and are designed with the popular brands of climbing boot in mind. Fit only tends to be an issue on the very largest and smallest sizes but it is still always worth checking in store. Make sure that the points run around the edge of the boot and that the foot will not be un-balanced as a result of points that are poorly positioned.

The step-in bindings should line up well with the binding attachments on the boot. You may wish to fit the crampon to different pairs of boots so a quick and easy length adjustment is an important feature. Note that some boot and crampon brands offer an integral compatible system that can be effective, providing the boot fits well and the crampon suits your climbing style. Crampon fit tends to be more of an issue on smaller or larger boots. In particular, the heels of small boots are prone to sliding too far through the rear posts of the crampon. Note that some crampon makes offer extra long or extra curved spacer bars to fit larger or more asymmetric models respectively.

Starting Out
Equipment
Mountain Safety
Ice : Style-Ethics
Ice : Techniques
Mixed : Style-Ethics
Mixed : Techniques
The Mind
Training
Destinations

Crampon sharpening

It is important to keep your crampons sharp for ice climbing, to improve holding power, minimise shattering and reduce the need for hard kicking. For mixed climbing it is equally vital to minimise the chance of a foot sparking off a sloping rock hold. Pay particular attention to front points, sharpening them the same way as you would your axe picks (see page 62). The secondary points are also very important and can be sharpened by taking the file to them at an angle of 45˚.

✔ Sharp point and front blade, rounded at top to minimise snagging

✔ Steeply inclined sharks tooth for grabbing down (created by filing away first tooth)

✔ Sharp secondary points

✘ Blunt end and top edge

✘ Front teeth badly wearing

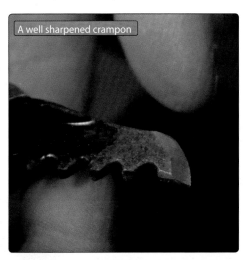

A well sharpened crampon

A blunt, poorly maintained crampon

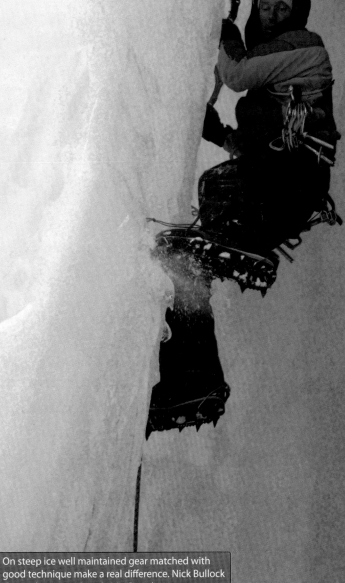

On steep ice well maintained gear matched with good technique make a real difference. Nick Bullock shows the way at Bear Spirit, Canada.

Starting Out

Equipment

Mountain Safety

Ice : Style-Ethics

Ice : Techniques

Mixed : Style-Ethics

Mixed : Techniques

The Mind

Training

Destinations

Protection

Ice screws

Ice screws are the main form of protection for icefall climbing. They consist of a solid tube with a serrated end and a sharp screw thread around its lower section. They are placed by being screwed manually into the ice often using some sort of winding handle (BD Express Ice Screws right).

The first priority for ice screws is that they must be sharp and the second is that they have a good wind-in system. Ice screws are blunted when they 'bottom out' on the rock, so it is worth carrying different lengths and assessing the ice thickness before you make a placement. Good ice screws are finely polished inside to reduce friction with the core of ice and some also have a slight taper to assist with this.

Ice screw features:

> Sharp teeth
> Polished interior with taper to reduce friction with ice core
> Wind-in system
> Different lengths

On standard 'fat' icefalls it is best to rack up mainly with medium length screws and to go light on both long and short screws. Long screws are good for belays but they can be tiring to place on the lead so it's usually worth carrying only one or two.

It may be worth carrying more long screws on days when the ice is soft or aerated. Short screws don't inspire much confidence, but they are the easiest to place and can be solid in compact ice. They are also essential on thin ice and on icy mixed routes. It can be worth racking a short

screw where it can be reached easily for a quick 'panic placement' on steep ice if you're dangerously pumped.

Starting Out

Equipment

Mountain Safety

Ice : Style-Ethics

Ice : Techniques

Mixed : Style-Ethics

Mixed : Techniques

The Mind

Training

Destinations

Ice screw sharpening

Some manufacturers offer a re-sharpening service (for a fee) but this is usually for their own screws. Only attempt to sharpen ice screws yourself if they are badly burred, as there is a chance you will make them worse. With a vice and an extremely narrow file, you can make them serviceable but you'll never restore them to their original glory. Some manufacturers offer detailed notes on sharpening or have video clips on their websites. It may be possible to track down a specialist engineer in your locality who will have an appropriate sharpening rig. If you're keen to climb as well as possible on steep ice routes then you may have to bite the bullet and accept that your screws will need to be replaced regularly.

Ice screw rackers

These usually come in the form of large plastic karabiners that can be fitted to thread loops on specialist ice harnesses. They sound gimmicky but if you've ever tried removing, with one hand, an ice screw from a standard karabiner clipped to a gear loop, you'll see just how essential they are. You may need up to four and a good system is to use 1 for long screws, 2 for medium and 1 for short.

The best screw rackers even have a 'shelf' for holding screws out of the way while you search for the one you need. A good variation on this system is a 'frame' which houses 2 ice screw rackers and slots over your harness. Ice screw rackers are also very handy for clipping your axes to when abseiling off. Holster-style systems for individual ice screws also exist but most find that these take up too much harness space.

Screw racking tip

A great system is to mark your blunter screws with tape and rack them on a separate racker, usually nearer the back of the harness. This way you can save them for belays or for placements when you're in a comfortable position. You can then rack your sharper ones nearer the front of your harness and use them mid-pitch when the going is tougher.

Double clipper ice screw racking system

Starting Out

Equipment

Mountain Safety

Ice : Style-Ethics

Ice : Techniques

Mixed : Style-Ethics

Mixed : Techniques

The Mind

Training

Destinations

Hand-hooks

A hand-hook is the ice-climbing equivalent of a sky hook. These stainless steel talons have serrated teeth like an ice pick and a clipping eye that is threaded with a sewn sling.

Hand-hooks may provide the only protection on very thin ice and they can also provide an emergency 'panic rest' by slotting them into a pick placement and tapping them home. Note that it is a far better idea to do this than clipping into an axe. If you need to leave a back-up anchor behind, hand-hooks can provide a cheaper alternative to an ice screw. Hand-hooks also have useful properties for mixed climbing such as driving into icy cracks or frozen turf.

When the ice is very thin a handhook may offer the only feasible protection.

Deadmen

We introduced Deadmen when talking about basic belay techniques on page 32.

Deadmen may prove to be essential on long Scottish style snow-ice routes that require belays on steep snow. Deadmen should be treated as precautionary anchors at the best of times, although they can be solid if sunk deep into solid neve. They are not needed on the vast majority of short technical ice and mixed climbs.

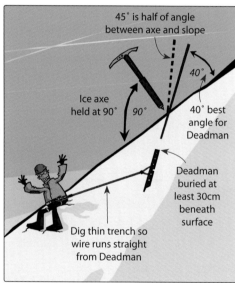

45° is half of angle between axe and slope

Ice axe held at 90°

90°

40°

40° best angle for Deadman

Deadman buried at least 30cm beneath surface

Dig thin trench so wire runs straight from Deadman

it might pull out. If and when the cable feels taught, dig yourself a snow seat and brace yourself constantly when belaying. In the event of a fall always attempt to absorb the weight yourself to minimise the loading on the anchor. A Buried-axe belay (page 33) may be used as an alternative, or to back up a Deadman. When using any snow anchor consider using a waist belay to give a dynamic belay and help reduce shock on to the snow anchors.

Placing a Deadman

Practise placing a Deadman before using one on a route. Assess the snow for soundness and depth and check that the placement site correlates with your intended belay position. Dig a hole, with a flat bottom and an open front. Place the Deadman as deep and far back as possible, sinking it at an angle of 40° to the slope. Cut a slot for the cable and bed it in. Take great care not to lose your footing when doing this and always suspect that

Practising placing a Deadman.
Photo by George McEwan.

"Ice screws do work!"
- Ian Parnell

I must have climbed over three-hundred pitches of ice but I'd never taken a fall, that was until an entertaining night out in Iceland. I'd travelled to this frozen isle for a week to check out the rumours of an ice climbing paradise. What we found was indeed something very special. Rising above the black sand beach of Kaldakinn stretches route after route of perfect ice.

We spent the first three days picking off first ascents under clear winter skies before Iceland threw us a curve ball. Perhaps we should have been expecting it. Within thirty miles of the Arctic Circle, Iceland has some of the World's most extreme weather. It was now one of those occasions: horizontal snow, driving winds and the thermometer dropping down to -25 meant no climbing that day. And the next as the drifts built up against our door. The following dawn, our last at Kaldakinn, saw temperatures drop a notch lower and with the snow showing no sign of abating, frustrations grew. Packing our bags we opted to set off for Reykjavik and the airport early concerned that the last three days of snow fall might have blocked us in.

We were right to be worried. Hours passed by as we crept across sheet ice and dodged the snowdrifts. Near the end of a full day of driving Ramón, our keenest team member, noticed we were within half an hour of Haukadalur, one of the first ice climbing areas to be developed on the island. Despite the late hour it seemed worth a look.

We weren't disappointed. The snow had stopped so we ignored the setting sun and minus twenty temperatures and grabbed our axes. In the gathering gloom I managed a long pitch of WI5 but to my left Ramon had snatched the real prize; a fragile metre-wide pillar. It looked fantastic I had to have a go at it myself. Psyche had got the better of any grip I might have had on reality. I ignored the fatigue I felt on the WI5, ignored the plummeting cold that was turning the pillar into a brittle bombshell and finally I ignored the darkness, donning a headtorch for my lead.

Everything went smoothly until about halfway up the pillar, rather than the usual expected pump, my arms felt numb. Pump I knew how to cope with but this new feeling drew a blank. This was the point at which I should have bailed. Instead I ran my feet up high, cranked up on my rubbery arms and pressed on. Hyperventilating now I spied one of Ramon's ice screw holes and desperately zipped in my own. There was none of the reassuring bite of a fresh screw placement but at least it was something to clip and now I only had three metres of pillar left to climb. Fighting for each placement I edged higher and higher. The further I made it from my wobbly screw the shorter my swings became and the more desperate became my footwork. I was now eyeballing the end of the pillar but there was no way I was going to make it. It felt like someone had flicked a switch shutting off all power. As my axes slipped between my fingers it dawned on me with a shudder of terror I was about to take a lob on ice and as the wobbly screw was bound to rip it would be a monster!

Slumped on the end of the rope I eventually calmed down enough to realise I was still in one piece and more surprisingly that I'd only taken a mere twenty footer; the dodgy screw had held! The monster had been averted, ice screws in solid ice really do work!

Starting Out

Equipment

Mountain Safety

Ice · Style · Ethics

Ice · Techniques

Mixed · Techniques

Mixed Style-Ethics

The Mind

Training

Destinations

Ian Parnell climbing an unnamed WI5 at Kaldakinn, Iceland.
Photo by Alastair Lee **www.PosingProductions.com**

Rock protection

For most trad mixed routes, especially the snowed up Scottish style, you will be racking up in much the same way as you do for rock climbing, with a full selection of wired nuts and cams.

For thinly-iced routes, that offer the potential for limited amounts of rock gear, you will be stripping your rock rack down and combining it with more pegs and a minimal selection of ice pro. Here are the must-know pointers for using rock gear in winter.

Cams

Cams are dangerous in icy or heavily snowed-up cracks because they simply don't work. You can usually clear the snow but it is rarely possible to chip away sufficient ice. Hexes provide an essential alternative.

Hexes

Hexes are a superb alternative to cams, especially on verglas days when the rock has a thin coating of ice. They can also be hammered into place (like old-school 'Bong' pegs) in marginal or icy placements.

Nuts

Two sets of nuts are standard for most trad mixed routes and these are usually racked in groups of small-to-medium and medium-to-large. A single or even a half-set may be okay for bold thinly-iced mixed routes and a half set (with alternate sizes) may suffice for ice routes with the possibility of the odd rock runner or belay. Beware that nuts will flick straight out of icy cracks so go the extra mile with cleaning.

RPs and micro gear

Small brass wires can be used as an alternative to knifeblade pegs, when the cracks are shallow, or you need to move fast. They can also be tapped or bashed into place with your pick, like placing a copperhead.

Pegs

A minimal selection of pegs will be useful on most trad mixed routes, especially the thinly-iced ones. A couple of angles, a couple of lost arrows and two or three knifeblades will usually suffice (see page 28 for an illustration). A peg or two may also be handy on a sport mixed route that looks like it has been sparsely bolted. Many rock climbers who come to mixed climbing for the first time have limited or no experience of placing and removing pegs so give it a go somewhere appropriate before you get involved.

Placing a hex in an icy crack with the aid of your axe.

Starting Out

Equipment

Mountain Safety

Ice · Style·Ethics

Ice · Techniques

Mixed · Style·Ethics

Mixed · Techniques

The Mind

Training

Destinations

Protection is the priority for Olly Metherell on *Didgeridoo* VII,6, The Cairngorms, Scotland.

Other gear

Quickdraws

Wire-gate karabiners work best because they are light, they don't freeze and their wide gate opening means you are less likely to trap your gloved thumb when clipping.

Thin tapes are also good, simply because they weigh less when water-logged and frozen. Take loads of quickdraws on trad mixed routes but carry the same number of quickdraws as you have ice screws on standard ice pitches, plus one or two more and a couple of single karabiners for slings.

Slingdraws

A slingdraw is a quickdraw made from a 60cm sling. By placing one karabiner through the other and clipping the bight that is formed, the slingdraw can be shrunk to 1/3rd of its length and used like a short quickdraw and easily racked. You may find it easier to use if one karabiner is fixed in place and designated as the rope end. Slingdraws are great for quickly adding extra extension without messing around with slings. Slingdraws are not sold as a complete product, you will need to buy the component parts separately and arrange them yourself.

Slings

Long slings (120cm) are handy for threading large icicles and short slings (60cm) are essential for extending runners on featured ice. Short slings are also useful for smaller ice-threads, or tying off short screws in thin ice. Many climbers prefer to carry slings on karabiners rather than bandolier style around their neck, seeing as they are prone to tangling with a hood and helmet during removal.

Shock-tapes

Shock-tapes, or 'screamers', are special quickdraws that soften the impact of any fall. They are great when ice climbing, especially for use with short screws, or for days when the ice is fragile or soft.

Harnesses

Adjustable leg loops are universally recognised as an important feature for ice and mixed harnesses, although some sport mixed enthusiasts may wish to spend half an hour feeding fixed leg-loops over their fruit boots (page 48) in order to save the weight of a buckle! When fitting, check that there is sufficient adjustment range to accommodate extra clothing although you rarely (if ever) need to put your harness over a down jacket.

A good ice and mixed harness will have at least four gear loops and attachment points for ice screw rackers. The better designs feature closed-cell foam padding, rather than the sweat-absorbent linings that are common on summer harnesses, and which suck up water in winter. They may even have a water-resistant coating or plastic cover to prevent them from absorbing moisture from the outside.

Belay devices

Winter climbing has similar requirements for belay devices to summer climbing, only there are a few specific considerations.

'ATC style' modern belay plates, with extra friction options for skinny, or icy, ropes are the best all-round option. Plaquettes or 'Reverso style' belay plates that can be fixed directly into the anchor are great for bringing up two seconds at once.

Sport mixed climbers may find Grigris more functional, especially for prolonged stints of project belaying (take care with skinny ropes).

Use simple HMS screwgates with a wide gate opening for stuffing slings and ropes in and out with gloved hands. Stay clear of the 'quick-lock style' gates which will not earn their name with gloved hands when frozen.

Starting Out

Equipment

Mountain Safety

Ice · Style · Ethics

Ice · Techniques

Mixed · Style·Ethics

Mixed · Techniques

The Mind

Training

Destinations

Starting Out

Equipment

Mountain Safety

Ice : Style · Ethics

Ice : Techniques

Mixed : Style · Ethics

Mixed : Techniques

The Mind

Training

Destinations

Ropes

Double ropes

Most ice climbs are best tackled with a double rope system, primarily for making abseil descents. It is also useful to be able to clip thinner ropes into screws to reduce shock-loading in the event of a fall. When climbing with less experienced partners, a second rope may prove to be a life-saver in case a stray ice axe or crampon damages one of the ropes.

Double ropes are also the best option for the vast majority of trad mixed routes where the line may wander and you'll need to clip different ropes in order to reduce drag. When the rock is loose or sharp, having two ropes in the system is also a wise move. Single ropes may be quick and clutter free for ice, but that's about all. Double, or 'half', ropes are usually between 8mm and 9mm in diameter and it makes sense to go for a minimum of 60 metres in length in order to have the option of making long pitches and for reaching abseil stations in comfort. Longer ropes are also a good idea in case they receive axe or crampon damage and need to be chopped. Dry treatments are essential to reduce water-logging and freezing.

Twin ropes

'Skinny twins' are lighter and narrower than double ropes (typically 7 - 8mm in diameter) and hence manufacturers only advise that both ropes are clipped into the same karabiner for each runner. Twin ropes create the possibility for a very interesting and versatile system to be used on ice.

If the leader is confident that a screw is good they will clip both ropes, but if they suspect it is poor they can clip only one, taking advantage of maximum stretch properties in the rope, but potentially bending the manufacturers rules a little (note that 'officially' this is not recommended).

In general, great care is required when handling ultra-slim twin ropes. They can be difficult to hold falls if the ropes are clipped separately, especially if they are frozen and the belayer is wearing thick gloves. Belay devices with extra friction options are essential. Take particular care when abseiling.

Single ropes

Single ropes are the best option for sport mixed routes owing to their ease of clipping and handling. If you go for a very light and narrow single rope (9.1mm to 9.7mm) then take care when using a Grigri, which is not rated for use with ropes under 10mm, and try to keep it dry to prevent it from freezing - skinny singles can be 'slick' to handle at the best of times. It's also vital to take extra care not to catch them with points or picks.

Most climbers feel that 9.8mm to 10.5mm is the best diameter range for general sport mixed use, but the very keenest may wish to use a thicker single rope for working a route and a skinnier one for redpointing. Go for a dry treatment, presuming you intend to encounter the odd icicle at some point! Single ropes are a poor option for the vast majority of ice and trad mixed routes, both for safety and practicality reasons.

Gear inspection and care

Drying your gear out always seems like a chore after a big day on the hill, let alone inspecting it, but you should always do both. With a brew at your side it's never such a big deal and you can use the time to reflect on the day and get psyched for tomorrow (before you hit the pub and put paid to it all!) If there's one thing you should never compromise on it's your rope - if it has sustained damage from crampon or axe then chop the end or discard it. A little furriness on the sheath may be fine, but if you suspect the core is damaged then don't chance it. The thinner the rope, the more this becomes an issue. Look for burrs on your ice screws and if you find one then mark it with tape or rack it separately. File your picks and crampons as described on pages 62 and 70.

A general point about gear inspection is that there are no clear answers to the shelf lives of products and the key is to use common sense and always to err on the side of caution. A mountain guide may wear out a product in a season whereas an infrequent user might get ten years of good use from the same product. In general it is the soft products: slings, ropes and harnesses that require the most scrutiny. Store them dry and away from bright light and keep them clear from oily or acidic substances. Change your harness as soon as you see signs of wear, especially on the tie-in loops and belay loop. Ropes should not be stood on, especially with crampons but if you do then check it immediately. The myth about invisible 'hair-line' fractures in karabiners, or metal products, that have been dropped from a height is indeed a myth. If you can't see the damage then it isn't there, but you are still advised not to lob your gear off cliffs.

Headtorches

Head torches are easy to forget, but oh so difficult to manage without - the chances of walking home, or finishing a route in the dark, are pretty high when ice or mixed climbing, so keep your headtorch permanently in the lid of your sack along with new spare batteries. LED bulbs give the longest supply of light and halogens burn the brightest. A torch that offers both is the most versatile, but any torch is better than none. On particularly cold days (below -15°C) it may be worth taking lithium batteries as a precaution. Super light and compact headtorches are great for slipping in your pocket and carrying on the route.

Tool storage bags

Crampon bags are the best way to avoid shredding the contents of your rucksack and some climbers also chose to throw their axes into tough storage bags and carry them inside their rucksack rather than fiddling with ice axe attachment points. Of particular use are the specialist ice screw carry bags that can be used to keep your screws from getting dented in your sack. Note that 'tool bags' exist for transporting all your ice hardware for flight travel, but if you show up with one of these on the hill then someone is likely to call the mountain rescue!

Starting Out

Equipment

Mountain Safety

Ice · Style · Ethics

Ice · Techniques

Mixed · Style·Ethics

Mixed · Techniques

The Mind

Training

Destinations

Starting Out | Equipment | Mountain Safety | Ice : Style - Ethics | Ice : Techniques | Mixed : Style - Ethics | Mixed : Techniques | The Mind | Training | Destinations

Rucksack

Tube-shaped sacks with compression straps and no side-pockets are best. Forty to fifty litres in capacity is usually adequate for most one day routes. Make sure the back-length is right and that the hip belt can be folded back on itself in case you need to climb with it whilst wearing a harness. A bit of padding is usually worth its weight in preference to the ultra-lightweight alpine style. Ice axe attachment points and an extendable lid are essential. Crampon attachments points are a good option especially if you don't have a crampon storage bag. The clean, simple, tough sacks are the ones you want rather than the teabags with loads of plastic clips and gadgets.

Streamlined shape, compression straps and extendable lid all go towards making up a good winter sack.

Expandable lid

Side compression straps

Crampon attachment points

Ice axe attachment points

Tip:
When climbing in a pair, make sure one rucksack is smaller than the other. Once you have geared up you can stuff the smaller sack in the now-empty larger sack. The leader can then climb unencumbered and the second can carry the two sacks as one.

Also on the check list

> Map and compass (especially in Scotland)
> Guidebook
> Water bottle (preferably wide-necked to enable clearing when choked with ice)
> Hydration system (beware freezing pipes when it's much colder than -2°C)
> Hill food (see page 255)
> Sunblock

Packing for the hill

Early morning blunders are all too common so pack your sack as best you can the night before and leave it close to any kit that is still drying. A general and more obvious point is to leave behind everything that you don't definitely need, especially for routes with long approaches. The only thing you might add are a few extra bits of protection, in case you change plans and go for a different route. Extra axes and other spare gear are out of the question unless it is a ten minute walk-in to a sport mixed venue.

Most Scottish winter climbers don't take a survival bag or much of a first aid kit with them, and whilst there are strong arguments for both of these seemingly life saving items, you have to think it through. While a few plasters and a light wound dressing may be advisable, remember you can shove someone's feet in a rucksack and put them in a down jacket and you have a make-shift survival bag.

The fast and light approach becomes more tempting, the further you are travelling from the car, but you have to think everything through before you make the call since having the right gear will often prove to be the difference between a good day out and a terrifying epic.

Gearing up fast!

Having chosen a safe place to prepare for the climb, a final point is to be fast when gearing up, both to maximise your time on the route and to inspire confidence in your partner. Less experienced climbers or those who aren't on top of their game are prone to 'faffing' with their kit at the base.

Andy Kirkpatrick aiming for a rapid kit-up in typical challenging Cairngorm conditions.

Starting Out · Equipment · Mountain Safety · Ice : Style-Ethics · Ice : Techniques · Mixed : Style-Ethics · Mixed : Techniques · The Mind · Training · Destinations

Starting Out

Equipment

Mountain Safety

Ice : Style-Ethics

Ice : Techniques

Mixed : Style-Ethics

Mixed : Techniques

The Mind

Training

Destinations

Equipment maintenance

How often have you heard winter climbers tell stories of how 'quite suddenly and out of the blue' their crampon fell off or the blade on their axe drooped as the attaching bolts fell out. While unforesee-able catastrophic gear failure does happen it is very rare. What is more likely to be happening in these no-doubt terrifying events is the result of poor maintenance and fitting of equipment. It is crucial that long before you stride out to the hills that you ensure all your equipment is working smoothly and that items like crampons are carefully fitted and checked.

The following check list is well worth following:

Ice tools

Have your picks been sharpened? Check all bolts for tightness. Check grip tape and any bolt on handles for security. If using leashes or lanyards check for any fabric furring or wear of parts.

Crampons

Ensure optimum fit to the individual boots you will be using. Ensure sharpness of the points, replacing any front points that have become too short. Check bails, attachment straps and anti-balling plates for wear.

Boots

Check for wear in particular eyelets or laces. Ensure they are dry - wet boots are cold.

Harness

Check for wear, in particular the belay loop and the areas of attachment to the waist belt and leg loops. Check for wear of gear loops and ice clippers (in particular the wire gates).

Moving hardware such as karabiners and cams

Damp winter climbing can take a similar toll as salty sea-cliff climbing on gear, locking solid moving parts. Wash and lubricate such gear after every trip.

Slings and quickdraws

Check the slings are dry and free of knots, damp gear quickly becomes frozen and unusable.

Ice screws

Check for sharpness of teeth.

Shell clothing and gaiters

Check that there are no rips or tears from your crampons from your last time out. A small tear can prove to be an accident waiting to happen.

Headtorch, mobiles and GPSs

Check that batteries in all these devices are fresh or fully charged, make sure to pack spare batteries for your headtorch.

Navigation

All winter climbers should aim to be competent in basic navigation techniques using map and compass. GPS systems are a very useful modern aid but it is crucial to carry map and compass as well in case batteries fail.

Being able to navigate in the mountains is as important as being able to swing an ice-axe or use a rope.

We don't have the space here to devote to navigation techniques but you should be familiar with the following skills:

> Orientating a map and comparing the map with ground features.
> Setting and following bearings.
> Measuring distance covered by pacing and timing (including the affect of height gained).
> Night navigation skills.

Starting Out

Equipment

Mountain Safety

Ice - Style-Ethics

Ice - Techniques

Mixed - Style-Ethics

Mixed - Techniques

The Mind

Training

Destinations

Starting Out

Equipment

Mountain Safety

Ice : Style-Ethics

Ice : Techniques

Mixed : Style-Ethics

Mixed : Techniques

The Mind

Training

Destinations

Leaving the car at 4am rewards Pete Benson with beautiful dawn light and maximum route time at Lochnagar, Scotland.

Mountain Safety

Winter climbing offers some of the biggest and best challenges in climbing but with those greater challenges come inevitably higher risks. Learning how to recognise, assess, manage and minimise those risks is the key to an enjoyable day on the hill. This chapter suggests a step by step approach for safer winter climbing.

Starting Out

Equipment

Mountain Safety

Ice : Style-Ethics

Ice : Techniques

Mixed : Style-Ethics

Mixed : Techniques

The Mind

Training

Destinations

Starting Out

Equipment

Mountain Safety

Ice : Style-Ethics

Ice : Techniques

Mixed : Style-Ethics

Mixed : Techniques

The Mind

Training

Destinations

Key assumptions

It is assumed that readers of this book are familiar with the basics of general climbing craft, such as how to put on a harness, belay safely and place protection. (Rockfax's **Trad Climbing+** covers these areas in detail).

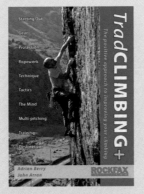

As winter climbers it is also assumed that you will be familiar with general naviga-tion skills such as map reading, using a compass and simple pacing and orientation techniques. If you don't feel confident in these areas then it is essential that you acquire these skills before you head into the hills.

Either read up and practise in a safe environment or get expert advice from a UIAGM Guide or instructor holding a Mountain Instructor Certificate (MIC).

Winter climbing, be that single pitch roadside ice climbing or a multi-pitch route in Scotland with a four hour walk-in, usually involves bigger challenges than typical summer rock climbing. With these challenges come higher risks. Whilst we have been careful with this book to avoid glaciated, traditional high mountain ter-rain, it is fair to say that all winter climbing should be classed as mountaineering. Developing a mountaineer's approach to even the most innocuous looking ice cragging is a good way of keeping aware of any dangers and managing risks.

Mountain safety starts long before you sink your first ice axe placement of the day. We suggest a step by step approach for safer winter climbing.

Every winter climber should know their basic navigation skills.

Freddie Wilkinson revelling in the commitment of a big Scottish route on *North East Buttress*, IV,5 on Ben Nevis, Scotland.

Starting Out

Equipment

Mountain Safety

Ice : Style-Ethics

Ice : Techniques

Mixed : Style-Ethics

Mixed : Techniques

The Mind

Training

Destinations

Starting Out

Equipment

Mountain Safety

Ice : Style·Ethics

Ice : Techniques

Mixed : Style·Ethics

Mixed : Techniques

The Mind

Training

Destinations

Preparation

Most accidents that occur during winter climbing are avoidable. In fact many calamities could have been avoided by decisions made long before the actual climb. Furthermore without the right preparation a small incident en-route can easily snowball into a full-blown epic. To avoid things spiralling out of control and for enjoyable stress-free winter climbing a small amount of planning ahead is required.

Conditions resources

Scotland

www.sais.gov.uk - Scottish Avalanche Service including Blogs from Lochaber, the Cairngorms and Creag Meagaidh.

www.mwis.org.uk/scotland.php - Mountain Weather Information Service.

www.westcoast-mountainguides.co.uk/blog/blog.htm - Ben Nevis, local alpine guide Alan Kimber's blog.

freespace.virgin.net/kings.house/ - Glen Coe webcam.

www.camvista.com/scotland/scenic/skye.php3 - Skye webcam.

www.cairngormmountain.co.uk/web-cam/ - Cairngorms Ski areas webcam.

France

www.ice-fall.com/ - Freissinieres, Fournel.

www.webcam-gavarnie.com/ - Gavarnie webcam.

Canada

www.gravsports-ice.com - Canadian Rockies.

USA

www.neice.com/ - North Eastern US, Eastern Canada.

Venue choice

This is perhaps the most important decision you have to make and will be based on a number of factors:

The ability of your team

If this is your first ever winter trip to Scotland there is no point rushing in to the Cairngorm's Shelter Stone, where there are hardly any easy routes. Instead choose a venue like the nearby Northern Corries or Stob Coire nan Lochan in Glen Coe, which have a wide range of introductory grade routes.

The fitness of your team

Venues such as Aonach Mor near Ben Nevis with a one hour approach are much more manageable for most than the three hour slog to Beinn Eighe. Remember climbing ability is one thing, but not everyone has the general fitness to cope with many of the long days needed for Scotland's wildest cliffs or the biggest multi-pitch continental icefalls.

Weather

There are three factors to consider. What the weather has been like over the previous few days will affect not only the condition of the ice and turf you plan to climb but also the approach to the cliffs. Heavy snow can bury paths doubling approach times and making navigation difficult. The weather forecast for that day is obviously crucial, if it's going to be a stormy battle, moderate your ambitions and choose a sheltered venue with easy approaches and descents. Snow, high winds and rising temperatures will all affect avalanche risk. Finally take note of what the weather forecast is for the following day as there is a good chance that a weather front could come in early, turning your well-planned day into an epic. See page 14 for more.

Route choice

You may have a route in mind that you wish to climb, however it is worth having a few other options nearby as a back up incase your chosen route is busy with other climbers or is out of condition. Try to research what conditions are like at your chosen crag. In Europe many mountain village's Tourist Information Centres can provide general conditions reports, local mountain guides are an excellent source of up to date information and there are an increasing number of websites and blogs that provide reports on the Internet (see conditions box opposite).

You should be able to make an educated guess on the likely condition of your route by keeping an eye on weather patterns over the preceding week or so. Ask yourself how much snow has fallen, is it enough or perhaps too much? Has the temperature been cold for enough time to enable ice to form? Is the wind in the right direction and of the right temperature to build up hoar frost or will it strip the buttresses bare?

A crucial part of route choice is not just the way up but also the descent. Many icefalls are descended by abseil (rare in the UK but very typical on the continent) which to some extent takes away this headache. However for most of the winter routes in Scotland you will have to read up and plot on the map the descent. Bear in mind possible avalanche risk, exposure to cornices and any alternative options if the weather or conditions deteriorate.

Leaving a route plan

It is well worth leaving a plan of your intended approach, cliff (with grid reference) and routes with a friend. Explain your intended day's itinerary and your estimated return time. Make sure they would be able to describe where you plan to be if they have to phone a rescue.

Having left a route plan with someone, it is vital that you make contact with them on your return, something that isn't always easy if there is no mobile phone reception. If necessary incorporate into your plans a detour to a pub or village to use public phones. It is also worth leaving a route plan and estimated return date and time in your car, as Police and mountain rescue are briefed to look out for abandoned cars in winter.

Starting Out

Equipment

Mountain Safety

Ice : Style-Ethics

Ice : Techniques

Mixed : Style-Ethics

Mixed : Techniques

The Mind

Training

Destinations

Avalanches

Many climbers assume avalanches only happen in high alpine areas and present more of a hazard to skiers or alpinists. But most places winter climbers head for are likely to have some avalanche risk. Many of the most famous winter climbing venues in Scotland or even the Lake District and Snowdonia have a well-catalogued history of avalanches. Though the art of assessing and forecasting avalanches is complex, it is possible for winter climbers to make themselves aware and assess basic avalanche risks with a few simple procedures.

Avalanche forecasting

The good news is that many winter climbing areas have daily avalanche forecasts compiled and updated regularly by experts. These are often available on the net (**www.sais.gov.uk** is the Scottish avalanche service website) and posted at ski areas, mountain stores and venue car parks.

Make yourself aware of the forecast and plan your venue accordingly, if there's a high avalanche risk then that decision may be which distillery you might be visiting rather than climbing that day.

The scale used is as follows:

Low

A well bonded stable snowpack.

Moderate

Well bonded snowpack. Avalanches possible with high additional loads.

Considerable

Moderate to weak snowpack. Triggering possible even with low loads on certain aspects. In certain conditions natural avalanches may occur.

High

Weakly bonded snowpack. Triggering probable even with low loads on many steep slopes. Frequent natural avalanches likely.

Very high

Weak and largely unstable snowpack. Numerous large natural avalanches are likely even on moderately angled terrain.

A shocked Nick Bullock having been swept by an avalanche in Canada. Photo by Nick Bullock.

This airborne avalanche was triggered by a serac collapse in the Argentière basin, France. Although a number of people can be seen very close by, no-one was hurt. Photo by Ian Sherrington.

Avalanche assessment

As well as reading the forecast you will need to know how to assess the avalanche risk yourself. Avalanches occur due to a number of factors. Here's what to look for and assess:

Slope angle

Avalanches can happen on terrain of almost any angle but commonly it is slopes between 25° and 45° that present the highest risk. This just happens to be the angle of a typical coire approach to a climb and also many hillsides that provide drainage above ice climbs. If a high risk is suspected avoid, where possible, open slopes of this angle.

Coire an T-Sneachda in the Cairngorms, Scotland. This area is prone to cornice collapses and ideal avalanche terrain.

Ridges can offer the safest approach but if this is not an option you might need to take a more circuitous route to avoid potentially dangerous slopes. Note that convex slopes present a higher risk than concave slopes.

Cornices

These are overhanging waves of snow that loom ominously over the tops of many winter climbs. Cornices are formed when high winds cause snow to be swept to the crest of a ridge or plateau. They can collapse through sheer weight and size and become significantly less stable in rising temperatures. As well as the danger of being hit by a breaking cornice, their collapse often triggers avalanches, with cliffs such as Creag Meagaidh notorious for late season cornice collapses.

Starting Out

Equipment

Mountain Safety

Ice : Style-Ethics

Ice : Techniques

Mixed : Style-Ethics

Mixed : Techniques

The Mind

Training

Destinations

"This photo was taken in March 2007 when the Ben was in fantastic condition. We raced up Tower Ridge. At the summit I saw this guy standing on the cornice trying to have a look at the climbers on *Indicator Wall* which was in top nick as well. I don't think he realised how bad the cornice was."
Photo by Henning Wackerhage.

Weather conditions

Be aware of the pattern of the weather over the last few days. Heavy snowfall is an obvious potential risk but it is vital to note that snow build-up can happen on snow-fall free days when there are high winds. For example a strong northeasterly wind can scour the snow on slopes facing into the wind and deposit it onto southwesterly slopes. This type of wind blown snow is known as 'wind-slab' and can be particularly susceptible to avalanching. The other issue is big fluctuations in temperature, which can create different layers of snow, which in turn may create instability in the snowpack. See page 14 for more on reading the conditions.

Underlying terrain

Smooth slabs of rock present a potentially more difficult surface for snow to stick to, therefore being more likely to avalanche. A boulder field will anchor snow better.

Snowpack

The snowpack is often built of many layers following different snow falls. Older snow can melt or freeze creating dangerous weak layers ready to slide and cause an avalanche. An advanced method of assessing a snowpack's stability is to chop out (or dig if you have a snow shovel) a pit into a slope (ideally not the main slope but a safer subsidiary slope of the same angle). Usually this will be two feet or so deep or down to the first layer of solid neve. Smooth away the back wall until it is vertical and then assess the different layers by poking your finger into them or brushing them lightly with your hand. Layers of ice, very soft snow, loose crystal snow, air or graupel (ball bearings of snow) all present potential hazardous layers.

Next you can assess the snowpack's stability by a simple test. Carve either side to create a block down to the first significant layer and then pull with your hands on the block see how easily it slides. Do this for each layer. A very poorly bonded snow-pack will slide almost without effort while a well bonded pack will stick together.

Obviously these tests are only very rough guides that give some indication to the stability of slopes of the same angle and aspect. In order to get more idea you may have to dig several pits on your approach and even then the test is still not very reliable.

The best idea is to make your decision based on a combination of all the various techniques and regard snowpack assessment as a last resort.

Mark Garthwaite examines a snow pit on the way up to the Stanley Headwall in the Canadian Rockies. Photo by Neil Gresham.

What to do in the event of avalanche

If you find yourself caught in an avalanche the following steps will aid your survival:

Shout out 'Avalanche!' partly as a warning to others in its path but also so that you attract the attention of potential rescuers.

Try to escape the pull of the avalanche - if you are close to the fracture line you may be able to jump above the break, if you are caught below advancing snow then run towards the edges of a slope, if you are swept up in the debris then try to reach the edges of the avalanche; a rolling or swimming motion may help.

As the avalanche slows down make a big effort to get to the surface or at least thrust your hand through so that rescuers can find you.

If buried - try to keep calm and conserve your energy, if possible keep hands in front of your face to preserve a pocket of air.

If you witness someone get caught in an avalanche then:

> Try to pinpoint where they entered the avalanche and the point at which you last saw them, this will help narrow down the search area.

> Scour the immediate surface debris for any signs such as clothing or equipment such as a rope which might lead to them.

> Probe potential burial spots with an ice axe, ski poles or better still avalanche probes.

> Send for help and begin a systematic search with a group of people, if possible probing along a line from top to bottom of the potential burial area.

While rarely used by climbers, avalanche transceivers are considered essential kit amongst off-piste skiers and snow-boarders, and there is a strong case for these being worn by climbers as they significantly assist rescue in the event of an avalanche.

The aftermath of an avalanche - chaos and disorientation. Nick Bullock happy to be alive.
Photo by Al Powell.

Starting Out

Equipment

Mountain Safety

Ice · Style · Ethics

Ice · Techniques

Mixed · Style · Ethics

Mixed · Techniques

The Mind

Training

Destinations

Safety while climbing

Safety while climbing is a combination of common sense, vigilance in spotting hazards and making good route choices.

Several points to keep an eye out for are:

Protect your belayer - if there is any flexibility in where to belay, opt for belays with:

> Multiple strong multi-directional anchor options.

> Shelter from the next pitch, either to the side of the line of fall or under overhangs or in caves.

> Ideally with a comfortable ledge for those long belay stints.

Hazards

Falling ice

Ice is a fragile medium and it should be expected that pieces will splinter off as you make your axe placements. Even a small fist-sized lump of ice can do a lot of damage falling from high on a pitch, let alone the bigger dinner plates common on cold brittle ice. While it is almost impossible to avoid these smaller chunks, bigger sections of ice usually take several swings to dislodge. If the ice gives a loud hollow crack on your first swing try other placements. If you have no other placement options, make sure your belayer and any bystanders are warned before you clean the loose ice away. Sometimes when an ice block breaks free it can still be possible to reduce its size before it falls. If any sizeable chunks do fall, the common warning to shout out is 'Ice!'

Just a matter of time or a quick change in temperature before this icicle falls.

It is not just while climbing that you should be aware of falling ice. Even seemingly safe bolted winter sport climbing areas have many hanging ice hazards for bystanders. There have been fatalities from icicles that have broken free (see photo belowcrushing those walking below. Note that falling ice will splinter and break on impact acting like shrapnel and scattering danger over a wide area, so stay well clear.

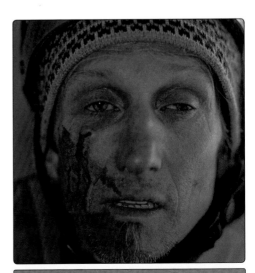

It could have been a lot worse Sandy Ogilvie who was glad he was wearing a helmet.

Loose rock

Winter mixed climbs often climb natural summer drainage lines, or vegetated broken ground avoided by summer rock climbs. This terrain is the natural home for loose rock. This is one of the most serious hazards confronting a winter climber, not just because of the injuries falling rock can cause but also because it is possible for falling rock to cut your ropes. If a route is known to be loose, then it is wise to only attempt it during cold conditions which may freeze blocks into place. If you are forced to climb through an unstable section then gently test every placement for any movement, climb slowly, don't lunge for placements. Spread your weight between all your limbs in case one suddenly rips.

If you do dislodge any rock, try to direct it away from your belayer. The common warning to shout out is 'Rock!'. If you break free a block but it doesn't fall and it isn't safe to throw it clear, then you may be forced to set up a sling to keep it safe until your second can dispose of it safely.

Unstable snow

On some routes snow can form into suspended blobs below overhangs known as Snow Mushrooms. These are very unstable and surprisingly heavy. One of the authors of this book had his ribs broken by one on a climb in Alaska and climbers have been killed when they are dislodged. Avoid going near or under these if at all possible. Cornices, although often more stable can offer a similar hazard particularly during rising temperatures.

Avalanches

Many climbs are threatened by avalanche from snow slopes above the climbs. The Argentière Basin Icefalls in the Alps, the Gavarnie Cirque in the Pyrenees and Cascade Falls in Canada are all famous examples. These routes should be avoided after heavy snowfall and in rising temperatures. Smaller avalanches can also happen in routes themselves, particularly easier gully lines (grade I-III). If in doubt retreat.

Flexibility in decision making

Sometimes no matter how strong your arms feel or how well you're climbing, a route can refuse to play ball. There are many reasons why it might be prudent not to continue; rotten ice, unfrozen loose blocks, conditions or weather deteriorating during the day, or perhaps simply that things are going slower than expected and you might be unable to complete the route in daylight.

Whatever the problem, learn to listen to your inner voice. If something doesn't feel right then there is no shame in deciding to back off. Obviously if you find that you are backing off more routes than you get up then you are either climbing on routes out of condition that no-one else would go near, trying climbs too hard for you or you need to turn to the mental chapter (page 224) and get your head in order.

ABOVE HERE
EXPERTS
ONLY!
VERY ICY!!
HAVE A NICE DAY!

Retreating

Once you've made the decision to retreat from a lead, discuss it with your belayer. If they are sufficiently experienced they may wish to try to lead the pitch. If so you may be able to just lower off or abseil off and leave the gear for them. If not then you have several options:

Down-climb

Only do this if you can do so safely and in control, in which case you should be able to remove your gear as you descend. Be very careful of descending hard ice as it is difficult to swing axes properly at waist level and easy to lift your heels and pop your crampon points off their placements. If forced to down-climb ice take things slowly making shorter moves than you would on an ascent. If down-climbing snow ensure you re-kick and reinforce any footsteps you made on the way up.

Lower from gear

If the terrain you have covered is tricky and you have good protection at your high point it will be safest to lower-off. Make sure you have good communication with your belayer. Don't be tempted to shortcut safety, double check your gear and leave a krab rather than abseiling from a piece of tat looped through your pro. If you have climbed less than half a rope length it is better to be lowered rather than abseil so that any lower gear you've placed will act as a back up. Similarly with double ropes, whether you are abseiling or being lowered, you can descend on one rope and have your belayer keep the spare rope tight to protect you if your top piece of gear fails - see diagram to the right.

A combination

If you are not absolutely certain about the security of your lower-off point, then you may need to use a combination of down-climbing while some of your weight is taken by the rope through your high gear. With double ropes get your belayer to take in one as a backup. Once you've down-climbed to a rock-solid piece you can then clip-in, pull your ropes through and arrange a safer lower off point.

Remember to keep an eye out for and note good anchor points as you climb. If you are forced into a descent perhaps in the dark then at least you will know what you are aiming for.

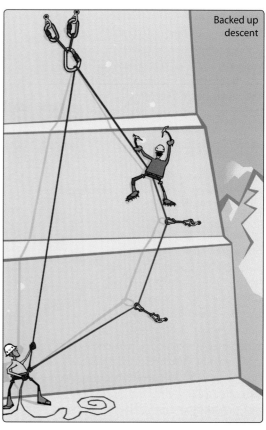

Backed up descent

Guy Roberston abseiling down Rotten Gully on Skye, Scotland.

Starting Out

Equipment

Mountain Safety

Ice : Style-Ethics

Ice : Techniques

Mixed : Style-Ethics

Mixed : Techniques

The Mind

Training

Destinations

Descents

Hopefully you will have planned ahead, identified your safe descent, found bomber anchors or topped out with plenty of time to spare before it gets dark, in which case your descent should be stress free. However things don't always work out as planned so bear in mind the following issues:

Fixed gear

Many ice and sport mixed routes have fixed anchor points to lower or abseil from. Due to the damp environment and the freeze and thaw weather of winter, these anchors can be under a lot more stress than anchors found on summer rock routes. As a matter of principle all fixed gear should be treated with caution. Always look for a back-up (that can then be removed by the second climber). Don't trust fixed gear such as slings that you can't see and assess properly. If you can get a good back-up then it is worth testing fixed anchors such as slings or Abalakovs by clipping a sling in as a foot stirrup and bounce testing them. Remember to clip this test sling loosely into your back up or you will loose it if the fixed anchor fails. If in any doubt, make your own descent anchors. A few more minutes in time is all it takes to prevent potential disaster.

Changing weather

A deterioration in weather can reduce visibility, increase avalanche risks and, as many have found in places like the Cairngorm Plateau, make walking almost impossible.

If this occurs during your climb be prepared to change your descent plans. On topping out, you might find that rather than take a previously planned exposed high-level path home, it is safer to regain your starting point by descending back down into the coire and then retracing your approach. In some cases it might be dangerous to summit at all and an abseil descent back down the route will provide the safest option.

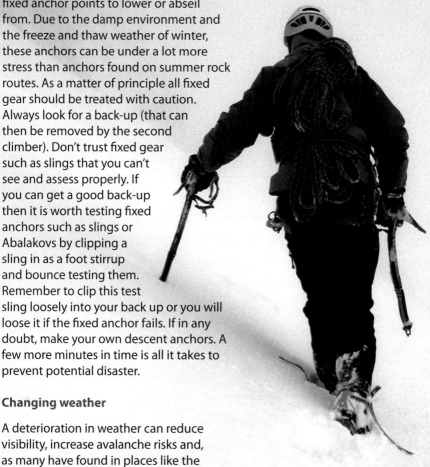

Andy Nisbet treading cautiously in poor visibility.

The onset of darkness

Climb enough in the winter and you are bound to get caught out by darkness falling at some point. Perhaps the route proved trickier than expected or heavy conditions slowed progress. Whatever the reason, once it becomes evident that darkness will beat you to the summit it is time to keep calm and make a plan.

Climbing into the dark can feel scary and can dampen spirits, so this is the time to work as a team. Prepare yourself; get out and attach your head torches well in advance. As a belayer you may wish to don that duvet jacket, as climbing in the dark is a much slower, and therefore colder, process. If there is tricky ground ahead and some time before nightfall left it might make more sense for the leader to push on, perhaps combining pitches to make the most of the remaining daylight. It is much easier to second a pitch in the dark than it is to lead. Once darkness is with you shorter pitches will make communication between you much easier. Keeping each other informed and the banter going amongst a team becomes much more important once you can't see what you are doing. If darkness is combined with poorer weather you have a potentially serious situation it may be prudent to abandon any plans of completing the route and descend if possible.

Inevitably darkness will make navigating your descent significantly tougher. Be especially wary of unseen hazards, keeping well clear of the cliff edge and cornices. If in doubt stay roped together with the leader descending cautiously while the last person on the rope is braced, axe at the ready for a slip. Utilise natural anchors such as rock spikes to provide protection in case of a fall. Your best plan will be to aim to rejoin your approach as soon as is safely possible so that you can follow features or footsteps recognised from earlier in the day. If navigating featureless terrain you can walk on a bearing by sending one of you ahead and directing their head torch in line with the bearing. While night time descents can be slow exhausting affairs, with care and calm they should become just another part of the winter experience. Finally, don't forget to inform those with whom you have left your route plan if you are late off the hill as you don't want to have the mountain rescue called out unnecessarily.

Keeping everyone informed during the challenge of night time navigation.

What to do in an emergency

In the event of an incident it is important to keep calm. This will aid clear decision making and avoid rash choices that could make matters worse. Clear communication is vital between all members of your party.

If you get lost

Often the simplest solution is to retrace your steps until you return to a point that is recognisable on your map. Once you know you are on the right track you can then commence standard navigation.

If retracing isn't possible (perhaps your tracks have been buried by driven snow) but you know the general area you are in, then you may be able to navigate towards big recognisable features e.g. a river, a major ridge-line or a large sweep of forest that you can then re-orientate from. These are often called 'catching features'.

If you do find yourself completely lost, or unable to complete the return back to your car due to extreme conditions then you may have to consider finding shelter. This should only be considered in emergencies as by continuing to move you will keep warmer, but if disorientation is so bad it feels unsafe to continue, then it might be best to wait for better light or weather.

If there is a fall resulting in injury

If it's possible to communicate with the fallen climber try to establish the nature of any injuries and the climber's level of mobility.

If the climber is on a rope then it may be possible to lower them, ideally to the base of the climb or a safer position such as a ledge or piece of protection on which

either they can secure themselves, or you can tie them off safely.

In some cases reaching the casualty can be tricky and it is important not to put yourself at risk in doing so.

If you are able to get to the injured climber talk calmly to reassure them and do an initial basic check of the first aid ABCs (Airway, Breathing and Circulation) and then breaks or bleeding - It is not the aim of this book to go into first aid details.

Having assessed the injured party you will have to decide whether you need to call for a rescue or if you can manage yourselves. In bad conditions you may need to get the injured party to a safer sheltered position, perhaps even a mountain hut or bothy, and then go for rescue.

If you do have to leave your partner to get help then make sure they are as sheltered as possible, perhaps by digging a snow hole, trench or snow wall. Wrap them in any emergency bivi kit you have or let them use any spare clothes you have as well as any food and fluids. Rucksacs and ropes can provide good insulation for the head and torso from the ground. Ideally leave them in an easily identifiable spot and look for features and take compass bearings to describe their position. Mark the shelter with spare ski poles, axes, ropes or brightly coloured ruscksacs. If you have a spare head torch then leave it with them to help signal rescuers. Make sure it is clear to them what you are planning to do and reassure them that help is at hand and you will return.

Digging a snow hole

A snow hole can provide the most effective form of overnight shelter. Even though it can take an hour or more to dig, the fact that it provides complete shelter from the wind makes it a real lifesaver. The crux of any snow hole is finding suitable ground in which to dig, this will need to have a minimum of one and a half metres depth of solid consolidated snow, ideally ice free as ice layers will take infinitely longer to excavate. Snow drifts and lee slopes offer the best potential.

If working in a pair, the quickest approach is to dig two parallel smaller caves which can then be connected by a tunnel, blocking one entrance after the hole is finished. While digging put on your waterproof shell clothing and mitts as you will find it can be a very damp process. Once inside pad out the floor with ropes and a rucksack saving your other sack to block up the door. If you have bivi gear you can change out of your wet outer layers before getting wrapped up. Be aware that if you shelter out a big storm you will need to check that the entrance doesn't become buried by snow.

Calling for a rescue

In the UK the mountain rescue service is made up of volunteers such as experienced climbers and medics, while in many other countries such as Europe and America it is a professional service. It is worth noting that in these countries rescue services can often charge for some or all of the rescue costs and it is assumed that all climbers will have full insurance that covers the mountaineering and climbing they are undertaking.

As well as insurance make sure you have the mountain rescue phone numbers before you set off for the hills. In the UK this is the standard 999 emergency services number. In other European countries the number is usually 112. When you make a call you will need to provide the following information:

> The number of people injured in the incident.

> The nature of their injuries, consciousness and responsiveness.

> Location details, grid reference, mountain features, route name etc.

> Any hazards that might confront rescuers i.e. if there has been a cornice collapse, is there any more cornice threatening the area?

Starting Out

Equipment

Mountain Safety

Ice : Style-Ethics

Ice : Techniques

Mixed : Style-Ethics

Mixed : Techniques

The Mind

Training

Destinations

Sandy Ogilve on the upper pitches of *Murchison Falls*, WI 4, Canada.

Ice: Styles and Ethics

Starting Out

Equipment

Mountain Safety

Ice : Style-Ethics

Ice : Techniques

Mixed : Style-Ethics

Mixed : Techniques

The Mind

Training

Destinations

There is something strangely compelling about waterfall ice. To be up there on a slender column, connected only by a few steel points must surely rank alongside surfing a giant reef break when it comes to feeling the forces of nature. Ice is beautiful but dangerous, allowing passage only to those who are humble and prepared.

Each time it will feel different, offering a joy ride one day and a horror show the next. A classic pillar may have ten ascents on a busy weekend and then the next day, with a slight rise of the thermometer, it will come crashing to the ground.

Staring Out

Equipment

Mountain Safety

Ice : Style-Ethics

Ice : Techniques

Mixed : Style-Ethics

Mixed : Techniques

The Mind

Training

Destinations

Types of ice

Anyone whose experience of ice goes no further than a skating rink, could be excused for imagining that ice climbing isn't a particularly broad skill. It's not until you start to venture out that you realise just how much ice can vary.

Not only are there different methods of formation: such as water ice or snow ice, but the same route may change dramatically in structure and consistency according to prevailing climatic conditions and time of the season. There are also a multitude of features to climb in addition to the stereotypical flat sheet of ice. It is important to understand the basic mechanisms of ice formation in order to predict the different climbing styles that you will encounter.

Water ice

The type of blue water ice which is found on frozen waterfalls is perhaps most commonly associated with ice climbing.

Water ice formation

Most large icefalls give the impression that they have been formed from major waterfalls, whereas it is minor dribbles of water that are usually responsible. In fact, the heavier and faster moving torrents are always the last to freeze.

The best conditions for water ice formation are when temperatures are well below freezing but fluctuating slightly. The rises in temperature will melt snow and mobilise drainage courses and regular snowfall will feed the system. The easier angled drainage lines that touch rock (providing the ice with a surface to adhere to) will always freeze before free-hanging falls. Most ice falls will freeze from the outside inwards, and it can be common to encounter ice 'skins' with water running behind them on the rock, or free-standing pillars that have a frozen shell but are still flowing on the inside. Needless to say it takes great skill to judge whether they are safe to climb in this condition.

Hydnefossen, WI 6, in Norway represents a formidable challenge owing to its steepness and complexity. The ice freezes in different ways over its length, creating a vertical obstacle course to which you must constantly adapt your technique.

The *Montmerency Falls*, WI 3, in Quebec City rarely freezes in its centre due to the speed and power of the water, but the peripheral water usually firms up to create a classic and straightforward climb.

Starting Out

Equipment

Mountain Safety

Ice : Style-Ethics

Ice : Techniques

Mixed : Style-Ethics

Mixed : Techniques

The Mind

Training

Destinations

Starting Out

Equipment

Mountain Safety

Ice : Style-Ethics

Ice : Techniques

Mixed : Style-Ethics

Mixed : Techniques

The Mind

Training

Destinations

Icefall features

When water ice runs down an easy angled rock slab it usually forms in flat sheets, with slight ripples, and with an even texture. However, when it comes cascading down a steeper cliff, all sorts of interesting things start to happen. As it drips it will start by forming aerated, glassy chandeliers. If the water is dripping across the width of a roof these will form as free-hanging sheets or curtains, but if dripping from a concentrated point it will form a free hanging pillar. These may later touch down, fatten up, and connect to form concave grooves.

As a pillar gains weight, horizontal fracture lines may appear where it breaks and then re-freezes: these are often the tell-tale signs of collapse. If the falls are tumbling more heavily or a long way they will create splash-back features when they hit rock, such as giant mushrooms and cauliflowers, the largest of which will present them-selves as ice bulges. These aerated features are often granular in texture and may prove particularly challenging to climb.

Surrounding these 'splash-features' may be solid ice ledges that provide welcome rests or belay points. But occasionally these fill up with sugary, unconsolidated snow whose crust may melt and then freeze over to form ice skins that are just waiting to be surfed by unsuspecting ice climbers!

At the base of a column there will nearly always be a cone that is infested with spray-formed scales that may vary from a few inches to several meters in size. The final and perhaps the most challenging type of water-ice is super-thin verglas which is formed by the very tiniest trickles of water on rock. The techniques for climbing these various features will be discussed later in this chapter.

Ice falls in Vail, Colorado.

Curtain

Mushrooms

Column

Eyebrows

Cone

Bridlevail Falls, WI5+, in Colorado, a heavily featured icefall.

Starting Out

Equipment

Mountain Safely

Ice : Style-Ethics

Ice : Techniques

Mixed : Style-Ethics

Mixed : Techniques

The Mind

Training

Destinations

Starting Out

Equipment

Mountain Safety

Ice : Style-Ethics

Ice : Techniques

Mixed : Style-Ethics

Mixed : Techniques

The Mind

Training

Destinations

Snow ice

Snow ice is formed on high mountain routes by the freeze and thaw of compressed snow, as opposed to running water. In good condition, it is soft and chewy and provides easy placements, but it is notorious for offering poor screw protection.

On cold dry days, snow ice can be 'sugary' and on warm, moister days it can feel like climbing ball-bearings. Snow ice is notoriously difficult to climb at the point where the angle changes from steep to less-steep and your axes are prone to 'butter-knifing' through the unconsolidated material above. Snow ice may form in sheets or in the backs of gullies. In Scotland, Ben Nevis and Creag Meagaidh have some of the finest examples.

Tower Ridge with the snow ice climbs of Goodeve's Buttress and Raeburn's Wall dropping down from the summit plateau, Ben Nevis, Scotland.

Glacier ice

The attraction of glaciers is that they offer hard, compact homogenous ice of all angles, including steep overhangs. It has been known for groups of climbers to 'train' by setting up top-ropes or pre-placing screws, but it should be pointed out that even the so-called 'designated areas' can be safe one year and lethal the next.

Glacier ice

Artificial or competition ice

Competition, or artificial ice is similar in structure to glacier ice, being hard and compact. It is formed by packing layers of wet sludgy snow on to metal frames that are encased in 'chicken wire'. Those who are planning to enter an ice competition are advised to familiarise themselves with the medium before the big day, seeing as artificial ice is prone to chipping away in layers in a way that is different to real water ice. Indoor ice walls provide a great way to get used to the real thing. Advice for getting the most from them is given in the Starting Out section on page 36.

Artificial ice

Ice and mixed combined

There are many situations where pure ice climbing and mixed climbing will be encountered on the same route. It is common to find multi-pitch routes that offer a pitch or two of ice, then a pitch of mixed, and so-on. There will also be single pitches that will require a combination of icefall and dry tooling skills. Here the test will be choosing tools, protection and clothing that will give optimum characteristics for both styles.

Ice and mixed

Top: The Torres del Paine Glacier, Chile. Photo by Scott Price/CelebrateBig.com
Middle: A competitor in the ice world cup.
Bottom: Nick Bullock on *Bear Spirit*, M7, Canada.

Ice climbing conditions

Microcycle variations

The same ice route will take on different characteristics from day to day, or even within the same day, according to variations in temperature and humidity. On particularly cold, dry days, with temperatures well below -8°C, the ice may be very brittle and prone to shattering, especially if the air is dry. Here, the need for good gloves and sharp picks should be apparent.

Perhaps the best temperature range for water ice climbing is from -1°C to -5°C where the ice will tend to be 'plasticy', accepting picks and screws readily without excessive shattering.

On warmer days, from 0°C to 2°C, the ice will be softer, which will make it easier to climb but may pose a threat to the security of screw protection or indeed the safety of the entire ice feature. It is also likely that the route will be running with surface water and you will be in for a soaking.

Pay particular attention where you can see water running behind as there is very real danger of a full-scale collapse. Look out for missing chunks or for major cracks. It may not give you another warning before it goes.

It is hard to say where the cut-off temperature for safe ice climbing lies. Clearly it is unwise to attempt thin or free-standing formations unless the temperatures are below freezing. However, a fat sheet of ice that is continuously bonded to rock could be climbable in temperatures around 3°C.

Macrocycle variations

Ice conditions will also vary considerably throughout the season.

Early season ice

Early season ice formations tend to be leaner, fragile and more brittle. Expect to find the easier angled routes in condition but the steeper pillars may still be forming.

Most routes will be fatter at the top and thinner at the base so take care when departing. Watch out at the very top, where the ice is often rotten or detached at the point where it meets the drainage course. Early season ice routes are usually 'chandeliery' and a lot of clearing may be required to get through to the solid ice behind. Routes may also feel steeper than the grade might suggest and there may be more features to negotiate than you'd hope for at the given grade.

Early season ice with typical fragile tapering icicles.

Mid season ice

As the season progresses, the effect of freeze and thaw allows the features to grow and consolidate. The ice crystals become more tightly packed and the layers bond togather to create a denser, more homogenous structure. Features are filled out and grooves may form in the front of pillars. Mid season is undoubtedly the best time to climb, but it's worth watching out on warm days because routes that have put on a bit too much weight may be prone to collapse.

Late season ice

Late season ice is often lean or soft and rotten. It can be easy to climb, accepting picks readily but difficult to arrange reliable protection. On warm days take extra precaution when surveying the ice.

So clearly there is an optimum range both for daily temperatures (-5°C or 6°C to -1°C) as well as a point in the season where conditions are likely to be at their best; which in the northern hemisphere, usually means mid January to mid February. Selecting routes or an area to fit the conditions and adjusting your equipment and technique on the day is one of the most important skills in ice climbing.

Above: right, by mid season the icicles have fattened and consolidated together.
Bottom right: towards the end of the season ice can become dangerously soft and rotten.

Starting Out

Equipment

Mountain Safety

Ice · Style·Ethics

Ice · Techniques

Mixed · Style·Ethics

Mixed · Techniques

The Mind

Training

Destinations

Starting Out

Equipment

Mountain Safety

Ice : Style-Ethics

Ice : Techniques

Mixed : Style-Ethics

Mixed : Techniques

The Mind

Training

Destinations

Ethics

On first acquaintance, the ethics of ice climbing can sound a little contrived and pointless. Surely all that matters is that you get to the top in one piece without knocking the route down?

The beauty of climbing is that we are free to do as we please. Of course it's no big deal if you take the odd rest on an ice axe or a screw, but if the only way you can get up an icefall is by clipping into your axes to rest, then quite simply - you are out of your depth and likely to hurt yourself.

Theoretically you could leave your axes behind and aid the entire route with étriers and an arsenal of ice screws, but where would be the challenge in that? The more time you spend on ice, the more likely you will be to gravitate towards the free ethic.

Free ethic

The free ethic in ice climbing is to lead with ropes but to place screws without resting artificially by allowing your harness to take the weight. In other words, you must hold on to an axe with one hand whilst placing gear with the other.

One of the reasons this ethic exists is to encourage people to respect harder climbs. If you aren't fit or skilful enough to climb WI 5s or WI 6s then serve your time on WI 3s and WI 4s and one day you will be! The other reason is to prevent accidents. Clipping into an axe is a bad idea as they have a habit of jumping out if loaded incorrectly. Ice axe rests should be considered an absolute last resort to get you out of a difficult situation (see 'getting out of trouble' page 167).

Alan Mullin soloing well within his Scottish grade IX limits.

Above all else it is important not to be so hung up about the free ethic that you jeopardise your safety. Falling on ice should be avoided at all costs. It's worth considering a quote from Canadian ice guru Joe Josephson here:

'If you must hang to divert disaster, that is considerably better style (and a lot smarter) than falling.''

Soloing

Soloing on ice is to climb alone, either without a rope, or with a rope that can be fixed to the ice as a backup, or used for abseil descent. Many of the world's most experienced ice climbers still refuse to solo, and with good reason - make a mistake and it will probably be your last. Never attempt to solo unless you are well within your grade and absolutely sure about what you are taking on. The unpredictable nature of ice should speak for itself.

Neil clipping the rope into his axe as a precaution while placing gear on *Patri Right-hand*, WI4+, Cogne, Italy. If you're facing catastrophe then such a clip into your axes to get a crucial piece of gear in could save you from a dangerous fall.

Starting Out

Equipment

Mountain Safety

Ice : Style-Ethics

Ice : Techniques

Mixed : Style-Ethics

Mixed : Techniques

The Mind

Training

Destinations

Leashed or leash-less?

Both the leashed and leash-less methods are considered ethical for free ice climbing, as long as you don't clip into your tools to rest. However, the use of leashes is gradually becoming a thing of the past for technical ice climbs unless you are climbing in the high mountains.

Not only have leash-less tools improved from the original prototypes, but the word is spreading that you don't have to be a super-fit rock-jock in order to benefit from their advantages. In fact, it is not uncommon for beginners to be introduced to ice climbing with leash-less tools, providing they are on a top rope.

Leashed

Climbing with leashes may save a marginal amount of grip strength on very steep ice, but this will be off-set by the fact that you are unable to shake-out or place protection without a considerable amount of 'faffing'. The use of leashes gives you the sensation that your hands are chained to your tools and this can feel pretty distressing when you are desperate to shake out, or warm your hands up.

If you insist on using leashes then detachable or 'clipper' leashes are a must in order to allow you to release a hand. Leashes are also prone to tangling with gloves, causing pressure points and restricting circulation. Worse is that they always seem to tangle with ice screws during placement. The perceived advantages of leashes when you're dangerously fatigued are a myth, if you totally pump out, you will still let go!

Ben Wilkinson using leashes on *Blade Runner*, IV,5 Sgùrr a 'Chaorachain, Applecross, Scotland.

Starting Out · Equipment · Mountain Safety · Ice : Style-Ethics · Ice : Techniques · Mixed : Style-Ethics · Mixed : Techniques · The Mind · Training · Destinations

Leash-less

Climbing leash-less on steep ice may require slightly more grip strength than climbing with leashes, but this is more than compensated by the fact that you are able to shake-out, swap hands and place protection unencumbered.

On ice that is less than 80° there will be little difference in the amount of grip-strength required because all the weight should be on your feet. Clearly care is required when letting go of a tool, although there are various methods for attaching the tools to your harness with lanyards to reduce the chance of losing them when dropped (see page 196).

Leash-less is undoubtedly the most natural method for rock climbers. Leashes may be a wise precaution for less experienced climbers to prevent a hand being ripped from a tool in the event of a foot slipping. More experienced climbers are less likely to slip. Ice is about staying cool and climbing within your limits - sketching is bad news, with or without leashes.

Andy Benson using lanyards to remain connected to his leash-less tools on *Para Andy*, VI,7 Glen Coe, Scotland.

Leash-less with lanyards

This is a popular method for longer, multi-pitch routes which enables the ergonomic advantages of leash-less climbing to be experienced without the fear of dropping a tool. The idea is to attach lengths of thin cord (e.g. 1.5m of 4 -5mm cord) or bungee elastic to the grip-end of each axe and then to the belay loop of your harness (or to a chest harness or bandolier). The cords should be just long enough to enable you to make full reaches.

Note that the cords are prone to tangling and this method is not quite as clutter-free as the pure leash-less style. It is also important to be aware that if you do fall off using this method, it is likely that you will have a nasty collision with your tools.

Starting Out

Equipment

Mountain Safety

Ice : Style-Ethics

Ice : Techniques

Mixed : Style-Ethics

Mixed : Techniques

The Mind

Training

Destinations

Leash-less with cord connectors

An interesting method to bridge the gap between full leash-less and the lanyard method is simply to connect both axes together using a piece of cord or bungee approximately 1.5m in length. This should be tied into the clipping holes on the spikes of the axes and not the heads. This method is less of a tangle than lanyards and the chances of you dropping both tools at once are very slim, but if you drop one, it will simply stay linked to the other. This method may also work well for trad mixed, where it can be difficult to manage your tools whilst placing gear.

One leash

A less popular system that is only worth considering if you favour placing screws with one particular hand, is to have this hand free and use a clipper leash for security with the hanging hand. You're likely to get more pumped with the hanging hand but you can detach from the clipper leash periodically to shake out. It's better to practise placing screws with both hands so that you are more versatile and won't need to resort to this system.

Which method for beginners?

If you are top-roping or seconding a short single pitch route then it's worth going leash-less straight away, especially if there are no crowds below you at the base. If you are leading and especially if it's a multi-pitch route then clipper leashes provide a safer option, until you are experienced enough to make the choice to go leash-less.

Avoid old-fashioned fixed leashes which make shaking-out and placing or removing protection extremely difficult.

Beginners are advised to go for the security of leashes in a multi-pitch situation, rather than attempting to use leashes or cord connectors.

Leash-less to leashed

Many ice climbers who are experienced with leashes are reluctant to surrender one of the oldest 'legal cheats' in the game. They consider that leash-less is only relevant to steep dry tooling and will have no advantage on ice. Some of those who do switch are put-off leash-less during their first encounter - they are so paranoid about dropping a tool that they daren't let go!

There is also a tendency to over-grip and to forget to shake-out. It is vital to practise on easier routes first or when seconding and to make a conscious effort to relax into the style. Imagine you are rock climbing and suddenly it all becomes clear! Leash-less really is easier, but only once you are familiar with the technique.

A leash-less ice tool.
Photo by Neil Gresham.

Starting Out

Equipment

Mountain Safety

Ice : Style-Ethics

Ice : Techniques

Mixed : Style-Ethics

Mixed : Techniques

The Mind

Training

Destinations

Freddie Wilkinson leash-less on *Gargoyle Wall*, VI,6 Ben Nevis, Scotland.

Starting Out

Equipment

Mountain Safety

Ice : Style-Ethics

Ice : Techniques

Mixed : Style-Ethics

Mixed : Techniques

The Mind

Training

Destinations

Leo Houlding on *Ghost*, WI 5. Photo by Neil Gresham.

Starting Out

Equipment

Mountain Safety

Ice · Style-Ethics

Ice · Techniques

Mixed · Style-Ethics

Mixed · Techniques

The Mind

Training

Destinations

'Un-leashing the Rock God'
- Neil Gresham

In Chamonix, in the winter of 2002, I had the pleasure of taking the great young hope of British rock climbing, Leo Houlding, on his first ice climb. Leo was used to being in the driving seat, but I revelled in the fact that this might be the only day I would ever share with him where I wasn't on the back foot. The concept of starting on something steady remained a concept, so we headed for a two pitch WI 5 called *Ghost*, which looms steeply above the Argentière Glacier.

The plan was for me to lead the crux second pitch, so Leo set off up the sustained grade 4 first pitch, which was no soft option for an ice virgin. He started well, with a few crampons glancing off here and there. Leash-less tools weren't quite in at the time, so we both had clipper-leashes.

Leo placed a screw on the lower slab and cursed the awkwardness of it all. 'This is shit. I prefer rock climbing'. Then he charged at the vertical step above, running out a good ten metres before realising that another screw might be a good idea.

He unclipped his leash and whipped his hand down to his rack and with an ominous clipping sound, hand-cuffed himself to his gear-loop with the 'easy-clip' crab on his leash. Some swearing followed. 'OK, what do I do now Neil?' This was one that I didn't have any answers for and the next few seconds seemed to pass somewhat urgently.

Leo frantically wrestled to free himself while his other hand slowly drained of all its energy. In the final seconds, our ice climbing Houdini released himself and lunged at his spare tool as the other hand uncurled. We both breathed out and chuckled. Lessons learned: practise new techniques on easy climbs and don't run it out when you're new to ice. Care should be taken with karabiner-style clipper leashes.

Grades

The standard grading system used for icefalls is the WI (water ice) grade. However, all ice climbing grades should be regarded as subjective. We have already seen in this chapter how the difficulty of the same route may vary dramatically according to conditions.

A WI grade usually consists of two separate components: the first is an optional Roman numeral from I to VII which assesses the seriousness, length or level of commitment required for a climb (including approach and descent). This is often omitted at easy-access low-level venues where it would be superfluous. The second grade component is a number from 1 to 7 that assesses technical factors such as gradient or presence of difficult ice features.

WI 1

An easy ice sheet or stream bed that would typically be from 40° to 50° in steepness.

WI 2

An ice sheet or river course that would typically be from 60° to 70° in angle, with perhaps a few very short steps of 80°.

WI 3

A long, sustained pitch of 70° to 75° ice with the possibility of short vertical steps.

WI 4

A long, sustained pitch of 75° to 80° with big gaps between rests, or a pitch with approximately 10 - 15m of vertical climbing. There will be a need to place screws on steep ground. The pitch may also have some complex technical features or chandeliers to negotiate.

Cascade Falls, a classic grade III icefall, Canada.

WI 5

A long pitch of 80° to 85° ice, or a pitch with approximately 20 - 30m of vertical climbing. There will be a high possibility of difficult, complex ice features.

WI 6

A pitch with approximately 30 - 50m of vertical climbing with the likelihood of technical features such as bulges. An alterative would be less vertical climbing, but thinner or poorer quality ice.

WI 7

It used to be popular for traditionalists to suggest that the WI 7 grade does not exist. However, pillars may overhang slightly throughout their entire length or be so fragile that an extra grade is undoubtedly warranted, compared to a long fat vertical pitch of WI 6. More recently, some incredible pitches have been climbed involving a combination of overhanging glacier ice and free hanging pillars. The grade of WI 8 has even been suggested.

Mixed grades

In some cases a third category for mixed climbing may be introduced if an ice route has a mixed pitch or a short mixed section within a pitch (see mixed climbing grades on page 180) In recent years a French rock grade has sometimes been awarded if the rock climbing to approach the ice was done with hands as opposed to tools. In the same way, an 'A' or artificial grade may also be used if the rock has points of aid in it. E.g. III WI 5+, M6, F6c or A1

You will also encounter an 'X' for a route that is particularly prone to collapse and an 'R' which refers to thin routes which, by definition are run-out.

An example of a route worthy of an R route is the mythical *Gimme Shelter*, VI, WI 7, R, about which first ascensionist Kevin Doyle wrote:

'Not really very assuring climbing this half to one-inch business, but fortunately I could breathe a little when it gave way to some really thick two-inch stuff after 20m'

Grades and conditions

A grade presumes that a route is in average but not exceptional condition. This means that a route that forms predominantly in WI 5 condition may occasionally form in 4+ condition, in which case it should be regarded as a lucky steal.

Equally, this same route could be in WI 6 condition at the start or the end of the season. Only you will know how it felt on the day! When routes form in 'fat' condi-tion, they are often slightly less steep and they may also become 'grooved', creating better opportunities for resting.

Tim Emmett on *Hydnefossen*, WI 6, Norway.

A route may feel harder with early season chandelier ice or on warm days when it is running with water and the screws are dubious. Similarly, on bitterly cold days the route will feel extra hard because every placement may be a struggle.

"The difference between grade 5+ and grade 6 is that you can't get up a grade 6 without good technique."

Tim Emmett

Starting Out

Equipment

Mountain Safety

Ice : Style-Ethics

Ice : Techniques

Mixed : Style-Ethics

Mixed : Techniques

The Mind

Training

Destinations

Icefall etiquette

One of the greatest safety considerations when planning to attempt an ice route is the presence of others. Although you should make every attempt to minimise the amount of debris you dislodge, it must be accepted that falling ice will always represent a hazard, which is magnified the more people there are in the vicinity.

It is dangerous to stand at the base of an ice route when people are climbing and it is down-right stupid to start climbing directly below them. On narrow icefalls, especially those inside a confined gully (which will have a funnel-effect) you will get hit by frozen missiles. However on wider icefalls it may be possible to take a multitude of different lines up the same fall, enabling more than one party to climb at the same time, without straying into each other's line of fire.

The difficulty comes when another party, out of frustration at being pipped-at-the-post or just out of sheer stupidity, decides to set off below you on a route that won't accept two parties. Astonishingly, this potentially lethal scenario is very common and most experienced ice climbers consider this to be one of the greatest hazards. It is advisable to shout loudly and clearly that the party below you climbs at their own risk and to advise them to retreat. If they fail to heed your warning then you can only do your best to minimise the amount of debris you dislodge (more about debris on page 148).

Working backwards from the problem of parties climbing above you, it clearly makes sense to get to the base of your route first! On popular climbs, you may need to start hours earlier than you would deem necessary and perhaps even do the entire walk-in by torch light.

On busy weekends or during holiday periods, it pays to head for more remote or esoteric routes, or at least to have a contingency plan. Regarding who goes first, it is generally accepted that both members of the team should be geared-up and ready to depart, so anyone who tries to bag the climb when their partner is still halfway down the snow slope is acting inappropriately! The important thing is always to show respect and courtesy to others if you're beaten, but equally to be assertive if someone tries to take unfair advantage.

Neil on *Repentance*, WI 6, Cogne, Italy.

'Repentant?'
- Neil Gresham

Ian Parnell and I had wanted to do *Repentance Super*, WI 6, the jewel in the crown of Italian ice, for over a decade. We had been to Cogne on numerous occasions and it hadn't been in condition, but this was the last day of our trip and we'd heard it was there. We set our alarm early and headed down for breakfast in the hotel, where plans were discussed briefly with a French guide. He was taking his client up a WI 4 called *Monday Money*, just to the right of our chosen route. 'Have a good one,' we said and set off into the darkness.

Two hours later, Repentance towered menacingly above us as we bust up the slope. I stopped to catch my breath and then Ian muttered, "Err I think we might need to put a bit of a spurt on". To our bemusement, the French guide appeared from nowhere and seemed to be charging to the foot of *Repentance*.

We arrived at the same time although his client was nowhere to be seen. "Hi, we thought you were heading for the 4?", "Plans change," he said and started gearing up. Ian and I exchanged glances and weren't going to take this sitting down.

"Err, your client isn't here yet and you said you were doing the 4!"

His response, "Look, I'm a guide, I go where I want in the mountains!"

I couldn't believe it. "Well if you can, then we can!" I said.

"If you climb above me and dislodge ice, I will pull your rope!" He said coldly.

Ian's face turned scarlet: "You pull my rope and you'll have a big problem on your hands!"

Our friend recoiled and we simply set-off in front. We were astonished when he tried to take a line to the right of us. Fair enough to jeopardise himself, but when I led through on the second pitch I found myself fifty metres directly above his client, who was resting on the rope on the easy lower section!

Our lines had converged and the guide was belayed just to my right, within arms reach of my ropes. I looked at Ian and we both imagined a perverse version of the 'Touching the Void' story, with him pulling me off instead of cutting my rope! I went for it, climbing twenty metres of vertical ice without dislodging as much as a crumb.

Ian led through and I ended up sharing the next belay stance with the guide, who started changing his tune a little and apologising.

"Your first time on Repentance?" He asked.

It transpired he'd done it six times before! His client was now experiencing a full meltdown and I asked if it was her first time on a grade 6. He said that it was.

"Good effort on your first grade 6," I shouted down to her, "Keep going!"

"My first WHAT?" She exclaimed, "I thought we were on a 4!"

It wasn't until the guide told me his name that I recognised his face and realised he was only one of the most famous Alpinists of all time...

Starting Out

Equipment

Mountain Safety

Ice : Style-Ethics

Ice : Techniques

Mixed : Style-Ethics

Mixed : Techniques

The Mind

Training

Destinations

Starting Out

Equipment

Mountain Safety

Ice : Style·Ethics

Ice : Techniques

Mixed : Style·Ethics

Mixed : Techniques

The Mind

Training

Destinations

Neil on *Montmorency Falls*, WI 3, Quebec, Canada.

Ice: Tactics and Technique

There is a popular misconception amongst rock climbers that ice climbing is easy. With jugs to hang on to and holds wherever you need them - how hard can it be? Of course, it is rarely the case that we have complete freedom of choice with tool placements, especially on steeper and more featured icefalls. But even if the ice is flat and compact, there is still the need to conserve energy with tool placements and movement. A pitch will always start off feeling easy, but with poor technique the fatigue soon kicks in. On steep ice it's your forearms that start to burn from gripping, or your shoulders and triceps from swinging, and on easier-angled ice there is the dreaded calf-pump to contend with.

Starting Out

Equipment

Mountain Safely

Ice : Style-Ethics

Ice : Techniques

Mixed : Style-Ethics

Mixed : Techniques

The Mind

Training

Destinations

Starting Out

Equipment

Mountain Safety

Ice : Style-Ethics

Ice : Techniques

Mixed : Style-Ethics

Mixed : Techniques

The Mind

Training

Destinations

Ice climbing ergonomics

The subtleties of ice climbing ergonomics compare almost exactly to those in swimming. These are both movements that almost anyone can do to some extent but very few people can do properly. A swimmer may spend months correcting a stroke that is a few centimetres or a few degrees out and this may ultimately make far more difference to their performance than working on their fitness. Technique drives the machine in ice climbing. Get the movement right and everything else will follow.

Crampon placement

Efficient ice climbing must start from trusting your crampons. First make sure they are sharp.

Front and secondary points are all engaged to form a stable tripod by dropping your heels.

✔ The kicking angle is crucial - keep your heels low (this often feels unnatural to rock climbers who are so used to standing on tiptoe).

✔ Kick from below the knee. Firmly but not too hard or you will shatter the ice. On average it should take no more than 2 or 3 light kicks, even on brittle ice.

✔ Be accurate and look where you're kicking, aim for footholds whenever if possible.

✔ Engage the secondary points and drop the heel slightly to form a stable 'tripod'.

✔ Test each foot placement by gradually applying more weight.

✘ Never move up on foot placements that you suspect to be poor: try again, test and then relax once you know they're good.

✘ Never try to stand side-ways or on tip-toe on ice unless you are on a good foothold. Try to keep your feet perpendicular to the surface.

✘ Don't pivot with your feet unless using monopoints.

Using footholds

Always aim for ice ledges or footholds as they provide a great way to relieve the strain of pumped calves. Try shaking out your free leg, or even swapping feet to give both calves a shake. Go carefully when swapping feet so as not to snag your crampons.

Enlarging footholds

Consider chopping ice bosses with your adze to enlarge them when they are level with your torso and out to the side. Don't be greedy in case you destroy the entire feature.

Monopoint technique

With monopoints you can aim between chandeliers and obtain a secure placement without shattering ice. You can also stand in tiny pockets or in your previous pick placements. This is an essential technique for climbing thin ice or fragile columns.

Learning tip

On ice that is less than 80°, try climbing with one or no axes on a top rope to learn just how much help you can get from your feet.

Advanced footwork

Top level ice climbers barely kick with their feet at all, especially when climbing featured ice. It is good to practise using natural ice footholds, no matter how small and to develop a style that is more akin to rock climbing. Even with the tiniest ripples you need only place your monopoint to make your foot stable. Try pivoting and using your monopoint as if swivelling on a rock foothold, but be careful not to over-do it! Heel-hooks with spurs can also be used on steep pillars or bulges (see advanced techniques for steep ice starting on page 158).

Mark Garthwaite making sure his crampon placements are secure on *Vollokula Right-hand*, WI 5, Norway.

Starting Out

Equipment

Mountain Safety

Ice · Style-Ethics

Ice · Techniques

Mixed · Style-Ethics

Mixed · Techniques

The Mind

Training

Destinations

Axe placement

The axe swing

✔ Hold the grip right at the bottom.

✔ A light, minimal swing is the true sign of ice climbing ability. Hit as softly as you can in order to get a secure placement. Better to under-hit and have to make a repeat swing than to over-drive.

✘ Don't swing just from the wrist or the elbow or shoulder. You need an equal engagement of all three.

✔ Aim high above you, but not so your arm will be at full stretch.

✘ Don't let your elbow drift too far out to the side.

✔ The wrist must flick the tool forward so it accelerates at the final part of the swing, you will need to slightly relax your wrist longitudinally to do this, but not laterally.

✘ Do not relax your grip until the tool is securely placed.

✔ Be accurate, and if you need to swing again, aim for exactly the same spot, but if the ice at the placement site is poor then look around for something better rather than hacking the same spot to pieces.

✘ Never place both axes really close to each other, especially on brittle or chandeliered ice.

✔ When mixed climbing or on steep, patchy ice routes with intermittent features, you may need to swing the axe out to the side or at an awkward angle to make a placement. This requires practice but it is also worth considering that some axes perform better at this than others.

The start of the swing

The end of the swing

The elbow drifting out too far to the side (chicken-winging)

Adjustments for leash-less tools

Certain leash-less tools (with a prominent high-tool grip) require a swing that is slightly different and feels less natural. The action required is a downwards 'jabbing' or flicking action that comes more from the wrist (and requires less engagement of the shoulder). If you don't swing like this then you will encounter clearance problems (the shaft will hit the ice before the pick). The first generation of leash-less tools offered such poor clearance that many climbers were put off using them on ice.

The pull-test

Pre-testing axe placements is a key skill and the secret to gaining confidence, reducing physical tension and improving safety. This works on the same principal as bounce-testing when aid climbing before committing weight to a piece of protection.

The worst thing is to place a tool and move up on it without being sure if it's good. This will naturally force you to tense your body in an attempt to hold it into the ice. You will also find it harder to make the next swing and may enter a downward spiral.

The answer is to test first with a light pull and a slight wobble of the shaft, and then to fully weight the tool while still holding securely onto the other axe. Then relax! You are now free to completely trust it and focus on the next placement.

'Swing, test, trust, forget' - Alex Lowe

Reducing pull-testing

Only when you are very experienced should you even consider reducing the amount of pull-testing. Most climbers quickly learn that if the shaft of the axe rings and reverberates after a swing then the placement is almost certainly bomber and may not need testing.

The ability to judge less obvious placements is a skill that takes a lifetime and one which goes as soon as you spend time away from the ice. Use your ears and try to develop a feel, but if in any doubt then a quick pull-test always wins.

What to aim for

Aim for concave features such as pockets, scoops, dishes, the back of grooves, or better still - other people's placements! Avoid convex features such as the front of thin pipes or bulges as these may shatter.

Aim for concave ice features that are less likely to shatter than convex ones.

Starting Out · Equipment · Mountain Safety · Ice : Style-Ethics · Ice : Techniques · Mixed : Style-Ethics · Mixed : Techniques · The Mind · Training · Destinations

Starting Out

Equipment

Mountain Safety

Ice : Style-Ethics

Ice : Techniques

Mixed : Style-Ethics

Mixed : Techniques

The Mind

Training

Destinations

Placement depth

One of the great skills of ice climbing is knowing how deep to place your picks. Too deep and you will waste un-told energy with swinging and removal, too shallow and you will jeopardise your safety.

The best ice climbers place their picks as shallow as they can, yet with a safety margin built in. The skill is to alter the depth of your placements according to the condition of the ice and other safety factors such as the quality of your protection. Ice climbing is not about being a macho hard-hitter and those who adopt this approach will burn out well before their time. A skilled ice climber is more of a craftsman - using their axes with care and precision.

The first time out on ice, the tendency is always to over-drive. Focus on shallow placements, but don't rush this process or you may give yourself a scare. If you're really struggling, go back to top-roping or ground-level traversing. Remember the geometry of a reverse curved pick is designed to push the pick ever deeper into the ice, and provided they are sharp, a pick will bite even when balanced on a tiny ripple. A little tap home is really all that you need.

A great tip when leading is to place your picks shallow when close to screws and then gradually to place them slightly deeper as you get further away on a run-out. Placement depth is always harder to judge when climbing an ice feature with surface chandeliers - if they don't feel secure when you pull-test, then chop them away and get to the firmer stuff beneath.

Neil on *Patri Left*, WI 4, Cogne, Italy.
Photo by Dave Pickford **www.davidpickford.com**

Starting Out

Equipment

Mountain Safety

Ice : Style-Ethics

Ice : Techniques

Mixed : Style-Ethics

Mixed : Techniques

The Mind

Training

Destinations

Number of swings

The other great skill of axe work is to reduce the number of swings. Always aim for a 'first time' placement, by holding fire for a second or two and scanning the ice to spot the ideal place to strike. With hard, brittle ice and fragile features you will need to chip away with several light swings. This is always preferable to one giant bludgeon which can destroy the available ice and limit further options.

Hooking

To take the issue of minimal swinging further, the best ice climbers often attempt to hook with their axes, especially when climbing heavily featured ice. Look for natural pockets and threads by probing with your pick, but be sure to pull-test them first. You can really explore the potential for this when seconding and then try to maintain it when leading.

Another tip is to hook when you are close to screws and then swing slightly more as you run out the rope. Avoid marginal hooks, but if you are forced to use them then treat them like mixed placements, never high-tool. If you maintain a downwards, directional loading and the hook blows then there's every chance that the pick will still bed in deeper.

Pick retrieval

If you do over-drive an axe, the natural instinct is to jerk the shaft of the axe violently from side-to-side to release it. This quickly causes you to fatigue and may even lead to a broken pick. Instead, a swift upwards blow with the palm of your hand on the hammer or adze will cause the pick to cut a slot above it. The pick can then easily be removed. Take care not to over-do this when leash-less climbing. A pick with a sharp top edge, a rounded nose and short, bevelled teeth will be less likely to snag (see pick filing page 62).

Neil hooking his way up the featured ice of *Patri Right*, WI 4+, Cogne, Italy.

Starting Out

Equipment

Mountain Safety

Ice : Style-Ethics

Ice : Techniques

Mixed : Style-Ethics

Mixed : Techniques

The Mind

Training

Destinations

Swinging when fatigued

On good, 'plasticy' water ice, one accurate swing when tired is far better than four poorly aimed or limp-wristed attempts. It is the times when you find yourself severely pumped that there is a tendency to abandon good technique and make things worse for yourself.

If you get the dreaded jelly-arm and find that your pick glances off with every placement, the first tip is not to panic and to be very systematic. Stop thrashing away with your axe. Leave your tool in the ice - it doesn't have to be in a placement that will hold body weight, just one that will safely take the weight of the axe. Now lower your arm down and shake it, relax and breathe deeply. If you're using clipper leashes then you'll need to detach in order to do this. The key point here is to leave the tool behind because if you are gripping it you won't recover anything like as well as if shaking a free hand.

When you feel a notable improvement, raise your arm and with a single confident and accurate swing - make your placement. As soon as you have it, relax your grip then shake the other arm. Repeat until you are out of trouble.

Sandy Ogilvie battling the pump on an un-named WI 5 at Kaldakinn, Iceland.

Starting Out

Equipment

Mountain Safety

Ice : Style-Ethics

Ice : Techniques

Mixed : Style-Ethics

Mixed : Techniques

The Mind

Training

Destinations

Body positions

The basic body position for low-angled ice.

Centre of gravity over feet

Not over-stretched

Grip relaxed

Heels down, secondary points engaged

Knees braced

Centre of gravity beyond feet

Tense and over-gripping

Over-stretched

Heels too high, front-points barely engaged and secondary points not engaged

The basic position for steep ice - the monkey hang*

Arms straight

Body relaxed and breathing deeply

Legs bent

Knees braced

Heels down

Starting Out

Equipment

Mountain Safety

Ice : Style-Ethics

Ice : Techniques

Mixed : Style-Ethics

Mixed : Techniques

The Mind

Training

Destinations

Neil on a WI4+ pillar at Gol, Norway.

* The term 'monkey hang' was coined by legendary American ice guru Jeff Lowe.

Upward movement

On flat homogenous ice it is possible to perfect an ideal sequence for movement and climb in a similar way to a lumberjack, pushing with the legs rather than pulling excessively with the arms. The key to doing this is to move with the axes at alternate heights rather than level and to roll with the body rather than pulling up and locking-off. Practise until it becomes relaxed, coordinated and subconscious.

The alternating sequence

❶ Arms straight with tools at slightly different heights. Bring feet up high, taking two or three small steps, bend knees and stick bum out!

❷ Stand-up straight using full thrust from the legs (minimise pulling with arms and maintain downwards, directional pull on tools. Pull on the lower tool as much as the upper tool).

❸ Replace tools, rolling the torso slightly rather than locking off (note line of symmetry down body for balance).

Maintaining balance

It can be surprisingly difficult to stay in balance when climbing steep ice, especially on pillars. The key is to maintain a pyramid shape with an axe at the point and crampons level at the base and not to step or reach too far outside it.

Watch out for the dreaded 'barn-door' - it's surprisingly easy to become off balance. Don't reach too high and never place your axes too close together - if the ice shatters then both tools will rip.

Climbing pace and confidence

It is holding static positions, especially with bent arms, that causes your muscles to cramp up when ice climbing. The faster you climb, the less fatigued you will become and the happier your second will be! Yet clearly there is still the need to be steady and cautious. You must strike a balance and avoid unnecessary delays.

If a placement is good then go! Try not to waste time faffing and move on at the earliest opportunity. If you are shaking-out then don't allow your mind to wander to negative thoughts about being cold, tired or scared - concentrate on getting a good recovery, or looking above at the next section.

Advanced tips, keeping a rhythm

On really sustained pitches, when the ice is good, try climbing to an approximate time rhythm so that your muscles never stay tense for too long. Count a beat in your head but don't worry if a placement goes slowly and you can't stick to it. You may also try co-ordinating your breathing patterns with your movement. Don't make thin, rapid gasps with your mouth, instead breathe slowly and deeply from your chest cavity. Exhale hard every time you stand-up or pull-up and then inhale. When you start to get this to work, ice climbing becomes quite meditative and highly absorbing.

Moving on complex ice

When climbing heavily featured ice it will be harder to get into a steady rhythm using the alternating sequence but you will be able to adapt certain elements of it to your movements. Moving on complex ice is more akin to moving on rock, where you look for handholds and footholds, as well as weaknesses such as ledges or bridging grooves for resting and placing screws. When the ice is really funky you need to probe with your pick to explore and test formations. Beginners may find this frustrating or intimidating but experts find featured ice the most fun and interesting to climb.

Starting Out

Equipment

Mountain Safety

Ice · Style · Ethics

Ice · Techniques

Mixed · Techniques

The Mind

Training

Destinations

Starting Out

Equipment

Mountain Safety

Ice : Style Ethics

Ice : Techniques

Mixed : Style Ethics

Mixed : Techniques

The Mind

Training

Destinations

Bridging

When climbing steep ice you should always be on the lookout for bridging positions to rest and place gear from. These are usually found in grooves rather than convex pillars or flat walls. Bridging on smooth walls will place strain on the calves so look out for ledges, bosses or scales where the foot can be placed sideways to relax your calves.

When moving, make small but secure steps and try not to get one foot too much higher than the other. On featured ice keep an eye out behind you for a large boss, fluting or mushroom. It's easy to get tunnel vision and miss these.

Beware of bridging out onto slim hanging icicles too early. A great tip is to kick the base off to relieve it of its own weight and also to see how strong it is. Kick it low and don't massacre it or you may lose the whole thing. Kick in gently with small taps and test the foot placement by easing weight over on to it before you commit. Take advantage of the rest position but have it in the back of your mind that your foot may blow.

Guy Willet bridged out between the columns of a WI 5 at Mauvoisin, Switzerland.

Resting

A rest can mean anything from a quick shake of a forearm on a vertical column to a bridge position or a 'hands-off' ledge. The dilemma with good rest positions is simple: if you don't make use of them you will risk burning out, but if you spend too long on them you could be there all day. The key is to prevent yourself from getting excessively pumped on the steep sections so you don't need to spend so long on the obvious rests. By shaking-out very quickly and intermittently on steep ice you can go a long way towards preventing a major pump from setting in. With leash-less tools you can have a quick 'flick' after almost every axe swing, but with clipper leashes you may need to enter a disciplined routine of unclipping every four or five moves and forcing yourself to shake. Always take the time to shake after tough axe swings or screw placements.

Even if there are no obvious bridge positions or resting footholds and you are on steep, smooth ice, shake out by stabilising your feet and straight-arm hanging your tools. Don't shake whilst holding a lock-off. Breathe deeply and try to relax every part of your body that isn't contributing to maintaining the position. It's surprising just how many unnecessary muscles are often tensed. If you have a trigger finger on your axe then milk this for all you can.

The key skill when trying to make use of a 'semi-rest' is to recognise the point to start moving again. Monitoring your heart rate and breathing are the crucial tips here. It can sometimes be hard to tell what the pump is doing but when your heart rate and breathing are as low as they can go then it's time to split.

When resting on steep terrain you can often lean-in just a few degrees more than is first apparent, even without a faint groove. Arm bars around scales or projecting ice bosses can provide a great way to relax your grip, but always test them first. Note also that bridge rests can be pretty tiring on your calves unless you have good ice footholds, so it may simply be a case of trading the lactic acid between your calves and your forearms!

Tim Emmett hanging straight-armed, hips close to the cliff in line with his axe and his weight equally balanced between both feet. Gol, Norway.

Starting Out

Equipment

Mountain Safety

Ice : Style-Ethics

Ice : Techniques

Mixed : Style-Ethics

Mixed : Techniques

The Mind

Training

Destinations

Starting Out

Equipment

Mountain Safety

Ice · Style·Ethics

Ice · Techniques

Mixed · Style·Ethics

Mixed · Techniques

The Mind

Training

Destinations

Traversing

Traversing on ice is much more awkward than it sounds and is worth practising at ground-level before you encounter it on a route. Keep your feet perpendicular and make small sideways movements with both axes and feet - overreaching will lead to more strenuous placements and the chance of barn-dooring out of balance. However, avoid placing your tools too close together.

The swing required to place your tool to the side is awkward and more of a 'jab'. For this reason it's always easier to go diagonally up rather than horizontally.

On flat sheets, don't be tempted to step-through or side-step like you would on rock. Only do this if the ice is featured and there are large footholds. Swapping hands on leash-less tools will make things much easier, but go carefully - be sure each placement is solid and make extra effort to load the tool downwards.

Down-climbing

Most people would think that climbing down on ice was the same movement as going up, but in reverse - not so! The swing is different (more of a 'jab' like traversing) and extra effort must be made to keep the heels down when kicking. Climbing down is also a useful skill for taking rests or making a forced retreat, so it's worth giving it special practice.

Unknown climbers on *Weeping Wall Variant*, WI 4, Canada. Photo by Neil Gresham.

Neil making the difficult transition to easier-angled ice on a WI 4+ in Norway.

Moving from steep to slabby ice

Never presume that you've got it in the bag as you approach the top of a steep section of ice. Pulling over the top can sometimes be the most treacherous point of the climb and it is common to find cruddy snow ice or brittle, delaminating water ice that forms dinner plates when you hit it. Avoid the tendency to leave your feet behind as you become over-stretched and impaled against the ice.

- ✔ Place a screw in the last good ice before you pull over.

- ✔ Keep your feet level, with your heels well down.

- ✔ Clear away any excess snow or rime over the top with your adze.

- ✔ Plant a high tool over the top.

If you encounter dinner plates, make several small carefully aimed swings. It is often possible to make safe use of moderate dinner plates because the pick punctures through the plate to the better ice below, however this takes skill to judge. If the dinner plate looks really bad then chop it away and try to cut down to the next layer of ice. Don't start bludgeoning or you will destroy everything. It is usually possible to cut a ledge that you can hook, even if you can't get a deep placement below.

The key to the entire sequence is to avoid over-stretching with the high axe and to lean back with your body to make it possible to move your feet. Run them up in small steps and then walk them over onto the slab. Never use a knee!

Starting Out

Equipment

Mountain Safety

Ice : Style-Ethics

Ice : Techniques

Mixed : Style-Ethics

Mixed : Techniques

The Mind

Training

Destinations

Clearing verses trundling

There is a big difference between 'clearing' away loose or poor ice, and knocking off blocks because you are being heavy-handed and careless. It is all too easy to enter your own world when ice climbing, especially when taxed to the limit, but it's vital to maintain a constant check on the presence of others. Position your belay away from the fall line, and remember that others may turn up at the base of the route at any time.

Minimising the amount of debris you dislodge is one of the great ice climbing skills. Not only does it make sense from a safety perspective, it will increase the amount of energy you save. Learn to read the ice and aim for solid, concave features rather than convex bosses or flutings.

One or two light and accurate swings will always disturb less than a clumsy bludgeon. If you need to trim curtains or clear loose ice, then let your belayer know what's going on. Keep your body clear and dismantle larger features in chunks rather than going for the full demolition job.

When climbing, if you do hit something big and see a stress crack - don't hit it again! Some people feel that it is the second's job to remove any obvious cracked ice blocks or dodgy 'hangers' but you can make of this what you will. Take particular care when the ice is either very brittle or soft. The largest dangers come from thin curtains or free-standing pillars (see techniques on page 160).

Ian Parnell clearing poor ice from *Monday Money*, WI 4, Cogne, Italy. Photo by Neil Gresham.

Avoiding hotaches

Maintaining warm hands is a crucial aspect of climbing technique. The mistake is to be too passive or to forget to prioritise it. Your glove systems and preparation tactics will play a vital supporting role too.

When climbing

Keep your arms as straight and your grip as relaxed as possible.

Shake out frequently, especially if you feel the onset of numb hands. A vigorous downwards flick of the arm will stimulate circulation.

Using leash-less tools makes it much easier to shake and the handle shape means your knuckles won't be chilled from touching the ice.

Mark Garthwaite dealing with hotaches. Photo by Neil Gresham.

Resist the temptation to sprint the pitch and deal with the hotaches at the belay - better to stop at rests and deal with them in a series of minor bursts.

When preparing

Keep your climbing gloves inside your thermal on belays and whilst gearing up.

Keep climbing gloves as dry as possible.

Never gear up with bare hands - wear liner gloves for fiddly tasks.

Keep hydrated (see also nutrition on page 253).

Try taking the supplement Ginko Biloba to improve circulation.

Be aware that you are most susceptible on the first route of the trip, especially when seconding the first pitch.

Before you set out, always hang on your tools first to get numb hands and then leave time for the blood to return.

Keep active on belays, try doing sets of squats (stomping is usually out due to the risk of stepping on the rope). Do shoulder circles with one arm at a time by swapping the breaking hand on the rope.

Dealing with hotaches

Having apologised to anyone in the vicinity for the language that is about to follow, the secret is to put your arms above your head. This will make it very slightly less excruciating.

Starting Out | Equipment | Mountain Safety | Ice : Style - Ethics | Ice : Techniques | Mixed : Style - Ethics | Mixed : Techniques | The Mind | Training | Destinations

Starting Out · Equipment · Mountain Safety · Ice : Style-Ethics · Ice : Techniques · Mixed : Style-Ethics · Mixed : Techniques · The Mind · Training · Destinations

Placing ice screws

Placing protection is nearly always the most difficult part of an ice climb. Modern equipment and systems have greatly improved the efficiency of this strenuous and scary operation. With leash-less tools and razor sharp 'express' screws, it is now possible to protect relentlessly vertical ice.

One can only marvel at the bravery of the early pioneers whose hands were chained to straight-shafted axes. The prehistoric ice screws were so blunt that the pick of the spare tool needed to be used to lever them in. The result was that screws could only be placed on easier angled ice or by somehow threading your elbow through your leash on steep ice in order to release both hands! These days it is much easier yet the method still needs to be practised and perfected. There are various different systems and it pays to see which one works best for you. Always start on easier angled ice and work up to using the same method on ice that is progressively steeper.

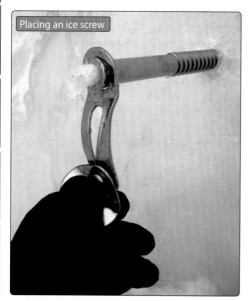
Placing an ice screw

Where to place?

First look for a rest place like a bridge position or a good foothold, then start looking for the best site for the screw. In perfectly formed ice you may have a free choice, in which case, place it between waist and chest height and not too far out to the side. A good method is to inspect the placement site when it is at eye level, look for hard, deep homogenous ice without air pockets or cracks. You may need to clear surface snow or rime, or trim away bosses or chandeliers. Chop a pilot hole with your pick approximately an inch deep. Now climb on a move until the placement is between waist and chest level.

Secure stance

Plant both tools deeply and securely above you and hang with straight arms and a relaxed posture. Keep your feet level and bed them in securely. Bridge out if possible. Engage the screw and make every attempt to get it to bite as soon as possible. This is always the crucial bit. Apply a few firm, careful turns, stabilising the shaft of the screw to prevent it from disengaging. As soon as you're sure it's bitten, use the ratchet handle to bury it as quickly as possible.

The crucial point is not to perform this entire operation without swapping hands and shaking out. With leash-less tools you have no excuse for allowing the hanging arm to get completely pumped. Keep shaking it out, even if the operation takes slightly longer. The big mistake is to focus on the placement at the expense of your arms. Take care to maintain stable posture and monitor your axe and foot placements.

Rope flick method

Placing screws on steep ice can feel frightening and precarious if you're new to it. A great method to increase confidence is to flick one of your ropes over the leash-less 'grip hook' on the base of your free tool. This will serve to protect you as you place the screw. Take care that the tool is well seated or it may be dislodged when removing the rope. The grip-hooks are rarely approved by manufacturers for withstanding high loads, but they may be sufficient to arrest a small slip. The old method was to flick the rope over the head of the axe but the risk of the rope sliding on top of the sharp blade ought to be enough to put most people off.

Clipper leash method

With clipper leashes, use the same overall method but detach one arm from one axe. If your axes have clipping eyes at the base of the handles, then you have the option of clipping the free one with a quickdraw and clipping the rope in to protect you while you place the screw. You can then simply transfer the quickdraw straight over to the screw (with the rope still clipped into it).

It is usually a good idea to swap hands mid-operation in order to rest the hanging arm, although this will require you to clip back in and then clip out. This method always seems frustratingly fiddly compared to using leash-less tools, but it may offer increased security to those who are new to the game. Perhaps a better option is to keep your clipper leashes permanently un-clipped and to use them only in an emergency.

Above: The rope flick method can provide some additional security when placing screws.
Below: A bridge or chimney position will always make it easier to place screws on steep ice.

Starting Out

Equipment

Mountain Safety

Ice · Style · Ethics

Ice · Techniques

Mixed · Style · Ethics

Mixed · Techniques

The Mind

Training

Destinations

Placing screws on snow ice and thin ice

Only the very best and boldest climbers will find themselves in a situation where they need to place screws on thin or poor quality snow ice that is also very steep.

One would hope to be able to lean in and stand on your feet in order to make the best of this harrowing task. With snow ice the issue is poor consolidation and hence long screws are a good idea. Many first-time snow ice climbers describe horror stories of their ice screws falling out below them as they led a pitch. The key is to chop away as much surface rime as possible and forage for better ice below. It could be worth placing two screws next to each other and clipping one rope in each, or alternatively, equalising both using a sling. Secure the sling to each screw with a karabiner and then tie a centralised over hand knot for the rope-clipping karabiner.

On aerated chandelier ice, pay particular attention to the resistance of your screws as you place them and listen carefully to monitor the 'bite'. It may be that the best you can hope for is half of the screw to be in contact with the ice - but at least half is better than nothing! Thread runners may provide a better option so keep your eyes peeled.

With thin ice, the key is to assess the ice depth - it may be the case that it is too thin to take anything other than a hand-hook. If you can get a short screw half way in or deeper then it may be worthwhile. Try to avoid hitting the rock and blunting the screw, but in an emergency you may have no choice but to maximize placement depth. Again quantity is quality here, and you may have to tie off protruding screws with a larksfooted sling.

Where and how many?

Try to resist the temptation to place too many ice screws. No matter how strong you are, it will always be more energy-efficient to keep climbing. The more experienced you become the more you can work on extending your comfort zone. Look at the pitch first and aim to correlate screw placements to cruxes or rest points. On steep sections try climbing up a few moves to place one and then reversing for a rest. Run it out when the ice is easier angled and plastic, but place gear if the ice is steep or untrustworthy. Above all else, always place one before you pull over the top onto easier ground as this is where you are likely to encounter dinner plates or poorly consolidated ice.

Paul Thorburn placing a screw on *Nemesis*, WI 6, Canada. Photo Neil Gresham.

'Placing screws the hard way'
- Neil Gresham

I hadn't expected this today - my first big lead on ice. My partner Ian Harrison and I had been slogging up the never-ending treadmill of *Gardyloo Gully* on Ben Nevis on our way to attempt a grade V called *Smith's Route*.

Ian was planning to lead, but his lungs were on the verge of collapsing so he sank a Deadman and sat down to spark up a fag. We were sat next to a short grade III ice step known as *Tower Scoop*, which we had planned simply to skirt around.

'You may as well lead this thing while I finish my Camel', announced Ian.

With the adrenaline flowing, I started racking my screws. My first ever experience of ice came only the previous day, when we had both had a total epic on a grade IV.

With hands clamped securely into my fixed leashes, I set off, kicking each crampon five times, just to make sure. At fifteen feet I looked down. The snow slope dropped off below like a perfect fairground ride landing, but the exposure kicked in and it felt best to place a screw.

I fumbled under my jacket, which was bulging over my harness. Frantic turning followed… it's bitte... no it hasn't... yes it has... axe knocks it out... I wobble... I'm sure my axe is coming out! I shove the screw in my mouth and lunge at the ice with my spare axe. Phew.

I remove the screw along with most of the flesh from my lips and throw it in the front of my un-zipped jacket. Where's that blood coming from? Better continue climbing, there's bound to be a rest soon.

Half an hour later I reached the snow slope at the top with eyes on stalks, no runners and a jacket full of ice screws! Things are easier these days with leash-less tools or clipper leashes but it's still worth practising before you play.

Starting Out
Equipment
Mountain Safety
Ice : Style-Ethics
Ice : Techniques
Mixed : Style-Ethics
Mixed : Techniques
The Mind
Training
Destinations

Reading the line

The first time you look up at a frozen waterfall it may look climbable by taking almost any line. Yet even the flattest and simplest falls invariably have better ice in certain places, subject to conditions.

When climbing complex and featured falls, route reading can take on a whole new meaning. As soon as you start climbing you will gravitate towards easier angled sections, grooves and lines of weakness. The trick is to check beforehand that these will not be blind alleys leading to nasty bulges or impassable sections of poor quality ice. A complex icefall can feel like a vertical frozen maze if you don't plan exactly where you're going before hand. Guidebooks usually offer minimal assistance so you must develop the skill for doing this yourself. Below are some pointers.

> Ice always feels steeper than it looks.

> Look for weaknesses - ramps, slabs, ledges and grooves.

> Avoid bulges, detached or fragile features with stress fractures.

> The ice on the sides of a feature is usually thin and poor.

> Look for blue ice first with a smooth, homogenous texture.

> Grey or white ice with a broken or bubbly texture is likely to be poor or chandeliered.

> Plan your belay points.

Where to belay

Plan belay points according to the guidebook description but remember that ice often forms differently and that fixed rock belays may be covered over by the ice in fat conditions or unreachable in lean conditions. Always look for ice ledges and only take hanging belays as a last resort.

When the ice is featured avoid climbing long pitches, as the rope is likely to drag or get snagged under icicles. Always position the belay away from falling ice. Hiding in ice caves, below bulges or around the back of icicles is a good tip if you are unable to move to the side. Your first belay at the base of the ice fall should be to the side of the fall line but not halfway down the snow slope so there is a load of slack in the rope. If possible place a belay anchor to avoid being dragged down the slope.

Belaying to the side of the fall line.
Mathew Tomlin on a WI 4/4+ at Arolla Tunnel, Switzerland. Photo by Adrian Berry.

Starting Out

Equipment

Mountain Safety

Ice : Style-Ethics

Ice : Techniques

Mixed : Style-Ethics

Mixed : Techniques

The Mind

Training

Destinations

Approaching *Nemesis*, WI 6, Stanley Headwall, Canada. A big undertaking where good route finding pays dividends. Photo by Neil Gresham.

Starting Out

Equipment

Mountain Safety

Ice : Style-Ethics

Ice : Techniques

Mixed : Style-Ethics

Mixed : Techniques

The Mind

Training

Destinations

"Blue Bombshell"
- Neil Gresham

In the winter of 2004 I was in Kandersteg in Switzerland with a team of talented young British sport climbers, most of whom were trying ice for the first time.

On the second day, I took fifteen year old Leah Crane (who had climbed an 8a sport route) up her first grade 4, but conditions were brittle and she wasn't enjoying the ice very much. Just to our left, setting out on a two pitch WI 5 was Chris Cubitt, who had made a dramatic impression on the world mixed climbing scene the previous season with an M11 flash and an M12+ redpoint. Chris had less experience on the ice, but he was keen to show Adrian Baxter the way. Adrian had onsighted numerous sport 8a+s but he was well aware that he was a beginner today.

I huddled in my jacket as Chris finished the first pitch. He had looked a little tentative on the long, steep slab and was foraging below some bulging cauliflowers for a belay below the final pillar. He brought Adrian up and secured him on the stance. Occasionally they would disappear from view below the mushrooms and then their heads would pop up again.

Soon Chris was picking his way up the final pillar but you could tell he wasn't entirely happy. The ice had been bad for us and I didn't envy him. He placed a screw and moved out onto the column. His swings were cautious, but for some reason he decided to hit, what looked from my vantage point like a vertical fracture line on the side of the pillar. With a loud 'CRACK!' a car-sized missile detached itself and plummeted towards Adrian's head and exploded on the mushrooms into a thousand pieces.

Chris swayed on his remaining tool, but Adrian was nowhere to be seen - for five seconds, ten, fifteen, twenty... and then just when we thought his time was up, a helmet popped out like a mouse from its hole staring at a tiger. As they abseiled off, I thought about the times when my belay had crept into the fall line and made a pact with myself that this would never happen again.

Neil climbing *The Candlestick Maker*, WI 5, in the Ghost region of the Canadian Rockies.

Warm-up and preparation tactics

Speed is sometimes described as safety in the mountains. With the clock ticking and your partner stomping his or her feet, there's hardly time to stop and perform a half hour yoga routine at the base of the route. It's easy to kid yourself that the walk-in has been more than enough to warm you up and that the best policy is just to get your breath back and then get going. If the route has an easy first pitch, then you're likely to get away with this, but if you think you can go from the snow slope straight to a super-sustained ice pitch without being hit by the dreaded 'flash pump' then think again.

It is also possible that you will scare your-self and get a major dose of the hotaches from over-gripping. The flash pump is caused by failing to build up the intensity of climbing progressively. Ice climbing is not user-friendly like sport climbing and it is always challenging to coax your body into the right state for action.

Ice bouldering

The best approach is some ice traversing or 'bouldering' if there is some steep ice at the base with an appropriate safe and flat landing. If the situation is less user-friendly, all you need to do are some pull ups and dead-hangs on your tools. Hang until your hands go numb and you get slightly pumped. Stay tied in if you are remotely concerned about the position.

Climb back down

An alternative is to climb up, place your first screw (with the full intention of getting slightly pumped) and then climb back down to rest and get the blood into your hands and forearms.

Quick stretch

Whilst resting, you may as well perform a quick and minimal stretching routine. If your partner complains then remind them that it will help you climb faster! If you hold each of the recommended stretches for ten seconds then this routine will take less than two minutes. Be sure that you are in a safe position to do this and stay on belay if necessary. More stretches are given in the warm-up section on page 252, but the best stretches for ice are given below in priority order.

> Shoulder circles and finger clenches
> Forearm stretch
> Calves
> Shoulder stretch
> Lats
> Groin
> Hamstrings
> Quadriceps

Tim Emmett improvises to warm-up for the Ice World Cup event in Quebec city 2001.

Starting Out
Equipment
Mountain Safety
Ice : Style-Ethics
Ice : Techniques
Mixed : Style-Ethics
Mixed : Techniques
The Mind
Training
Destinations

Dealing with different ice features

Complex icefalls may require a large repertoire of techniques:

Steep snow

This is commonly encountered when approaching the base or between ice sections on a climb. The basic approach should be common sense for anyone with a bit of winter experience. Keep front-pointing and kick as deep as possible. Plunge the shafts of your axes if the snow is soft, but if it is firmer then use the picks but swing hard and try pressing on the head to reduce 'butter-knifing'. Alternatively try using the adze.

If you are unfortunate enough to encounter one of those evil snow slopes that can't decide when it is merging with the ice route, then the trick is to revert to good old fashioned step cutting. Dig deep and chop them when they're above your head. Note the point above you where the ice looks good enough to take a screw and then make a very careful risk assessment. Never underestimate these situations. We have memories of a WI 6 in Norway where the 85° snow slope at the base was the crux!

The cone

The cone at the base of an icefall is created from the upwards splashing of water. Cones usually look easy due to their angle but may feel weird and insecure to climb if you're not prepared for what's in store. If the cone is heavily scaled you need to hook rather than swing with your axes. Similarly, you will be standing on the top of the scales rather than kicking with your feet.

On small scales, try placing your feet slightly sideways to engage more of the crampon. Small scales will be easy to climb but difficult to protect. Simply hook, pull test and move through. It's usually best just to run it out, but if the cone is huge or if it's warm, or very cold and brittle you may need to smash through to find solid ice beneath the scales for placing screws.

Neil hooking and side-stepping up the huge cone of *The Fang*, WI 5+, Vail, Colorado.

Shaft plunging in deep snow. Photo by Neil Gresham.

Starting Out · Equipment · Mountain Safety · Ice : Style-Ethics · Ice : Techniques · Mixed : Style-Ethics · Mixed : Techniques · The Mind · Training · Destinations

Giant scales, cauliflowers and mushrooms

Giant scales may look terrifyingly fragile but they can be welded-in and safe to climb in good conditions. Chopping them down simply isn't an option so hooking with your axes is the only way. There will still be a lot of leverage so be sure to pull-test every placement, keeping your body well to the side if possible!

Cauliflowers and mushrooms are fatter than scales and have broader bases, but all three features present themselves as overhanging obstacles when climbing. It's always best to weave your way diagonally between them rather than pulling straight over. Leg flexibility is useful for high-stepping and rocking over and it's well worth stretching first. Make sure your axes are well seated over the back and watch out for rime or poor bubbly ice over the top.

Screws placements may be found around the base of the features but avoid placements in the steep front faces as the ice is often brittle and striated. Never place screws in the top of giant scales, due to the threat of leverage forces, and instead place a sling over the top as a spike runner. Only place screws in the top of mushrooms if they are huge and well bonded and if you can dig through to find good quality ice. Rope drag can be an issue so take extra slings for extending screws.

Neil manteling onto a mushroom on an unnamed WI4+, Gol, Norway.

The classic WI 5+ pillar of *Stone Free*, Rifle, USA.

Pillars

Steep pillars usually provide the crux of ice climbs and all the techniques described in this chapter for efficient movement, resting and placing ice screws will need to come together for you to be successful. In particular, balance will be an issue, so be careful to stay within the pyramid shape.

Take deep breaths, relax, don't over-swing, keep your arms straight, look for footholds, shake-out intermittently and minimise screw placements. A good tip for getting started is to place an axe sideways or an arm or hand round the back in order to lean out and gain height. You may also place a high screw and come scurrying back down for a breather before you commit.

Fragile pillars

With thin or free-hanging pillars, the first step is to assess that they are safe to climb. Use the following checklist but remember to incorporate the 'X' factor - If you aren't feeling lucky then walk away!

Conditions

> Too warm or too cold and brittle?

> Too early or late in season?

> Missing chunks or stress fractures?

> Water leakages?

> Shape? If the pillar is free-hanging then it needs to be widest at the top and narrowest at the bottom. Heavy bases or weird wind-blown geometry are a no-go.

> Length? Note the length relative to the attachment point - 20m telegraph poles are out.

> Bonding? Check that it looks sufficiently well bonded at the top (i.e. it joins to a decent amount of rock or ice).

Starting Out
Equipment
Mountain Safety
Ice : Style-Ethics
Ice : Techniques
Mixed : Style-Ethics
Mixed : Techniques
The Mind
Training
Destinations

Climbing pillars

If you've given yourself a green light then the only approach is one of supreme confidence. Climb with razor sharp picks and points. Fix a screw on the cone or, better some rock gear as a high side runner. Pre-plan your exit dive in case it goes when you first tap it. Do not clear the thin pipes at the very base as these may still give it a degree of structural support if they connect.

Stretch as high as possible and 'build' two or three hooks by chipping very lightly. Never swing your axes. See how it 'feels' and go back down for a re-think if necessary. When you commit, avoid stepping on the thin icicles at the base, and press your points in rather than kicking. In extremely fragile cases you will have to wrap your legs around the column and 'shimmy' up.

If the pillar doesn't touch down then a one-arm lock-off is a much safer but more strenuous option than a figure-of-four.

Once you're established on the pillar, continue to use hooks and footholds or stand in your pick placements wherever possible. Try climbing with your axes round the back and leaning out, lumberjack style, as this will mean that you don't have to hit it so hard. It is crucial not to be tempted to hit harder as you get higher. Remember it's not an axe ripping that is the concern - collapsing pillars don't give warnings!

Fracture points are unpredictable so don't place gear until you're above the bonding point. Always remember that the last part is usually the most dangerous because you are highest and will be most tired. Forget the theory that if it holds you when you're on the bottom part then it will hold when you're on the top part - instead remember that it's more likely to break the more you mess with it, especially when close to the bonding point. Pat yourself on the back only when your second arrives at the belay!

Tim Emmett monkeying up a stick on a fragile icicle at Pont Rouge, Quebec.

Ice skins

Ice skins are thin crusts or sheets of ice that are loosely bonded to soft cruddy snow. If they are on flat ledges then they present no major obstacle, although care should be taken to sink your picks deep when pulling over. If they are at a steeper angle then you may be in for a toboggan ride unless you punch right through and bed your points into the snow behind. This type of terrain always feels bold and requires a confident approach. See climbing steep snow on page 158.

Thin ice and verglas

Thin ice can feel particularly intimidating and the temptation is to panic and start smashing it with your picks or blunting your screws. If you only need to pass a brief section of thin ice, then it may not prove to be a big deal if you can place good gear below. However, a full pitch of thin ice is another story. Know what you're letting yourself in for and be prepared to back-off.

A golden rule is that you should always be able to down-climb, as you can't rely on worthwhile protection being available. Your picks should at least start off razor sharp and the technique is to make tiny, light chips and never swing. Look for places where the rock below eases in angle as the ice on the top side of these angle changes will usually be thickest.

Try to hook wherever possible, especially if the ice contours a small edge or pocket. You can also try dragging your pick over dimples in the ice so it catches. Beware the 'tool tapping' method where the head or hammer of the other tool is used to bang your pick into place. If you get this wrong and the placement blows then there is no other tool in the ice for back-up. Best only to use this on slabby terrain when the weight is firmly on both feet.

An advanced tip is to chip a small edge and to place the pick sideways on the ledge in order to obtain more purchase, you can then use this to stand on with your feet. Sharp monopoints are essential and you should try to stand in your previous pick placements. Move slowly and carefully, spreading your weight evenly, and maintaining a downwards directional loading on both your axes and your crampons.

Hand-hooks and tied-off short ice screws provide minimal ice protection (see placing screws on thin ice on page 152) but it is always best to look out for rock gear. (See rock protection on page 78 and placing gear on trad mixed on page 220).

Verglas technique: the left axe has been placed slightly sideways to maximise placement depth and the right axe is hooking a small edge that has been chopped out.

Hanging curtains on ice routes

Free-hanging curtains or icicles are always strenuous and gymnastic to swing on to. In this section we will presume you are approaching the curtain from ice. Curtains on mixed routes will involve additional tactics that are given in the sport mixed section on page 206.

> Find a stable position first in order to rest and place good gear.

> Bridge or back-and-foot rests nearly always appear at the point where the ice meets the curtain.

> Trim away any fragile chandeliers at the base of the curtain (after checking all is clear).

> If you need to make a long reach then plant one tool in an undercut position and lean out on this. The aim is to plant the next tool in the near side of the curtain itself. Use this tool to get your body round and then plant another as high as possible in the front face of the curtain.

> Bring your feet out and try to bridge.

> Beware the fragile pipes at the base, but don't get your feet too high until your low tool is removed.

> In extreme cases where you can't step low or bridge then a figure-of-four may be required (see sport mixed techniques on page 202). It may also be useful to match one pick over the other to avoid the effort of making two placements.

> Check your rope as you move up and flick it round any snagging icicles.

> Don't place a screw until you reach the point where the curtain is joined.

Ben Wilkinson on the outrageous hanging icicles of *In der Wurze liegt die Kurze*, WI6, Kiental, Switzerland.

Starting Out

Equipment

Mountain Safety

Ice : Style-Ethics

Ice : Techniques

Mixed : Style-Ethics

Mixed : Techniques

The Mind

Training

Destinations

Starting Out | Equipment | Mountain Safety | Ice : Style-Ethics | Ice : Techniques | Mixed : Style-Ethics | Mixed : Techniques | The Mind | Training | Destinations

Advanced moves for steep ice

When the ice gets really steep and bulging or discontinuous then dramatic measures may need to be borrowed from the domain of sport mixed climbing.

Cross-overs

A cross-over is when you reach across one arm and axe with the other. They can be used to move between isolated ice features, although swapping hands is usually a better method.

Twist-locks

If you have to make large reaches between steep ice bulges or pull round ice roofs then twist-locking or even figure-of-fours can be employed. See sport mixed climbing on page 200 for further ideas on body position.

Undercuts and side-pulls

Undercuts and side-pulls work well for spanning between patches of discontinuous ice, as well as for moving onto hanging curtains. Chip a deep inverted slot or place your axe side-ways around the back of the pillar, lean back and stretch up.

Neil using a side-pull on an ice pillar.

Neil demonstrating a cross-over move on steep ice.

Heel-hooks with or without spurs

Spurs are worth experimenting with on ice for heel-hooking round the back of columns or for pulling over bulges. Most climbers consider the risk of colliding with a spur to outweigh their advantages.

If you don't have spurs then wrapping your leg around the back of a column may be almost as effective. Anything goes to help you save energy.

Ian using a heel-hook on *Stone Free*, WI 5+, Rifle, Colorado, USA.

Egyptian / drop-knee

When climbing very steep and featured grooves, try dropping the knee on the same side as the arm you're reaching up with. This will cause your hips to twist in at 90° to the ice and help to create opposing force between feet, equivalent to a bridging move.

Neil demonstrating the drop-knee.

Flag

For counterbalance on steep featured ice when standing on one foot, as an alternative to swapping feet, try swinging the free leg behind you and locating the balance point. The free leg can also be passed inside the active leg but take care not to snag your crampons.

Starting Out · Equipment · Mountain Safety · Ice · Style-Ethics · Ice · Techniques · Mixed · Style-Ethics · Mixed · Techniques · The Mind · Training · Destinations

However much hassle it feels to make a flask when you are rushing to get out of the door in the morning, you will never regret it on really cold days.

Dealing with difficult conditions

Cold showers

Some routes never stop running, but on warmer days you may have to deal with a torrent of water coming down the line. The old-school approach is just to put up your hood and go for it, but common sense should always prevail over machismo and every climber should recognise the point where enough is enough. The main point is not to get yourself in a situation where you are too cold or wet to climb safely. Wet, numb hands are not so good for placing screws.

The Canadian ice guru, Joe Josephson, recommends bin-liner inner gloves, but taking at least two spare pairs of normal gloves ought to be a minimum requirement. Take a good look at the falls from below and note which parts are running heaviest. You may opt to take a slightly more challenging line or use alternative belay points in the interest of staying drier. It's also worth having a full dry set of clothing in your sack for when you get down.

Cold brittle days

On particularly cold days, hand and toe warmers may provide a glimmer of comfort. Belay jackets and extra mitts may prove to be the best clothing system. See also tips for avoiding and dealing with hotaches and staying warm on belays earlier on page 142. Change out of wet thermals before you start.

Be hydrated and take a flask. Make sure picks and points are razor sharp and adjust your swing by using several small 'chips' rather than a big swing. Monopoints will be better than duals. Short screws will be easier to place and may be less prone to shattering the ice.

Rotten ice

Treat rotten or sun-baked ice with extreme caution and don't be afraid to back off. Has it been way too warm recently? Are you approaching the end of the season? If you're on the upper pitch of a route that always gets caught in the sun then be disciplined enough to make the call and retreat.

If you are forced to continue, then place your picks and feet deeply, move stealthily, load axes downwards and use body tension. Look for threads in preference to screws for protection. Equalised long ice screws are another option.

Sunny conditions

On sunny days it is vital to move fast as ice screws can be prone to melting out. Take long ice screws and look for additional forms of protection. Screws with metallic hangers are less prone to absorbing heat than black hangers. A less serious issue is to remember your sun-block!

Getting out of trouble

Retreating from steep ice

If the ice is simply too steep and you are too pumped to climb down or place a screw then you have three options:

1) Place a hand-hook in a previous axe placement and clip into this.

A hand-hook in a previous axe placement.

2) Clip the clipping eye on the bottom of your axe with a quickdraw. Never clip your leash or the top of the axe.

3) Flick the rope over the leash-less hook on the grip of your axe. Note that these are rarely designed to be fully load bearing.

Ask your belayer to take tight, but do NOT sit straight back on the rope. Instead gently apply the minimum amount of weight, making every attempt to keep weight on your feet. Attempt to place a screw as soon as possible, taking care not to move around excessively and dislodge your aid point. When you have two good screws you can then decide whether to lower off these or build an Abalakov (see page 34).

Retreating from poor ice

If the ice becomes too poor to continue then it is always best to climb down while protected on one rope from above. Sink as much gear as you deem fit and equalise it with a sling. Giant threads will usually be more secure and cheaper to leave than screws. Your belayer can then take in on the lead rope and keep you tight, but pay-out on the top rope as you reverse back down.

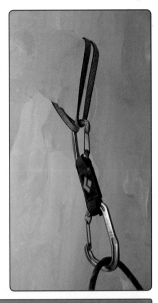

Above: threads in ice are secure, low-cost gear for bailing off.
Below: When screws protrude in thin ice they can be tied off and equalised to provide more security.

Starting Out

Equipment

Mountain Safety

Ice : Style-Ethics

Ice : Techniques

Mixed : Style-Ethics

Mixed : Techniques

The Mind

Training

Destinations

Ice trip tactics

Weather and conditions are always the deciding factors when it comes to planning your days during a trip, but if conditions are settled then you may have the luxury of working things so you can get the very best from yourself.

Watch out for the dreaded pre-trip 'trophy headlights' - where you run the risk of burning out at the start by being over enthusiastic. Pace yourself and build up to the big climbs on your tick list.

Another important tip is to get plenty of sleep and eat well prior to the trip and during the first few crucial days - winter climbing is particularly taxing on the immune system when you are out of practice and colds or flu are all too common at the start of trips.

On longer trips, rest days should be taken tactically before you blow yourself completely and have an epic that will take two days to recover from. Combining hard mixed routes with ice climbing can also be a challenge and it usually works best to do mixed on day one, ice on day two and then rest.

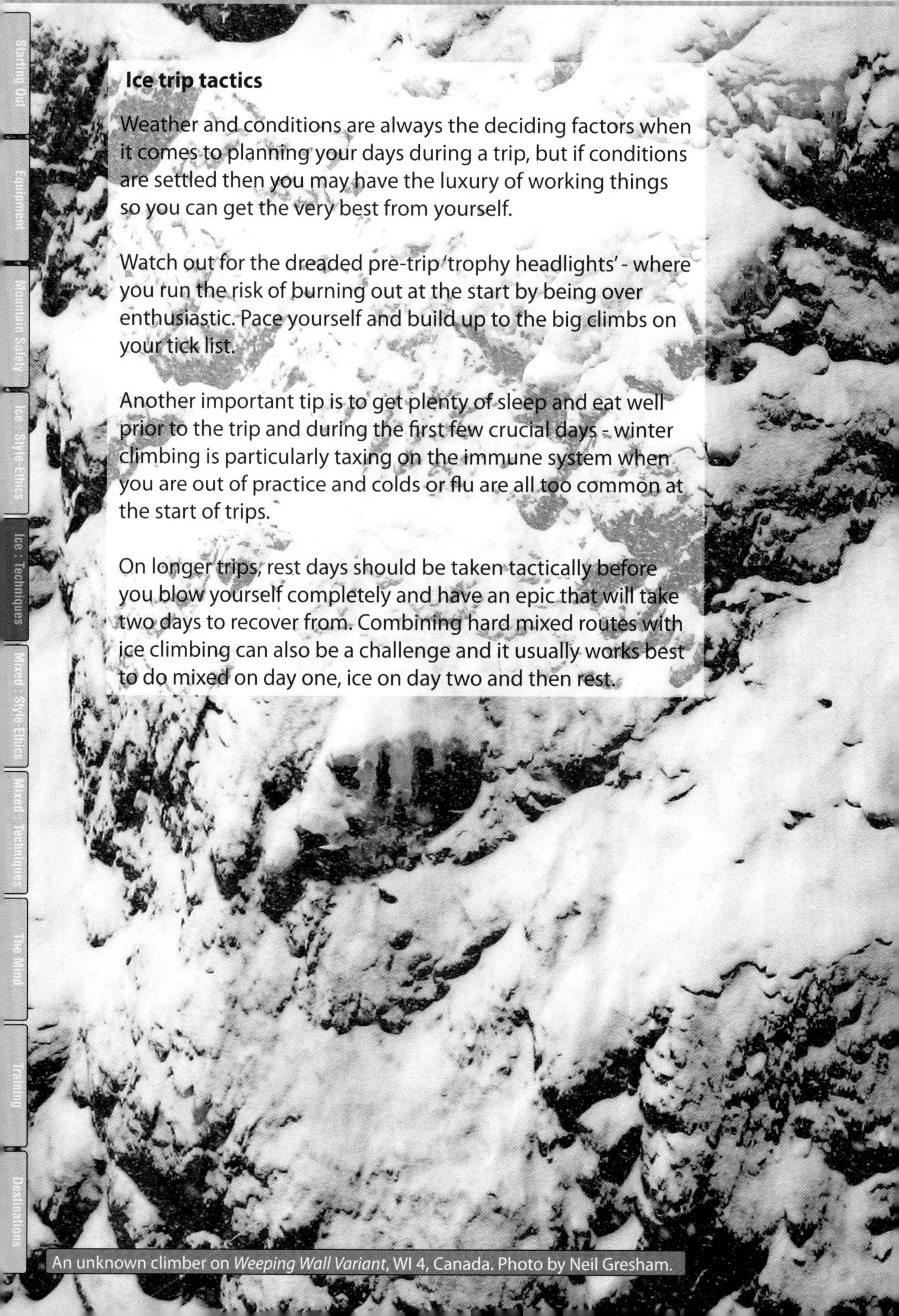

An unknown climber on *Weeping Wall Variant*, WI 4, Canada. Photo by Neil Gresham.

Starting Out

Equipment

Mountain Safety

Ice : Style-Ethics

Ice : Techniques

Mixed : Style-Ethics

Mixed : Techniques

The Mind

Training

Destinations

Starting Out

Equipment

Mountain Safety

Ice : Style-Ethics

Ice : Techniques

Mixed : Style-Ethics

Mixed : Techniques

The Mind

Training

Destinations

Jon Winter on the Scottish mixed classic
Savage Slit, V,6 Cairngorms, Scotland.

Mixed: Styles and Ethics

Starting Out

Equipment

Mountain Safety

Ice : Style-Ethics

Ice : Techniques

Mixed : Style-Ethics

Mixed : Techniques

The Mind

Training

Mixed climbing is surely one of the great tests of all-round climbing skill. The idea of hauling your way up a rock face with axes balanced precariously on tiny edges and crampons skating around on verglas is one thing. Add to the equation the need to clear thick hoar frost from the holds and place protection as you go, or transfer your weight onto a fragile hanging icicle and you have a major challenge on your hands.

Today mixed climbing has evolved into a diverse activity, with styles ranging from roadside crags with short bolted 'power' routes, to multi-pitch, traditionally protected, endurathons in the mountains.

Trad mixed

Traditional mixed routes are protected with natural gear, which is most commonly placed without using aid or resting on ice axes. Trad mixed routes may be on dry rock that is thinly iced or coated in verglas, or they may be on rock that is coated in thick rime or hoar frost. Frozen turf may be common to both styles.

Climate conditions will dictate the style of mixed climbing that is found in a given area. In Scotland, for example, there is a tendency to encounter icier mixed routes in the Western Highlands and snowier routes in the Eastern Highlands. Note that in some areas, the same route may come into condition either as an icy mixed or a snowy mixed route.

Icy trad mixed routes

Icy trad mixed climbs are rarely climbed as rock routes in summer, as they would be wet, loose and vegetated. These routes are often bold owing to the difficulty of placing gear in iced-up cracks. The main gear options are either to chip the ice away and attempt to place nuts or pegs, or to bang in a hand-hook or warthog into clumps of frozen turf. Cams are rarely safe in cracks that are heavily iced.

Snowy trad mixed routes

In general the snowy, 'hoared-up' mixed routes are less commonly found owing to the very specific type of climatic conditions that create them. In the Eastern Highlands of Scotland, cold, moist Easterlies blow in from the North Sea and plaster thick layers of hoar frost to the buttresses of high mountain crags. Many of the classic mixed routes of this area are also popular summer climbs.

Alan Mullin on the snowy trad mixed line of *Stirling Bomber*, V,7 Cairngorms, Scotland.

Snowy trad mixed ethics

Climbers sometimes raise the issue of whether it is legitimate to climb a summer rock route with axes and crampons in winter. Most consider it to be fair game as long as it is on designated crags and the route is in 'acceptable winter condition'. This latter point often attracts furious debate. Having made the drive and the long walk-in, it can be all too tempting to bag a snowy mixed route when it has minimal cover and is barely different to a summer rock route.

Those who are used to dry-tooling at sport mixed venues may find the idea of deliberately waiting for a route to be covered in snow to be extraordinary. But without snow cover, these are not mixed routes and the technical difficulty will be substantially less. This type of discussion often sounds ridiculous to outsiders, but the more you climb in snowy mixed areas, the more you start to realise that a very special set of ethics have been preserved in order to enhance the challenge of the activity.

Rich Cross earning full ethical brownie points but also tired arms from cleaning *The Deviant*, V,6 in deeply hoared condition. Cairngorms, Scotland.

Everyone has their own ethical boundaries but it also pays to respect the traditions. Only you will know whether a climb felt wintery on the day.

Starting Out · Equipment · Mountain Safety · Ice : Style-Ethics · Ice : Techniques · Mixed : Style-Ethics · Mixed : Techniques · The Mind · Training · Destinations

Sport mixed

Sport mixed routes are bolt protected throughout the rock sections, although some will require screws for ice sections. A small selection of trad gear may also be required if the bolts are well spaced. The most common style is for the rock to be 'dry' or dotted with the odd patch of ice or verglas. The intention of a true sport mixed climb is to head for a suspended ice feature or to connect a series of discontinuous hanging features. Many climbers feel that a degree of ice is necessary on a climb in order to justify the term 'mixed', and to make the use of axes and crampons feel appropriate.

Dry tooling routes

Today many bolted dry-tooling climbs exist which involve no ice at all. These are either found in between other routes that do have ice features, or at dedicated 'all-dry crags' where none of the routes have ice. Whilst representing fun gymnastic challenges, and great training options for warmer days, many winter climbers feel that the 'all-dry' mixed climbs lack a certain aesthetic quality in comparison to their icier neighbours. Theoretically, these routes could be attempted with ice tools on summer days as winter conditions are not required in order to make an ascent. At all-dry crags the 'D' grade (for dry) or even French grades are sometimes used instead of the 'M' grade in order to make a distinction from mixed routes.

Ian Parnell on *Puma*, M9+ at the Haston Cave, Cogne, Italy. Photo by Neil Gresham.

Ian Parnell on *Easter Rising*, M8, Ouray, USA. Photo by Neil Gresham.

Starting Out

Equipment

Mountain Safety

Ice : Style-Ethics

Ice : Techniques

Mixed : Techniques

Mixed : Style-Ethics

The Mind

Training

Destinations

Evolution of sport mixed

Sport mixed is a relatively young branch of climbing that evolved in answer to the long-standing dilemma of how to reach suspended ice features that never touch down. The early pioneers used aid on the rock to gain the ice and from then on, normal ice techniques would be employed.

It was climbers like Stevie Haston in Europe and Jeff Lowe and Will Gadd in the USA, who first experimented by using dry-tooling techniques as an alternative to aid in the 1980s. This was done at first with a combination of pegs, slings and a variety of different forms of fixed rock pro. But as momentum gathered, soon the drills came out and a whole new way of climbing emerged. The first routes of their generation were Jeff Lowe's *Octopussy*, M7 in Vail and Stevie Haston's *009*, M9 in Cogne. The first sport mixed climbers used standard ice tools with leashes, as no alternatives existed, but lighter boots and clothes were de rigueur. Standards rose and Gadd added *Amphibian*, M8 to Vail, and Pete Takeda and Jeff Lowe established *Fatman and Robin*, M9. Haston responded back in Europe with the incredible *X Files*, the World's first M10.

The touch paper was lit at the turn of the century when the potential for creating ice and mixed climbing competitions was realised in Europe, and suddenly an arms race to develop superior tools and techniques was on. The leash-less tool was born and a new repertoire of moves became the norm. The result was that mixed climbing grades went, literally, through the roof.

A few of the top French rock climbers like Francois Lombard and Daniel Dulac took to the mixed and their superior fitness levels showed. But Stevie Haston stayed in the frame with his multi-pitch M11, the *Empire Strikes Back*, which finished up a very serious hanging icicle. Meantime, Italian mixed master Mauro 'Bubu' Bole added *Mission Impossible*, M11 to Cogne and Robert Jasper also added a string of impressive M routes with double figures, including *Vertical Limits*, M12 in Kandersteg, Switzerland.

At the same time things were hotting up at the Cineplex in Canada with Will Gadd's *Mushashi*, M12 and Ben Firth's the *Game*, M13. On the whole, these routes were steep with good hook placements, but Gadd's 2007 Cineplex route, the *Steel Koan*, M13+ was notable for being marginal and precarious as well as preposterously strenuous.

Use of spurs

The technological advances in equipment for sport mixed climbing seemed to race ahead of themselves around the year 2003. Suddenly climbers were hanging upside down from heel spurs in the middle of roofs and taking hands-off rests in the middle of cruxes. 'Good luck to them!' was what most people thought, but then ethical awareness started to close in around the mixed cowboys. The new notion was that if you can rest anywhere then the challenge is greatly reduced. It seemed that heel-hooks with spurs were now the utility move and that figure-of-fours were needed less and less. Ultimately, the choice rests with the individual, many routes are now given a grade for spurs and a grade without. Now that many of the top sport mixed climbers have hung up their spurs, it will be interesting to see if others follow suit.

Starting Out

Equipment

Mountain Safely

Ice : Style-Ethics

Ice : Techniques

Mixed : Style-Ethics

Mixed : Techniques

The Mind

Training

Destinations

Stevie Haston in action making the second ascent
of *Mission Impossible*, M11, Valsavarenche, Italy.
This was the first ascent without the use of spurs.
Photo by Laurence Gouault Haston.

Some terminology

Onsighting

An onsight ascent of a mixed route is where the climb is led successfully on the first attempt, without falls or resting on the rope or ice axes, and without prior knowledge (or beta) of the moves or protection. You can still claim an onsight of a sport mixed route if the quickdraws are in place although it is undoubtedly slightly harder to place them yourself. On trad mixed routes you will need to place all the runners yourself and if you encounter any in-situ gear then treat it as a lucky bonus!

Onsighting can be especially difficult and frustrating on mixed routes. Sometimes it only takes a little pocket or 'nick' that is half the size of a fingernail to support a pick and full body weight. Add to this, the presence of snow cover on the route, and suddenly route reading becomes the key skill. Many traditional mixed climbing areas such as Scotland have a strong onsight ethic where working routes is still frowned upon.

Flashing

A flashed ascent is where a route is completed on the first attempt but with the aid of prior knowledge (or beta) of the moves and protection. On trad mixed routes, note that you will still have to place the protection yourself in order to qualify for a flash.

On mixed routes, beta can make an enormous difference to the feel of the climb. At sport crags you can watch someone to see where all the pick placements are or have the moves shouted to you as you climb. If you are just told one small snippet of beta before a climb then it will be up to you to decide whether it made a crucial difference to the ascent. Most will probably still claim the onsight!

Beta can be obtained verbally or by sight, whether live or on film, but if you actually abseil down the climb, and especially if you clear snow away or test hook or gear placements then it definitely does not count as a true 'flash' because you have actually been on the climb. Looking at a climb from an adjacent route is perhaps as far as you can bend the ethic!

Andy Nisbet heading into the unknown on the first ascent of *White Horses*, V,6 Aonach Mor, Scotland.

Mark Garthwaite following a well rehearsed sequence on an M9 at Pont Rouge, Quebec.

Redpointing

A redpoint ascent is the term given to a successful ascent of any climb that has been attempted previously. Even if you have only tried a climb once before and you are then successful on your second try, that is still a redpoint.

On a true redpoint ascent you must clip all protection as you go, though on sport routes, it is perfectly acceptable to have the quickdraws in place. Redpointing is less commonly applied to trad mixed climbing, although most would consider that you should try to place the majority of the protection on lead if you do go for a trad redpoint. Note that in-situ wires or pegs are sometimes used on routes that have heavily iced cracks.

A popular strategy on redpoints is to climb up to the first or second bolt, or protection point, and then reverse back down to the floor - this way you can leave that piece of protection pre-clipped for the full redpoint ascent. On trad routes, every attempt should be made to place protection on the redpoint. If some protection is in place an ascent is sometimes referred to as a 'pinkpoint'.

Working a route

You don't need to work a route in order to red-point it but it helps! Having fallen off a flash or an onsight, you may just wish to lower straight to the floor and try for a redpoint. Alternatively, you can hang on the rope to practice and perfect moves. The more you work a route, the more you will increase your chances of redpointing it quickly and for this reason, many purists are still uncomfortable about the idea of working mixed routes, especially the trad ones. With mixed climbing it makes a huge difference to work a route just once before doing it, seeing as so much of the skill is about finding and trusting placements.

Starting Out | Equipment | Mountain Safety | Ice : Style-Ethics | Ice : Techniques | Mixed : Style-Ethics | Mixed : Techniques | The Mind | Training | Destinations

Mixed grades

The 'M' system is widely used throughout the world for grading both trad and sport mixed routes. Note that 'M' grades take into account a combination of the technical difficulty and strenuousness of a climb but they do not take into account danger.

Trad mixed grades - the Scottish system

When 'M' grades are used for trad mixed routes then an 'R' is sometimes added to reflect big run-outs or poor protection; but whether the added difficulty of placing trad gear is reflected in the 'M' grade is a grey area. For this reason, many prefer to use the Scottish system, which consists of a two-part grade

1) A roman numeral indicating the overall difficulty of the route encompassing technical difficulty, length, sustainedness, strenuousness and boldness .

2) A number which describes the technical difficulty of the hardest move or crux sequence on the route (not pitch).

For example, VII,5 may be very bold or sustained, but with low technical difficulty, whereas V,7 is likely to be well protected and with a short hard crux section.

The only limitation with this system comes when assessing what constitutes the hardest 'move' on the pitch. Many climbers will disagree over this and what usually happens is that the numerical grade often gets used like an M grade, to reflect the 'overall' difficulty of the moves on the pitch.

Andy Kirkpatrick on *The Seam*, a classic Grade IV,5 in Scotland.

Sport mixed grades - the M system

'M' grades lend themselves perfectly to sport mixed routes by working in exactly the same way as French sport grades. For example, a long route with relatively easy moves may be given the same 'M' grade as a shorter route with harder moves.

A plus or minus is sometimes used to split 'M' grades, although some consider this to be a little pedantic. The issue of whether or not heel spurs are used is sometimes dealt with by offering 2 separate grades, although this will only effect the very steepest routes. 'M' grades usually start at about M4 or M5 because they were originally based on the 'WI' scale and sport mixed climbing is rarely any easier than this! M13+ has been established and the system is open ended.

Moving from bare rock to thin ice - a typical situation on a sport mixed route. Tim Emmett on an un-named M8 at Gol, Norway.

'M' grades and Scottish grades compared

Note that when comparing 'M' grades to Scottish grades, if the physical and technical difficulty were isolated then there would be an approximately two grade difference between the routes. In other words, a Scottish VIII,8 would be like doing an M6 without the bolts, but placing your own protection. The result of this means the 'overall' effort of onsighting a Scottish VIII 8, (hanging on to place fiddly traditional gear) is probably equivalent to onsighting a bolt protected M8 and hence the grades do actually compare.

Starting Out

Equipment

Mountain Safety

Ice : Style-Ethics

Ice : Techniques

Mixed : Style-Ethics

Mixed : Techniques

The Mind

Training

Destinations

Starting Out
Equipment
Mountain Safety
Ice : Style-Ethics
Ice : Techniques
Mixed : Style-Ethics
Mixed : Techniques
The Mind
Training
Destinations

Andy Kirkpatrick needing all his skills in full Scottish conditions on *The Seam* IV,5, Cairngorms.

Mixed: Tactics and Technique

Starting Out

Equipment

Mountain Safety

Ice : Style-Ethics

Ice : Techniques

Mixed : Style-Ethics

Mixed : Techniques

The Mind

Training

Destinations

The tricks for conserving energy on mixed climbs share many similarities with rock and ice climbing, but there is a further set of skills to master. The thing that shocks most people when they first try mixed climbing is how insecure everything feels and the result is that massive amounts of body tension and grip strength are squandered.

You only have to feel the difference between an onsight and a redpoint to realise just how much we are prone to over-compensating. This chapter will examine body positions, anchor points, and upward movement technique as three separate components in the mixed climbing chain and then put them back together so they function smoothly.

Mixed climbing ergonomics

Basic body position for slabs and vertical

The basic position for low-angled mixed terrain is similar to ice, except that you won't be able to place axes or crampon placements wherever you need. The result is that it will be more challenging to maintain balance and stability. Careful foothold selection and weight distribution provide the key.

Downwards pull maintained on axes

Arms relaxed, straight but not over-stretched

Head no higher than picks

Body relaxed

Centre of gravity over feet and central below picks

Legs slightly bent

Heels down with secondary points engaged for stability

Starting Out

Equipment

Mountain Safety

Ice : Style-Ethics

Ice : Techniques

Mixed : Style-Ethics

Mixed : Techniques

The Mind

Training

Destinations

Wrong body position for slabs and vertical

Avoid over-stretching, or stepping too high. Keep your weight over your feet. Pull directly down on your axes. Make every attempt to relax your body although your ability to do this will depend entirely on the security of your tool placements. If they are poor then maintain maximum tension.

Arms bent

Levering up and outwards on picks

Body too far out and head too high

Legs too straight

Ankles too high

Starting Out

Equipment

Mountain Safety

Ice · Style-Ethics

Ice · Techniques

Mixed · Style-Ethics

Mixed · Techniques

The Mind

Training

Destinations

Basic hanging position for overhangs

To save energy when mixed climbing on overhangs, keep your arms as straight as possible and try to relax your grip. Not only does bending your arms require bicep strength, but it will restrict the circulation to your forearms and cause you to get cold hands and pumped forearms.

Grip relaxed

Arms straight

Centre of gravity directly below axe

Legs bent

Attachment points

Crampon placements

It's all too easy to become over-reliant on your axes when mixed climbing, but if you can place your feet securely you will save on grip strength. A sudden sparking foot will cause you to hang on like crazy to compensate, and it's vital to remember that your feet will misbehave just like your axes if you don't give them the same level of attention.

Study every foothold before you place your points and position them with care and accuracy. Hook your front-points over in-cut edges and on larger holds you can slide your foot forward so that the secondary points engage just below the edge.

On slabby terrain you can sometimes drop your heel slightly so the secondary points engage to create a stable tripod. Mono-points give more options for thin cracks and narrow pockets. If you're used to rock climbing then the trade-off is simple - you won't be able to smear, but you can edge on literally anything, provided you maintain stable posture.

The big mistakes are raising your heels too high or simply forgetting to maintain a fixed angle with your feet, while you're concentrating on something else like an axe placement or a clip. The key is to be creative with footwork and to employ every trick you've learnt from rock climbing like pivoting on footholds, side-stepping, outside edging, flagging, back-stepping and Egyptians. These techniques have already been described in the ice chapter but they actually have far greater relevance to mixed climbing.

Lastly, it's vital to have a bit of faith in yourself - the tiniest foothold will work, provided it is positive and you are accurate and willful.

Footwork and body tension

Body tension is required in many ways when mixed climbing. First there is the need to keep your feet in contact when climbing overhangs. Then if they do swing off you'll need to lift them back-up, or perhaps hoist your legs in position for a figure-of-four. But the final need is for climbing vertical walls or slabs that have marginal footholds or ripples - in this case, you will have to use abdominal strength to keep your knees up high and prevent your feet from sparking off. You will also need a great deal of body tension to use vertical side-pull type footholds which are usually held in tension with opposing axe placements.

A mono-point placement on rock.

Axe placements

When rock climbing, we rely greatly on the sensation of touch to help us use each hold, but when mixed climbing for the first time it feels like your hands and fingers have been anaesthetised. With sensation removed, we tend to squander copious amounts of energy as we desperately 'will' each placement to hold.

Learning to trust your placements and relax are the key skills in mixed climbing. You can never hope to gain the same level of tactility that you experience when rock climbing but you can certainly develop a new sense for placing and trusting your tools. When learning these techniques on sport mixed routes, it may be a good idea to tape your adzes and hammers or remove them altogether to avoid a nasty blow to the face if a tool rips.

Hooking

This is the simplest and most frequently used method of obtaining a secure placement. A hook on an edge will work best when a unidirectional downwards force is maintained.

The key to using hooks is to keep your body low and to resist the temptation to lever the shafts upwards as you move up. A deep incut pocket or tapered crack will always provide a more secure hook and will place less demands on careful body positioning than balancing your pick on a flat or sloping ledge. A pick can sometimes be placed sideways on a thin edge but this will require extra care to prevent outwards drift of the shaft. The slightest rotation and the pick will spin-off. See page 194 for tips for hooking side-pulls or diagonal edges.

Driving

For awkward sized or parallel-sided cracks that are choked with mud or turf, try driving the pick, adze, hammer or axe head with force in order to obtain a placement. Occasionally a light tap on the back of the head of your axe with your other tool can help seat a placement and this shouldn't be confused with hammering your picks into blank rock which will cause permanent damage and is considered the lowest form of cheating.

Hooking

Driving

Pick torquing

If the previous method doesn't feel secure, another method for ascending parallel-sided cracks is to insert the pick and apply a torsional force. Pick torques will work for most cracks from pick-width to 2cm wide, but for larger cracks you may need to switch to torquing with the head or shaft of the axe.

For diagonal cracks, simply hold the axe in the usual way, but for plum vertical parallel cracks you may need to go for an inverted pick torque. This is where you turn the axe upside down, insert the pick and rotate the shaft. The key to torquing is to maintain even and continuous pressure throughout the duration of the move and only to release a torque when you are sure that the next one is good and loaded.

All pick torques place major strain on the blades but a great tip to minimise this is to shift your grip higher up the shaft of the axe. Note that B-rated picks have lower torque strength than T-rated picks (see page 60) and that stronger heavier climbers have to exercise particular care.

Torquing

Andy Benson torquing up *Central Buttress* VII,8 Glen Coe, Scotland.

Starting Out

Equipment

Mountain Safety

Ice : Style-Ethics

Ice : Techniques

Mixed : Style-Ethics

Mixed : Techniques

The Mind

Training

Destinations

Head torquing

Head or shaft torquing is another essential technique for climbing cracks that are wider than a few centimetres and they are especially useful techniques for the Scottish style of mixed climbing. The easiest option is simply to cam the shaft into a horizontal bedding plane, but more skill will be required for laybacking up corner cracks or giant flake systems. Feel around inside the crack for a flat secure surface - if the tool hits an irregularity mid-move then it may come skidding out. Be slick with your footwork and keep the shafts perpendicular to the crack. If the crack is too wide then your final option is a can-opener.

Can-opener (Steinpuller)

This technique relies on a camming force between the pick and the head of the axe and this can be created in three ways:

For a standard can-opener, the pick hooks on an edge and the head levers up against a capping roof or overlap - an upwards force is then applied to the shaft of the axe. These placements allow the climber to lean out further and gain more height than is possible merely with hooking.

A can-opener

The next method is to invert the axe and insert the pick into a downward pointing flake or undercut and then cam the head of the axe into the wall below it. The grip must then be held with your thumb towards you in order to maintain a downward force. This is notably different to undercutting seeing as you must pull down on the placement to maintain it rather than pulling up and leaning back.

An inverted can-opener

The third method applies to corner cracks that are too wide for head torquing. The axe is inserted with the pick facing away from you and the shafts perpendicular to the crack. This technique requires precision tool arrangements and the constant use of body tension in order to maintain the direction of loading.

Matching picks

If you can only find one secure placement then try matching your axes together by hooking one pick over the other (or the high grip). This is also a good technique to use when hanging from one arm when you need to pull back up.

Matched picks

Improvisation

Anything goes when it comes to trusting tool placements, so be as devious and inventive as possible. Experiment by using any number of the above methods in order to obtain a placement. With time it will become more obvious which one to go for.

High-tooling

With leash-less tools, a great way to swap hands or increase your reach is to use the high-tool grip. Avoid high-tooling on marginal hooks as this is prone to levering

High-tooling

the shaft upwards and causing the pick to skid off. Be sure to maintain a downwards loading, even when high-tooling on good hooks.

Use of hands on rock

If all else fails, don't be scared to use your hands on a jug or in a good jam if the territory permits. This is an essential technique for Scottish-style trad mixed routes. The best way is to leave an axe dangling from its clipper leash, but take care if you're leash-less. For a move or two, you may get away with a tool over your shoulder, but for longer sequences use a holster.

Using hands on rock

Some sport mixed climbers are reluctant to use their hands but a good jam or flake may provide a great means of resting on steep terrain by bringing you up closer to the rock and effectively reducing the gradient. It may also allow you to use your grip in a different way and hence relieve forearm strain. If it's a spike or flake then try hooking your wrist around it. Remember that your axes are nearly always the best option, unless a handhold or jam is really positive.

Starting Out

Equipment

Mountain Safety

Ice : Style-Ethics

Ice : Techniques

Mixed : Style-Ethics

Mixed : Techniques

The Mind

Training

Destinations

Developing a feel

It takes a lot of practice and experience to develop the sixth sense that is required for trusting axes when mixed climbing. It is always best to start by seconding if you are in a mountain environment and to build up a broad base of experience before moving on to easy leading. However, a great way to short-cut the learning process is to visit sport mixed crags where you can push harder in relative safety.

Dry tooling on old stone walls or disused buildings is also good for this purpose. The key is to keep pushing until you start ripping placements, but in a safe environment, as it is only then that you will learn what you can get away with and where the margins lie.

Alan Mullin refining the feel of tools on marginal hooks by dry tooling on a stone wall.

Placement rating system

When testing and using mixed placements, it may help to use a rough grading system in your head from 1 to 3, with 1 being the sinker hooks and 3 being the ones that will rip if you breathe at the wrong time! You can then adjust your climbing technique according to your assessment of the quality of the hook.

1) Sinker hooks

If your pick sinks into an in-cut hook and feels immediately secure then pull-test it by yanking hard and wobbling the shaft of the axe - this will tell you whether or not you can get away with relaxing and moving up without maintaining full body tension and a one-way directional force on the pick.

Use this placement to shake-out, clip or place gear if necessary. You may also match hands, use the high-tool grip or make aggressive moves like figure-of-fours.

The cups of tea model

When attempting to trust hooks that are average or marginal, it works well to imagine that you are carrying a full cup of tea in each hand. In other words, you can move your centre of gravity around below the cups as long as they stay level and completely still. It was the legendary master of modern mixed climbing, Will Gadd, who proposed this great little analogy in the first year of the Ice World Cups in 2000, which he then went on to win.

2) 'OK' hooks

If a feature appears less obvious, run your pick around it and attempt to locate the most incut part. Dig your pick into this precise point and pull-test the placement cautiously at first, and with a very slight wobble. If it rips or feels marginal then replace it, attempting to find a slightly different position or angle of pull. Test again with minimal wobble by pulling harder in a single direction. If you get a result then this hook will probably be fine to move through on. However avoid clipping, don't shake-out on it all day or attempt a figure-of-four! Be sure that you maintain the directional loading when you move through. Use the high-tool grip only if necessary and take great care not to lever the shaft of the axe upwards.

3) Marginal hooks

When you can tell that a placement is poor and likely to rip then use the previous procedure but never high-tool and make sure that your face is clear from your axe when you make the move. Keep your hips stable and move stealthily avoiding erratic or jerky movements. Breathe before you commit to the hook but not while you're making the move. Tense every muscle to maintain maximum body tension. Reach for the next good hook as quickly as you can.

The lower tool often blows just as you latch the next hold so be prepared to take the strain on the upper arm. Note that marginal hooks can sometimes work well as intermediates to assist with making longer spans between good hooks.

Raphael Slawinski using the most marginal of hooks on *Les Vacances des Monsieur Hulot*, M7, WI 6, on Stanley Headwall, Canada.

Pick orientations

The key to expanding your repertoire of mixed moves is to remember that your axes can be used in any number of different orientations in the same way that a rock climber will use holds. To do this you'll need to make the appropriate shifts of body position to maintain balance and stability.

Remember that the optimum body position is always found when the axe is perpendicular to the hold. When using side-pulls and undercuts you will also need to apply continuous tension to prevent your tools from popping.

Undercuts

Undercuts

Undercut moves may sometimes be started with Can-openers if the flake is good and deep. Use the Can-opener to gain initial height by pulling directly down on the shaft. Then switch to a more conventional undercut position by pulling and leaning out on the axe in order to gain height. This way a giant amount of height can be achieved from one axe placement.

✔ Body tension maintained
✔ Body in line with axe shaft
✔ Axe perpendicular
✔ Directional loading maintained

Side-pulls

Side-pulls can be extremely awkward to use with axes if they are too close to your body, but if they are at full-stretch and diagonally above then they may be worth taking on!

Carefully place a high foot for lay-backing and then use body tension and try placing an opposing axe to avoid barn-dooring. Side-pulling with axes always feels strenuous and precarious.

✔ Axe perpendicular
✔ Directional loading maintained
✔ Feet positioned for laybacking
✔ Body tension to avoid barn-dooring

Side-pulls

Reverse side-pulls

Reverse-side-pulls (a.k.a. Gastons)

If a side-pull is closer to your body then it may be better to bring the left axe through, across your body and use it as a 'reverse' side-pull. You can then roll with your torso to assist the move mechanically rather than laybacking strenuously. This option usually feels less prone to barn-dooring than using a side-pull.

- ✔ Axe perpendicular
- ✔ Directional loading maintained
- ✔ Body tension maintained
- ✔ Body roll

Stevie Haston on *The Empire Strikes Back*, M11, Cogne, Italy. Photo by Laurence Gouault Haston.

Starting Out

Equipment

Mountain Safety

Ice · Style-Ethics

Ice · Techniques

Mixed · Style-Ethics

Mixed · Techniques

The Mind

Training

Destinations

Axe stashing techniques for leash-less clipping

Knowing what to do with your spare axe when you are clipping or placing gear can be one of the trickiest parts of mixed climbing. A number of options exist, all of which have their strengths and limitations. It is worth practising all of them to get a feel for which one works best in different situations.

❶ On the rock

This is the fastest and easiest option if the axe can be left hooked in a tight crack, pocket, or in a deep in-cut flake; but if the hook is flat or shallow then you stand a strong chance of losing the tool.

❷ Over the shoulder

This method is fast and lends itself to clipping on sport routes. You must keep your body absolutely still and be very aware of your resting axe as you raise your arm for the clip. Beware using your shoulder on very steep routes or the axe may drop off the back and instead, rest it across your chest.

The shoulder-resting method is not recommended for placing gear on trad routes where there's a strong chance that you will dislodge the axe.

❸ Thumb pinch

Pinching the pick of your spare axe between your thumb and the grip of the active axe is perhaps the best all-round method for stashing a tool seeing as it is fast and relatively secure. However, make sure you don't let go during a long gear placing operation!

❹ Holster

A large plastic karabiner with no gate or a wire gate that stays open will work well as a holster for clipping the eye on the head of the axe. If the gate snaps shut you may never get the axe off again! This method is more secure than the previous two, but it may take longer to locate the axe in the holster and remove it. This is a great technique for trad mixed.

John Varco improvising on *Babylon* VII,8, Ben Nevis, Scotland.

Movement

In this section we will make a loose distinction between the moves that are most commonly required for trad mixed and those that are found on sport mixed routes. Of course there will be some overlap, but one would hopefully never need to dyno or make a figure-of-four on a trad route!

Similarly, most sport mixed routes will avoid corner cracks and chimneys in the interest of climbing the smoother steep walls.

Airlie Anderson on *Stirling Bomber*, V,7 Northern Corries, Cairngorms, Scotland.

Regardless of the style, the key is to think how your movements will affect your pick and crampon angles and to maintain an angle of 90 degrees between the shaft of the axe and the placement. Use as much body tension and stealth as it takes to stick to this rule.

Trad mixed moves

Laybacking

Laybacking is frequently used for climbing corner-cracks or flakes. The picks can be simply hooked in the back of the feature or the head of the axe can be torqued if hooking feels too marginal. Good foothold selection is vital as you certainly won't be able to smear to create an opposing force!

Chimneying

Chimneying is unavoidable if you want to complete a true trad mixed climbing apprenticeship, so squeeze in and let the struggle commence!

Axes with clipper leashes may be the best plan as leash-less tools may be pretty difficult to manage. Rack gear on the sides of your harness rather than the back to avoid snagging, or try using a bandolier which you can simply shift out of the way. When back-and-footing, build your feet in small steps and never allow them to get too high or too low. Take your time and allow intermittent periods of rest between all the thrutching!

Body bars

On trad mixed routes you should always be on the look out for knee and arm bars to give your forearms a rest from gripping your axes.

How's your flexibility? Mark Garthwaite making the most of his, sorting gear out from a wide bridge on the first pitch of *The Secret*, IX, 9 Ben Nevis, Scotland.

Snow clearing

Whilst this may not be a type of move, it is the first thing you will have to do on snowy trad mixed routes before you can actually move! The traditional approach is to use tools with large, classic spade-like adzes, but those opting for stripped-down leash-less tools may have to settle for using the side of the head. Note that this will be fine in light snow but less effective in hard-packed rime or hoar-frost conditions.

The key part is reading the rock and using its contours to guide where you clear. Remember to clear footholds as well as axe placements. Clear from rest positions wherever possible - the classic error is to clear in the middle of a hard move when there was a bridge position just below. All this makes following the moves feel easier!

Bridging

On any mixed climb, you should always be on the look out for an opportunity to bridge, especially when resting or placing gear. Many routes follow strong corner lines and bridging should be regarded as one of the utility moves. Bridging will also be vital on mixed routes involving hanging ice curtains or pillars.

Good inner thigh flexibility is useful and always stretch your legs before embarking on a corner. If the footholds are small then pumped calves will be a big issue. Always side-step on larger footholds and shake your calves out periodically, especially after standing still to place gear.

Starting Out

Equipment

Mountain Safety

Ice : Style-Ethics

Ice : Techniques

Mixed : Style-Ethics

Mixed : Techniques

The Mind

Training

Destinations

Sport mixed moves

Twist-lock reach

Twist-locks are the most important energy savers for moving on overhangs. The essence of this technique is to avoid keeping your hips parallel to the wall as this necessitates a strenuous pull-up and lock-off, which usually feels out of balance. Instead, twist in to the wall so your hips are perpendicular and roll with your torso to gain height without having to bend your arms. If you do this dynamically you can use momentum to propel you upwards, by twisting your body like a corkscrew. You can even cam your arm against your torso to assist with the final reach. The key to obtaining stability on overhangs and initiating this move is to take off the opposite leg to the arm that you are reaching with and to hold it out behind you at the balance point. (i.e. remove the right leg if you are reaching up with the left arm).

✔ Body balanced
✔ Arm straight as possible and cammed against torso
✔ Hips perpendicular
✔ Torso rolling
✔ Body balanced - opposite foot to hand

Starting Out

Equipment

Mountain Safety

Ice · Style · Ethics

Ice · Techniques

Mixed · Style · Ethics

Mixed · Techniques

The Mind

Training

Destinations

Neil halfway across the modern desperate *Musashi*, M12, Canada.

Figure-of-four

For the very steepest overhangs where you need to make long reaches between good hooks, figure-of-fours may enable more height to be gained and feel less strenuous than twist-locking.

The aim is to pass the opposite leg over the wrist (e.g. left leg over right wrist) in order to lock the arm in a bent position and reduce the need for bicep strength. The lower leg can then be used for upwards propulsion, providing the wall isn't too steep.

On roofs where the lower leg can't make contact with the rock, the feet can be hooked around each other to lock the legs together and maintain stability. Note that the most common error with figure-of-fours is to pass the leg over the elbow instead of the wrist - this makes the move feel much more strenuous as well as causing you to lose height. The middle of the forearm is the cut-off point.

Note that spurs do not go well with figure-of-fours as they are prone to snagging on your clothes or even slicing your forearms. Figure-of-fours require a lot of practice and plenty of abdominal strength. Specific exercises are given in the training chapter on page 245.

The best way to release from figure-of-fours is to let go of the lower tool rather than unthreading your leg, but only use this method if the lower hook is good and stable. It is also really important to note the difference between figure-of-fours when the tools are close together and when they are widely spaced.

Chris Cubitt using perfect figure-of-four technique to onsight *Reptile*, M10, Ouray, USA.

Figure-of-four with close tools

If your axes are next to each other in the same hook then it will be very difficult to pass your foot between your forearms without snagging your crampons on your sleeve. Instead, throw the leg over both forearms and then let go of the axe that you are about to reach up with. Unthread your arm and then grab the tool and make the reach.

Figure-of-nine

Similar to a figure-of-four, the figure-of-nine is to pass the same leg over your wrist (in other words, left leg over left wrist). This method sometimes suits certain body positions and tool configurations more than figure-of-fours, especially if your axes are wide apart. It is important to be aware of both options and to be able to switch between the two on super-steep terrain.

Figure-of-four with widely spaced tools

If possible, try to avoid making excessively long reaches from a figure-of-four by propelling yourself to full stretch with the lower leg. If you do this then you will find it almost impossible to get into a figure-of-four on the higher axe. If you have no choice but to do this then the way to get out of trouble is to make the high reach and then cut loose and match picks on the high axe. Then repeat the method given above to get into the next figure-of-four. An alternative is to attempt a figure-of-nine which will feel easier if your tools are widely spaced.

Neil using a figure-of-four to maximise his reach on *Puma*, M9+, Haston Cave, Italy.

Starting Out · Equipment · Mountain Safety · Ice : Style-Ethics · Ice : Techniques · Mixed : Style-Ethics · Mixed : Techniques · The Mind · Training · Destinations

Toe-hooking and linking axes

In an attempt to rest on roofs with no footholds, a popular technique is to toe-hook the high-tool grip of an axe. This technique was originally designed to work in conjunction with heel spurs where it will be much more effective. A more extreme and usually less viable option is to link both axes together (by hooking the clipping eye at the base of the grip) and to toe-hook the lower axe. *See photo opposite.*

Leg rests on can-openers

A technique which may at first sound preposterous to traditionalists, involves sinking in a bomber can-opener and then to throw a leg over the top in order to shake-out or lever the body up in order to gain height. Just be sure it's a good placement!

Use of spurs

Spurs may offer the opportunity for 'thank God' rests on steep terrain, especially if there are deep in-cut breaks to hook. For this reason, many climbers consider them to be unethical. If traversing a break, simply hook the spur next to your axes and shuffle along. When moving up, pull with your hamstring and use the spur to gain height. You may also attempt a full-blown 'bat hang' by securing both feet (usually one either side of your axes in a good break) and then cutting loose in order to 'rest'.

Dynos

The idea of leaping for a hold with an ice axe sounds pretty extreme, but dynos are becoming increasingly common on routes with double-figure M grades. Spy the hold, crouch as low as you can, spring hard with the legs, and hook with your tool at the dead-point. Be prepared for the strain as it's common for the tool to be ripped from your hand when it catches. A common mistake is to jump too far backwards - try to trace a curved trajectory so that your hips finish directly below the target hook. This way you will minimise the swing. Dynos are very hard on your shoulders so be sure to warm-up thoroughly first.

Neil making the most of his spurs on *Captain Hook*, M10, Cogne, Italy.

You won't see many of these at the crag - a dyno at a World Cup competition.

Daniel DuLac sneaking a rest by hooking his own axe handle during a World Cup competition.

Starting Out

Equipment

Mountain Safety

Ice : Style-Ethics

Ice : Techniques

Mixed : Style-Ethics

Mixed : Techniques

The Mind

Training

Destinations

Moving onto the ice

The most common mistake is to go for the ice too low. This often causes it to break off, or at the very least will force you into a strenuous crucifix which may be impossible to get out of, especially if you lose your feet! Stay calm and make another move on the rock if possible.

Once you're a little higher but still on the rock, you may decide to trim the lower part of the ice to relieve it of some of it's weight and prevent you from breaking it with your feet later on. Always notify your belayer. The next howler is to hit it too hard! On thin curtains it is always best to hook existing placements or gently tap out new ones. One careless bludgeon and you'll be without a route to climb.

Anyone who has climbed vertical ice will know how strenuous it can be, so how can you ever hope to climb a free-hanging pencil once you've blasted up all that overhanging rock? The answer lies in the fact that there is nearly always a hands-off rest (in the form of a bridging position) at the point where ice meets rock. You should milk this for all it's worth.

Don't attempt to place ice screws until you are high on the ice. If the rock is really steep then a rest probably won't appear, so go straight for the ice and try to arrange a rest later: aim for good mushroom footholds or better, a bridge between two icicles. It's always best to make a few moves until you reach the point where the ice is thicker and a little less steep. Kick your feet in securely, sink your axes and relax into a hang position to get a shake before you go for the remainder of the ice. More specific techniques for getting onto hanging ice features are given in the ice chapter - see page 158.

A classic mistake is to go for the ice too early. Neil gets himself into an awkward crucifix on *Slaughterhouse*, M8+, Canada.

A calm and confident approach is always required, and above all else - keep a constant eye on conditions and the actions of others. Horrendous accidents have happened when icicles have dropped at mixed crags. You may be sport climbing but this is not a sport climbing environment.

Tim Emmett resting before moving onto the ice of *La Grand Wazoo*, M7, Freissinieres, France.

Starting Out   Equipment   Mountain Safety   Ice : Style-Ethics   Ice : Techniques   Mixed : Style-Ethics   Mixed : Techniques   The Mind   Training   Destinations

Using ice hooks on popular mixed routes

If there are hooks in the ice on a popular mixed route then use them rather than risk making your own. If the feature is fragile then it may break, leaving you without a route to climb. Even if the ice is thick, why waste energy swinging when you can simply hook. Pre-made hooks in thin ice have a habit of deteriorating with use, but it's usually best to re-chip them, rather than making another and shattering the feature.

Neil Gresham topping out on *Critique de la raison pure*, M9, Freissinieres, France.

Starting Out | Equipment | Mountain Safety | Ice : Style-Ethics | Ice : Techniques | Mixed : Style-Ethics | Mixed : Techniques | The Mind | Training | Destinations

Ropework for sport mixed

If you have sport climbed on rock you will be familiar with most of the ropework techniques that are used for sport mixed climbing, namely: single rope belaying, clipping and threading the chain. There are a few variations on these themes that come into their own when crampons, axes and large icicles are involved.

Stick-clips and spotting

The first bolts on sport mixed routes are often the scariest to clip - if a tool pops you will be flat on your back. Receding snow slopes and nasty scree landings add to the problem so many sport mixed climbers clip the first bolt with a stick-clip. These can be purchased from most climbing shops or DIY'ed from an extendable walking or tent pole. If you don't have a stick-clip, be very wary of spotting someone as they go for the first bolt. Only do this up to the point when you can still physically reach them. If they fall, grab their waist and guide them to the ground, taking care to avoid their crampons. Otherwise, run!

Belayer positioning

The belayer should be very wary of colliding with the leader's crampons when they are on the first part of the route. Standing to the side is only a good idea if you are able to tie yourself securely to the ground

Ben Gilbert comes a bit too close after falling off *Boyd Mystery*, M8, Haffner Creek, Canada.

or the base of the cliff, otherwise you will be ripped off your feet. The belayer should also be extremely attentive at the point when the leader commits to a large hanging ice feature. Debris can ricochet, so standing slightly to the side is no excuse to relax. It's also worth guarding the base so that others don't walk through the fall line.

Advanced technique tips
- maintaining breathing

It is very difficult to maintain a continuous breathing rate on steep sport mixed climbs. The need for body tension means that your stomach muscles are constantly contracting and it is common for the breath to be held for long periods. The other bad habit is to suck the air in with thin gasps from the mouth as opposed to deep breaths from the chest cavity.

The first step is to constantly remind your self to breathe. If you forget to breathe mid-move then do so at each clip point or whenever you get a good hook. The secret is to start by exhaling more deeply than normal (in order to fully clear your system of CO_2) and then a deep breath from the diaphragm will follow as a reflex response. Not only will deep, continuous breathing help you to reduce your lactic acid levels but it will help you to stay calm and focused too.

Mark Garthwaite relaxing on *Slaughterhouse*, M8+, Canada. Photo Neil Gresham.

Starting Out

Equipment

Mountain Safety

Ice · Style·Ethics

Ice · Techniques

Mixed · Style·Ethics

Mixed · Techniques

The Mind

Training

Destinations

Holding falls

Tight ropes break ankles. The old-fashioned method of trad belaying where the belayer resists the fall by leaning back or taking in will cause your leader to catapult hard into the rock. A little slack combined with running in slightly will soften the fall and save you both from a piggy-back ride down the snow slope and an afternoon in casualty. See **Trad Climbing+** for more depth on dynamic belaying.

If your leader bottles a run-out and asks to be taken tight or, worse still, pulled off - don't do it. Only take tight when the bolt is above or level with them. The shortest falls

are the worst for this type of unnecessary accident. With a belay plate, you may be able to let a small amount of rope run through (this requires care and practice) but with a Grigri the best technique is to run forward. A skilled belayer will spot the moment to actually pay out rope in the event of a fall to help the leader clear a protruding ledge or obstacle. Clearly this is not the approach on some trad routes where the aim might be to arrest the fall before the leader hits a ledge.

Smart belaying

A skilled sport belayer will predict the leader's clipping points and will move in to pay out the slack fast and aggressively, so that they don't encounter any resistance. They will then step back slightly once the clip has been made to take in the rope and attain a better viewing position. Never step back too far in case you are pulled off your feet. Three or four metres will do the trick.

A tip for redpoint belaying: when your partner is working a project and needs to rest at a bolt, really help them by taking tight aggressively - sitting back hard on the rope as soon as they've clipped a draw. There's nothing more infuriating than sagging back down a few metres after all that effort. The same goes for when they are climbing back up the rope after a fall - lean back and really give them a hand!

A general point is that mixed climbing falls can be sudden and unpredicted. Many belayers fall into the bad habit of only really concentrating when the leader is looking pumped or sketchy. But with a mixed fall it can happen at any point. It is during clips where you need to be especially prepared for an axe to blow.

Attentive belaying is particularly crucial in the lower part of a route to avoid groundfall.
Ramon Marin belays Mark Garthwaite on *Slaughterhouse*, M8+, Canada. Photo by Neil Gresham.

Taking falls

Sport climbing falls are only safe if both you and your belayer use correct practice. Try to make a continual risk assessment as you move up the climb - if you're a long way up a steep route then you will be fine to pitch off, but if you're above the second or third bolt then be cautious, especially when clipping. Be particularly careful not to get your leg twisted round the rope when climbing and watch out for crampon tangles.

If you're pumping out and sense that a fall is imminent then be ready to flick your tools out so that they don't get left stranded. If they do get stuck then you may need to clip in and haul up someone else's tools in order to retrieve them, or better still, use a stick-clip to knock them out.

Ian Parnell seconds away from pitching off *Puma*, M9+, Cogne, Italy. Photo Dave Pickford.

When making hard or dynamic moves, or when moving on marginal hooks, you should always have it in the back of your mind that you might lob. If you do fall, try to push yourself clear of the wall, but don't jump back too far or you will swing in hard. Be prepared to ditch your axes if you're climbing leash-less and brace yourself to make a clean contact with your feet on the rock.

Never make your body completely rigid, or hold your legs out straight - the key is to absorb the fall on impact; or better still, to have a good belayer, so you don't touch the rock at all. If you do come off at a weird angle then work like a cat in the air to right yourself. In general, sport climbing on rock greatly prepares you for taking falls. If you're not happy about taking leader falls then you will be seriously limiting yourself. The only way to cure your fear of falling is to take regular falls using safe belay practice.

Clipping positions

Clipping is one of the toughest parts of mixed climbing. An important issue is where to stash your axe and this is covered on page 196. The next dilemma is where to clip from. A poor choice of position will disrupt your flow and cause you to waste energy or even take a fall. The secret is to resist the temptation to clip from too low, unless you are on a bomber hook and can't see a good one higher up. Clipping from too low will necessitate a big lock-off and may cause your pick to jump out if you lever outwards on your axe to make the reach. Worse is that if you do fall mid-clip you will go a lot further than if you'd simply climbed on a move or two. Better to spy out a good hook higher up and to press on to it, and then to find the most stable body position to clip from, keeping your arm straight.

Climbing with ice axes makes the bolts harder to reach, so you will need to climb higher to compensate for this, or use the high-tool grip when you're on a good hook. As a rule of thumb bolts are usually placed near to good hooks so if you're on a bad hook then you're probably in the wrong place.

Clipping technique

Fumbling clips is all too easy when mixed climbing, so use thin gloves and wire-gate karabiners - see page 80.

There are only two ways to clip a bolt - with your palm facing the gate (like a forehand stroke) or your palm facing away from the gate (like a back-hand stroke). Make sure you practise both methods with both hands and stick to them in the heat of the moment.

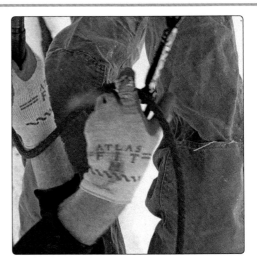

For a forehand clip, take the rope diagonally across your palm, trap the back of the 'biner with your thumb and use the nose of the biner to capture the rope. To make a backhand clip, pinch the rope

between thumb and forefinger, capture the apex of the biner with your index finger and twist the wrist to flick the rope home.

Lowering off

Most sport mixed routes have trees at the top with slings round them for lowering or abseiling off. Occasionally you will find an Abalakov if the route finishes on ice, but you should be prepared to make your own.

If the route doesn't involve ice and there are no trees then look for a bolt belay. If there is a maillon or ring on the belay then thread this using the conventional sport climbing method (see **Sport Climbing+**) and simply lower off. However, you should always take an abseil device with you in case you only find an Abalakov or a sling without a maillon at the top. Never lower off by threading a sling.

Ben Gilbert stripping *Boyd Mystery*, M8, Haffner Creek, Canada. Photo by Neil Gresham.

Stripping routes

When stripping steep routes, never use your axe to hook the rope or the webbing slings on your quickdraws. If you must use your axe to pull yourself in then hook the bottom karabiner on each draw, or better still the bolt hanger. Clip yourself to the rope using a quickdraw from the belay loop of your harness as shown in the photo.

Take care when removing the first quickdraw (it's easy to make contact with your belayer or even the ground when you swing off) - the best method is to clip directly into the second bolt and then reach down.

Bolts and bolting

A visual inspection is usually sufficient to see whether or not a bolt is good. Tighten the hanger if it wobbles when you clip it. If a bolt looks rusty or poor then test it with a careful pick torque. Never hit a bolt with your hammer.

If you bolt yourself, avoid wet streaks, detached blocks or stress-cracks. Go for solid, flat rock and check by tapping it first with a hammer. Check also that the bolts wont' be obscured by ice, and that the rope won't drag over roofs or icicles. Use a power drill as hand drills are desperately strenuous and do a poor job.

Stainless steel 'thru-bolts' are best (preferably 10mm in diameter) and go for longer lengths (100mm +) in softer rock-types. Practise at ground level first. You will also need to get your aiding systems sorted because getting into position is always the hardest part, especially on steep cliffs.

Placing a long quickdraw before the ice will reduce rope-drag. Photo by Neil Gresham.

In-situ quickdraws

Far riskier than deteriorating bolts are the in-situ quickdraws at popular sport mixed crags. These very quickly become unserviceable as a result of people hooking them with their picks. If you are working a route then inspect every 'draw carefully as you go and take plenty of your own so you can back them when needed.

If you wish to onsight a route with in-situ draws then it is highly advisable to get a partner to back the draws up first. Alternatively, back-up alternate draws as you go. Note that it will be very hard to inspect the quickdraws for wear as you are onsighting, so be aware and don't chance it. A final point is to resist the temptation to hook the draws with your picks as you will be contributing to this dangerous problem.

Ethical issues

Be ethically aware and never bolt in trad-only areas like the Scottish mountains. Don't over-clutter sport areas by squeezing lines in the gaps. If it's a good line and it adds something to an area without spoiling something else, then go for it.

Avoid creating dangerous run-outs at popular sport crags but it's up to you how you space the bolts if you bolt a more independent climb.

Regarding placement enlargement, this tends to happen naturally as popular routes see more traffic, but the big issue comes when making a first ascent. Most climbers consider that excavating rubble from a crack or a pocket is fair game but if you deliberately hack a placement out of blank rock then this is no better than chipping, which should be deplored.

Starting Out

Equipment

Mountain Safety

Ice · Style · Ethics

Ice · Techniques

Mixed · Style · Ethics

Mixed · Techniques

The Mind

Training

Destinations

Beware the condition of in-situ quickdraws at sport mixed crags such as the Caveman area at Haffner Creek, Canada.

Preparation tactics

Warming up for sport mixed

The importance of warming-up correctly for sport mixed climbing can not be stressed enough. Not only are you likely to rip an arm out of it's socket if you jump straight on a hard 'M' route, but you will get so unbelievably pumped that you can put paid to the day's climbing.

The key is to build-up the pump gradually over a period of at least half an hour. The best way to do this is with boulder traverses, interspersed with cooling off periods and stretching. Trees can make good leaning posts for stretching or pull-up bars.

After at least three or four traverses, do some pull-ups, leg raises and some harder boulder problems to get your power up. It is always best to try to replicate the same warm-up that you do for training so that your body is familiar with the build-up sequence (see page 252). If you are at a sport crag that has user-friendly warm-up routes then take advantage of these. A good example is to do an M5 or 6 before getting on an M7 or an M6 or 7 before getting on an M8.

Warming up for trad mixed

It is nearly always harder to warm-up for trad than sport mixed, but the effects of not doing so can be even more dramatic! If you haven't time to do a warm-up route then try to find a place to traverse, even if it means moving further across the base of the cliff. Aside from this, one of the best tactics is to go up and place the first few pieces of gear and reverse to the floor. Maybe even do this a few times. It is vital to get a moderate to hard pump and then take a good break before going for it. Stretch and visualise while you're resting.

The hand warming technique

Above all else, the most user-friendly warming-up technique, which can be used at the base of any climb, is simply to hang from your tools until the blood drains from your hands and they go numb. It makes sense to do a few pull-ups while you're at it, but the main thing is then to release your hands and lower them to allow the blood to come back.

Neil warming up with a few ice axe pull ups at Kaldakinn, Iceland.

Reading the line - onsighting

The more time invested in planning your route from the base, the more time and energy you will save. On dry sport routes the sinker hooks, cracks, pockets and flakes will be apparent, but try to spy out some of the more hidden placements. The big tip here is to look out for tell-tale scratch marks.

View the route from different angles - you will see undercuts from the base and side-pulls from the sides. Step well back to check out the top. Be wary of standing under icicles when you are doing this.

Bolts should be easy to see but try to work out where you might clip them from. On snowed-up trad routes you may only be able to pick out a line of weakness beneath all the rime, however, turf poking through is a good thing to look out for. Look for ledges, bridge positions and rest points.

The guidebook may tell you where the crux is so plan how you're going to protect it and climb it. Look for rest points to climb back down to. On dry routes where things are more obvious you can sometimes plan a pretty clear sequence but don't get anything too rigid in your head or you may be caught out. Consider your options and keep them open. If the route finishes on an icicle then plan how you're going to protect it and move onto it and work out where the rope will run.

Pete Benson onsighting the first pitch of *Link Direct*, VIII, 7 Lochnagar, Scotland.

Resting between attempts

It can be a constant battle to stay warm when resting between attempts at a sport mixed route or a hard single pitch trad route. Keep on the move with stints of jogging around and light shoulder circles but don't wear yourself out. It's important to strike a balance.

After long rests it is essential to repeat a condensed version of your main warm-up prior to making an attempt (e.g. do a light traverse and a few pull-ups). The amount of time you rest for will vary according to your fitness levels, the style of route and how far you got on the previous attempt. If you pinged off at the third bolt you may only need ten minutes, but never get straight back on out of frustration. Even a few metres of mixed climbing will take it out of you. A good rule of thumb is to rest a minimum of five minutes per bolt reached.

On trad routes, it is more difficult to make these rules but it's usually best to rest a minimum of double time (e.g. if you were climbing for ten minutes then rest for at least twenty) but if possible, rest triple time. There is always a fine line between resting and cooling right down. The main thing is to communicate your wishes to your partner as early as possible to avoid clashes of agenda.

Redpointing

Sport mixed climbing lends itself well to climbing very hard projects, and at some point, most are tempted to take on something pretty challenging. When selecting a route, pick a good one as you're likely to be on it a while. The grade should reflect the amount of time you're prepared to spend on it. A grade or two above your onsight limit might yield in a day, but 3 or 4 grades harder might take anything up to 4 or 5 days. If you're going for something really hard then it's best if it suits your climbing style.

Bolt-to-bolt

The classic error is to see how high you can get on your first go - this will only mean that you burn out and learn very little about the route. Resist the temptation, instead 'dog' up the route, getting all the quickdraws in place using whatever means you can. It's fine to grab them as long as you work out the best place to clip them from afterwards.

Practise the route in short sections at a time. Don't just stick to the first sequence you find - be sure to review it and consider other options. Take plenty of rests on the rope and use the time to re-examine tool placements and commit your sequence to memory. Make sure that the gates on the quickdraws are facing the right way and that the draws are the right length. Only when you've got every last tool placement and body position completely dialled should you then return to the ground for a good rest.

Links

Next up don't be tempted to go for it straight away. Instead try to link larger sections of the climb together, paying particular attention to the top half as this is where you're likely to make mistakes when tired. Use this time to really get into your flow and only if you do really well on your links should you go for the redpoint. See also 'visualisation' on page 237.

Neil redpointing *Pink Panther*, M9+, Ueschenen, Switzerland.

Starting Out

Equipment

Mountain Safety

Ice : Style-Ethics

Ice : Techniques

Mixed : Style-Ethics

Mixed : Techniques

The Mind

Training

Destinations

Redpoint

A common tactic is to have the first or even the second bolt pre-clipped - there are no prizes for hurting yourself when sport mixed climbing. If you're really ethical then climb up and then reverse back to the floor. Take deep breaths and remember to focus entirely on the climbing and not the end result. Get into your flow and rely on auto-pilot as much as possible. It's a great feeling to climb something very hard in complete control and with redpointing that's often the only way it can be. If you need to correct a minor mistake then do so calmly, but if it's a major blunder low down on the route then you're sometimes better of lowering-off and trying again rather than carrying the energy deficit with you. Lower back down, take a rest and have a better go.

Gear placing on trad mixed

Placing gear whilst mixed climbing can feel incredibly awkward unless you have your systems completely dialled. Detailed information about usage of each type of trad protection is given in the gear chapter - see page 72. Below is a selection of pointers to help you get the most from your game.

> Pack a little more hardware than you need - you can always leave some in your sack. Tune your rack to each pitch on multi-pitch routes and give the surplus to your second.

> Be disciplined and don't take too much - not only will the excess weigh you down but it will clutter your rack, which is a big issue with gloved hands.

> Rack editing is a key skill. If you really must take extra then go for wires and quickdraws which weigh less and take up less space than cams.

> Spend time tucking your jacket into your harness and getting everything straight and orderly before you set out.

> Consider a bandolier for use in confined chimneys, or for ease of changeover on belays.

> If you make changes to your leash system or purchase some new kit then try it out on an easy route first or when seconding.

> Wear the thinnest and most sensitive gloves you can get away with.

Andy Benson slotting in the gear on *Redemption*, VI,6 Church Door Buttress, Glen Coe, Scotland.

> Take the time to place good gear. The nature of mixed is such that a pick could pop on easy ground. You'll also move a lot faster and more efficiently once it's in. Trad mixed climbing is not the place for gung-ho heroics.

> Place extra gear on loose routes.

> On poorly protected routes equalise the load on your runners.

> Tension gear down if necessary - for example a nut or hand-hook can be tensioned down by connecting it to other pieces below. Long slings or a spare length of thin cord can be good for this.

> Inspect fixed gear (pegs can be tapped with your hammer) and always back up old tat and rusty *in situ* wires.

> On multi-pitch routes, consider carefully how you will divide up the pitches. If it is agreed that one person will lead the crux pitch then it may be worth the other person leading all the other pitches in order to split the effort more evenly, or more fairly! Practise your negotiation skills as many parties have fallen out over this one!

> Don't forget belay jackets, mitts, flasks and extra food. Trad mixed can be a slow business.

Jim Keeley making the most of rock protection on *Red Gully*, II/III, Cairngorms, Scotland.

Starting Out · Equipment · Mountain Safety · Ice : Style-Ethics · Ice : Techniques · Mixed : Style-Ethics · Mixed : Techniques · The Mind · Training · Destinations

Loose mixed routes

Mixed routes are often found on loose crags that are slowly crumbling away under the effects of freeze-thaw. The odd loose flake is a common occurrence, but some crags give the impression that they are on the verge of collapse, with hideous rubble filled bedding planes carving their way across piles of tottering shale.

The technique for dealing with the former is obvious - test suspicious looking flakes and if they creek then don't pull on them! A flake may be welded in place with a smearing of ice one year but the next it may be dry and will come off in your face!

The methods for dealing with rubble take practice and a fair amount of nerve. Those who come to loose mixed climbing from rock climbing are usually appalled that you would use something as destructive as an axe to make progress. The technique for loose rock climbing is to spread the pulling forces around, rather than to concentrate them on a single point! But with axes you can approach things differently. Place your picks deep into the back of loose holds or breaks rather than hooking the edge of them. Pull test every placement as if you were dealing with fragile ice. You should then try to keep the weight spread evenly between both axes and both feet. Move stealthily with loads of body tension. Make sure you inspect the rock around every bolt, bearing in mind that bolts have been known to pull out, still attached to fridge-sized blocks of shale. You're advised not to treat these routes like the average sport climb!

If you're placing trad gear then it's a simple case of safety in numbers. Look for the deeper cracks that are joined to the soundest looking features. Take loads of slings and quickdraws and try to build clusters of equalised runners wherever possible.

Starting Out
Equipment
Mountain Safety
Ice : Style-Ethics
Ice : Techniques
Mixed : Style-Ethics
Mixed : Techniques
The Mind
Training
Destinations

Clearing loose rock, Jon Bracey on *Redemption*, VI,6 Glen Coe, Scotland.

Starting Out

Equipment

Mountain Safety

Ice : Style-Ethics

Ice : Techniques

Mixed : Style-Ethics

Mixed : Techniques

The Mind

Training

Destinations

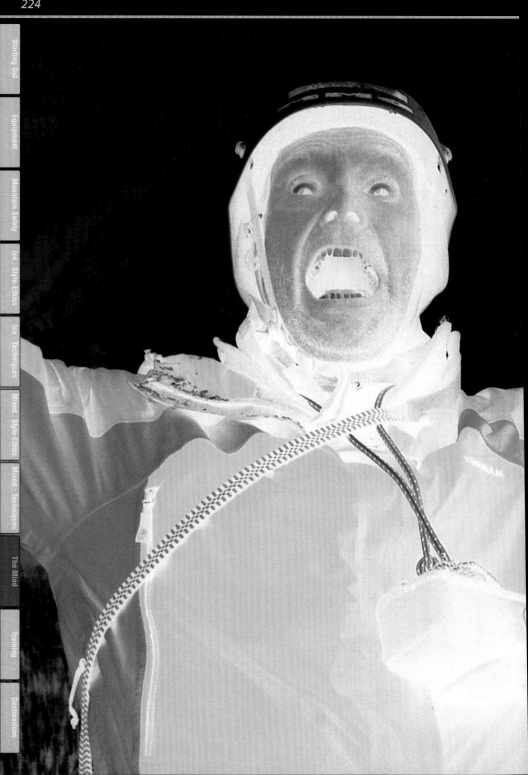

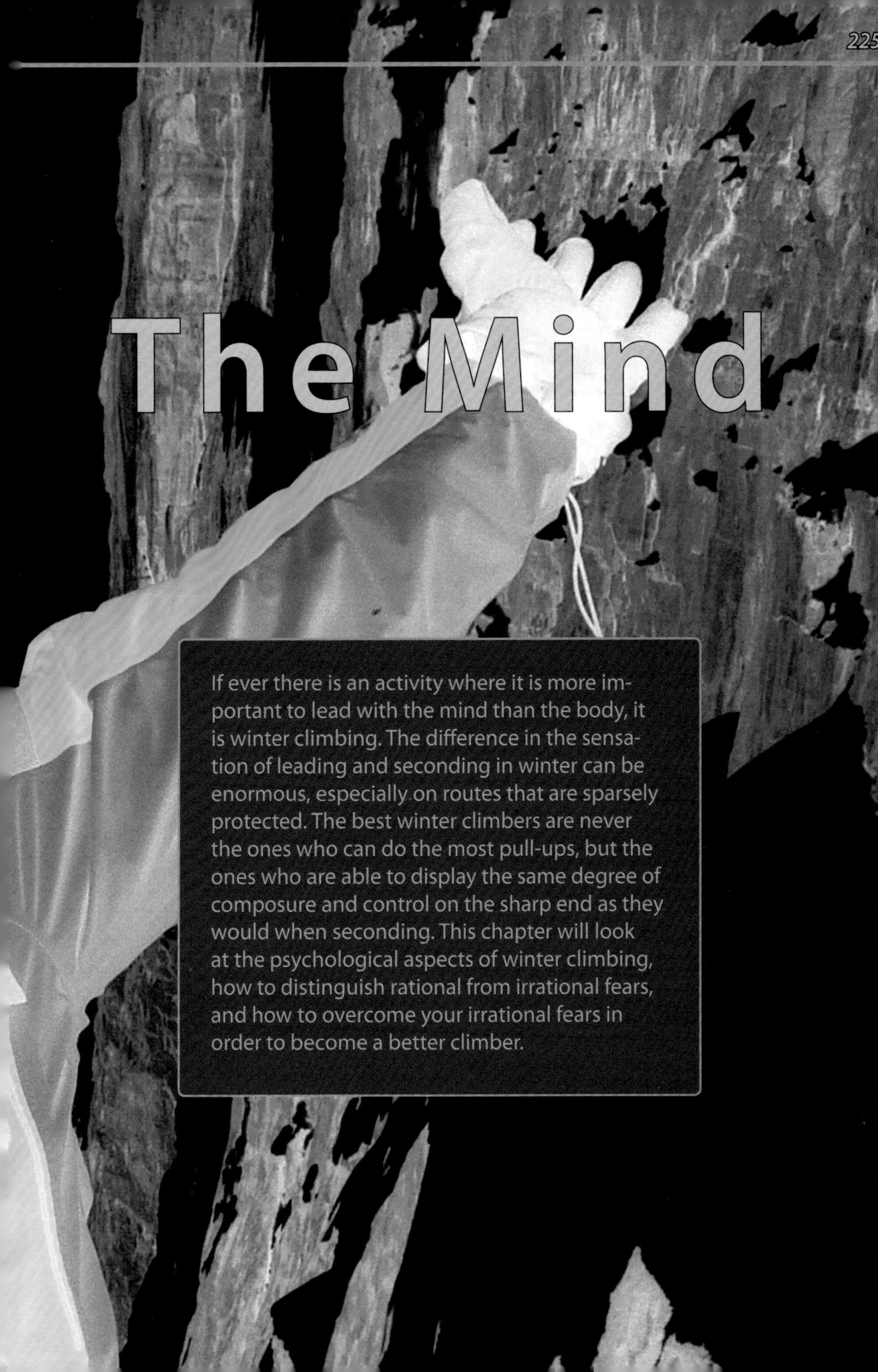

Starting Out

Equipment

Mountain Safety

Ice : Style-Ethics

Ice : Techniques

Mixed : Style-Ethics

Mixed : Techniques

The Mind

Training

Destinations

The Mind

If ever there is an activity where it is more important to lead with the mind than the body, it is winter climbing. The difference in the sensation of leading and seconding in winter can be enormous, especially on routes that are sparsely protected. The best winter climbers are never the ones who can do the most pull-ups, but the ones who are able to display the same degree of composure and control on the sharp end as they would when seconding. This chapter will look at the psychological aspects of winter climbing, how to distinguish rational from irrational fears, and how to overcome your irrational fears in order to become a better climber.

A state of mind

The ideal mind state for winter climbing may take a lifetime of experience to acquire, and even then some of the world's best find that their mental ability will fluctuate throughout a season. So what hope is there for those mortals who are unable to spend half their lives in the mountains? Many reach the conclusion that they simply aren't wired up for the extreme levels of effort and boldness that are required to push your limits in winter climbing. It only takes a succession of bad experiences in the early days to cause many to become demoralised or to hang up their tools altogether. The purpose of this chapter is to prove that anyone who is sufficiently passionate can get their head into gear for the vast majority of winter climbing challenges, provided they follow a few important guidelines.

In this chapter we will make a basic distinction between the two main aspects of psychological performance that are tested in winter climbing. The first is boldness, which is required to some degree by anyone who aspires to lead, even on well protected climbs. The other is the ability to stay focused under extreme pressure and concentrate only on the relevant techniques to aid the ascent. It tends to be the case that these two factors are intrinsically related, after all, most people are so busy worrying about falling that they are unable to devote sufficient head space to good use of technique - such as breathing correctly, maintaining a relaxed grip, and so on. However, even those who are sport mixed climbing and who are happy to take to the air will often find that it is easy to forget what they are doing under the influence of extreme fatigue, or to worry about it all being over instead of staying true to the moment. There is

a third factor, upon which the other two are crucially dependant and as such lies right at the core of mental performance for winter climbing, and that is motivation. Let's look at this first.

Motivation

Without motivation you will never be able to run it out above dubious runners into unknown terrain. Without motivation, you will never be able to hang onto your axes to the point where you are almost sick with fatigue. Without motivation you will not be able to push into the darkness when your hands and feet are numb and your clothing is soaked. The main reason why good winter climbers are good is because they are ridiculously psyched. Their level of motivation is colossal.

Ask yourself the following questions: Do you spend a lot of time reading guidebooks and have a hit list of climbs at key destinations? Do you know much about the history of winter climbing? Do you train for winter climbing, or at least for rock climbing, more than twice a week? Is this training more than just dabbling or socialising at the climbing wall? Do you make every attempt to arrange trips, in spite of all the obvious expenses and time constraints? Do you make sure that your gear is updated each season if you can afford to do so? If the answer to all these questions is no then you may as well forget the rest of this chapter. We don't believe it is our duty to help you to love winter climbing! But if it is yes to most of them, and you're prepared to give it your best shot, then it's time to take a journey into the margins of the mind.

Starting Out

Equipment

Mountain Safety

Ice : Style-Ethics

Ice : Techniques

Mixed : Style-Ethics

Mixed : Techniques

The Mind

Training

Destinations

The sixth sense for backing off

The key mental skill in winter climbing is learning to gauge when to back off, and to use what some climbers call 'the sixth sense' to assist with this. Many climbers who have a highly developed 'sixth sense' will describe it as a feeling, or a form of intuition, rather than a part of their conscious mind. When it comes to climbs that are blatantly too dodgy or oviously in good nick, there will be no need to consult the sixth sense. But this inner voice comes into its own when the amber light starts flashing, either at the base of a climb, or on the route, in the middle of a run-out, or at a belay stance when contemplating whether to push on.

In these situations the facts alone may not be sufficient to clinch the decision and it's the feeling in your stomach that must be consulted in order to make the final call. Many experienced climbers will describe days when conditions were perfect, they felt fresh and raring to go, but for some weird and inexplicable reason, they decided against the route on the day. Equally, you will hear tales of lousy weather and aching limbs and the original plan of an easy route being aborted in favour of an assault on the testpiece of the crag.

The key point is that beginners are well entitled to make decisions like the first example but they must never make decisions to go for it if things are looking way less than ideal. If you are in any doubt during the early stages of your winter climbing then the answer is to back off. But the experience of backing off the routes with a question mark, combined with completing the routes with an obvious green light, will slowly but surely, enable you to raise the bar and develop a sense of judgment that is based on reality, which you can then feel entitled to trust.

The more experienced you become, the sharper and clearer the red line will seem. If the decision making process currently feels like Russian roulette, then you are very definitely doing something seriously wrong. The grey area should be minimal, and the purpose of developing the sixth sense is to minimise the level of uncertainty in your winter climbing situations. Be like a Jedi master, or as Yoda himself said, 'Do or do not do. There is no 'try!'

Starting Out

Equipment

Mountain Safety

Ice : Style-Ethics

Ice : Techniques

Mixed : Style-Ethics

Mixed : Techniques

The Mind

Training

Destinations

Risk assessment

Rational verses irrational fear

Winter climbers often find it useful to do a basic risk assessment of a climb, firstly to decide if it is on, and secondly to summon the appropriate mind state for the challenge. This can also help you to differentiate between rational and irrational fear sources, which may be clouding your judgment on the day.

For example; a typical steep and well-bolted sport mixed route will generally be suitable for pushing your physical limit with less consideration for danger, although it is vital to note that sport mixed routes are rarely completely free from potential hazards. The average sport mixed route might earn a risk score of 1 out of 5, although this may be promoted to a 2 or a 3 if the suspended ice features are unsafe on the day or if the bolts are well spaced. Clearly, the type of mind state required for these routes generally has less to do with boldness and more to do with the ability to push yourself and concentrate on the moves while tolerating extreme levels of fatigue.

A steep, smooth, but well protected trad mixed route may represent the same type of challenge, provided you know what you're doing with your gear, although if the cracks are icy, this score could easily be raised to a 3 or a 4. In general, these routes are more about coping with fatigue, but you should be prepared to switch to a bolder mind state if you suddenly face a run-out.

A typical icefall in good condition might also score a 1 or a 2, depending on your ability to judge the soundness of the ice on the day, and use ice protection ap-propriately. However, thin or badly formed icefalls might score a 3 or a 4, along with poorly protected mixed routes. The mind state required here evidently has less to do with coping with extreme fatigue or working out desperate moves, and everything to do with staying calm and composed in a situation where a fall could have serious consequences. These are the routes where backing off must always be considered along the way. You must also embrace the likelihood that you may (inadvertently or otherwise) find yourself in a situation of extreme commitment, and be prepared to accept everything that this entails.

A category 5 risk assessment should perhaps be reserved for big routes in the mountains that may be under threat from additional objective hazards such as avalanche or cornice collapse. The presence or absence of an X grade in the guidebook will prepare you for what's in store.

This type of risk assessment may seem obvious to veteran winter climbers but it can help those who are newer to the game straighten their thoughts. Yet there are still many climbers who may think that this approach is all very well on paper, but they still have an irrational phobia of falling onto bolts or bomber protection. For these climbers, it isn't as simple as splitting routes into red, amber, or green categories and then simply getting on with it. We all know that falling off can still feel scary, even on so-called 'safe' routes. Sometimes you just 'get the fear'. And that is what the next part of this chapter is all about.

Fear of falling on safe trad mixed routes

If you simply don't trust your gear on well protected trad mixed routes then it is well worth setting up some test falls on an appropriate trad rock route in summer, or at the very least, clipping into pieces of gear and weighting them at the base of the cliff. If you wish to attempt some falls, pick a wall that is flat and smooth and make sure you back-up your top runner with as many bombproof runners as possible just below. This procedure should only be practised by experienced parties. It is not advisable to conduct this type of experiment in winter, because most trad mixed routes tend to be vertical or slabby and a collision with axes and crampons is likely. If your problem is trusting the gear or the physical sensation of flying through the air then summer routes will suffice.

Fear of falling on sport mixed routes

If you simply can't get it together to lead even the safest sport mixed routes then it is likely that you need to take some leader falls in a controlled environment. It is a popular myth that the way to cure your fear of falling is to lead more. In fact, this may actually make you more fearful. The only way to reduce that sense of panic is to gradually desensitise yourself to the experience of letting go and dropping. It is best to practice at an indoor climbing wall or an appropriate summer sport cliff first.

Pick a line that is gently overhanging and that doesn't have too many large projecting holds or features. Those who are particularly anxious should practise on a slack toprope before eventually working up to taking leader falls. Don't miss out clips and always use a dynamic belay to soften the fall. The belayer should move in slightly rather than leaning back

and resisting the fall. Contrary to popular misconception, it is actually desirable that the belayer gets pulled slightly off the ground, but beware of major weight differences - in these cases the belayer can be tied to the ground, with a meter or so of slack in the ground anchor. You can then work towards taking leader falls on sport routes outside. There are no fancy mental training rituals that can be performed on the ground as a friendlier alternative. It is essential to go through this process if you are ever to sort out your leading head.

Ian Parnell not too fazed by falling on *The Hardline*, M9, Ouray, Colorado, USA. Photo by Neil Gresham.

Starting Out

Equipment

Mountain Safety

Ice · Style·Ethics

Ice · Techniques

Mixed · Style·Ethics

Mixed · Techniques

The Mind

Training

Destinations

Dean Dorrel falling from *Capitaine Courageux*, 4/4+, Fournel Valley, The Écrins, France.

'Dean was using his new leashless axes with very thin picks and despite getting them stuck all the way, he opts for the last pitch. Dean got about 2-3 metres up the first steep bit and stuck his axes. He's bunched up with awkwardly placed feet and just can't shift his axes. He got one out and planted it again before falling off. He fell between 5-10 metres with a bounce in the middle and the first ice screw popped. He was stopped by the snow slope at the top of the third pitch. He escaped with a bruised elbow and bashed family jewels.'

Photos by Toby Whitely.

Starting Out

Equipment

Mountain Safety

Ice · Style·Ethics

Ice · Techniques

Mixed · Style·Ethics

Mixed · Techniques

The Mind

Training

Destinations

Fear of falling on ice

Falling off on ice is not something you need to become acquainted with and practice falls are an extremely bad idea. In an ideal world, you should pass through your ice climbing career and never take a fall, so if you are getting scared on ice then it has less to do with an irrational fear of taking leader falls. It is more likely that you don't trust your tools or screws, or simply that you are pushing too hard too soon. The answer is to drop your leading grade and focus on consolidation. You may also benefit from top-roping or seconding harder routes in order to focus on tool skills.

Boldness

The extent to which boldness can be nurtured has always been a contentious topic of debate amongst climbers. Some believe that they are inherently disadvantaged by not being brave from the word go; but many experienced climbers who climb boldly will report that they were very timid during their apprenticeship. In the same breath, those who perform daring deeds during their early exploits are probably fool-hardy rather than brave. Tales of reckless decisions that have led to epics are nothing to brag about. If you possess a healthy sense of self preservation and are essentially reluctant to take whippers with axes and crampons in a mountain environment then this is a much better starting point upon which to build!

Developing boldness

The time to learn to be bold is not during the early stages of your winter climbing career. While many of the easy routes you do during your apprenticeship may involve steep snow or low-angled ice with poor protection, you should never feel at any point that you are in a position where you are likely to fall. Of course, we all know that you can be caught out by rogue conditions, but if you are having near-misses regularly then it is time for a rain check.

Drop your grade and focus on climbing calmly and with a composed style. Once you really start to feel more competent and have a list of routes to prove it, then you may choose to slowly start winding things up. Once you start pushing your grade you may find yourself in a situation where you need to reach for some advanced strategies for keeping your fears at bay.

Speak to good climbers and they rarely admit to 'mental training' but they will still rely heavily on a series of mental processes which they tweak as their climbing develops, so that they can apply them to greater effect each time. Less experienced climbers will attempt to apply diluted versions of the same processes, but there will be gaps and attention leaks. It is not the case that the better climber can just tell you what to do and you can copy them straight off and go for the lead of your first unprotected Scottish Grade VIII.

Mental training is just like physical training - there are no overnight cures, you need to practise to make perfect, so if you can't go winter climbing every week then you need to incorporate it into other routines.

Rational boldness

You won't be bold if you know you're unfit or your technique is rusty. Being fit and technically competent will give you the best chance of being bold.

Process focus

Never wish to be at the top of the pitch when you are in the middle of it, or waste time wishing you hadn't set out on it. Instead, focus everything on making the very best possible job of the current task, whether it is digging out the next runner or re-adjusting your balance to get more weight on your feet.

As soon as you project yourself away from the current task you will reduce your effectiveness and increase your anxiety. If you decide to bail out then calmly focus on arranging protection - there is no point in panicking until you realise that you can't find any! But even then, you should focus every inch of your brain on slowly and carefully climbing down - remind yourself that taking your mind away from this process for a second will put you in greater danger.

Simultaneous focus

Many climbers find that they spend too much time obsessing about the distances between protection points. Of course, you must keep a continuous check on this, but the key trick is to focus on the moves and the climbing in order to push thoughts of the run-outs slightly further back into your subconscious. Thus you must sustain two simultaneous levels of focus - the moves in your conscious mind and the run-outs or other factors (such as objective hazards) in your subconscious.

Connective breathing

It is understood both in Eastern practices such as Zen, or indeed in mainstream sports psychology that the way we breathe plays a crucial role in determining our emotions and our ability to concentrate.

Breathing erratically or in fast thin gasps, causes more adrenaline to be produced, making us physically tense and edgy. Breathing slowly, deeply and regularly lowers adrenaline and helps us relax and focus. Keep a constant check on your breathing as you make your way up the pitch. It will also help you lower your lactic acid levels and reduce fatigue.

Conscious calming

If you have one of those rare total melt-downs, don't keep fighting it or you will become increasingly ineffective. Try projecting yourself away from the situation just for a few seconds. Shut your eyes if possible and breathe deeply, then slowly and methodically start gathering the facts. Consider your options and communicate with your second if possible. Things will start to get better once you have hit a psychological lowpoint and you can gain some strength from the plan as it starts to form. As soon as you start moving again and doing something to help you through, you can gain some comfort from that too. And if nothing else, try smiling - some of the most psychotic climbers swear by that one when all else fails!

Summary

An agreeable level of boldness can be nurtured, providing you do a lengthy apprenticeship on easy routes and slowly work towards increasing your grade. But if you rush the process you will become known as a reckless climber and find that you struggle to get partners.

Starting Out

Equipment

Mountain Safety

Ice : Style-Ethics

Ice : Techniques

Mixed : Style-Ethics

Mixed : Techniques

The Mind

Training

Destinations

Mental training and preparation for hard mixed climbing

(Coping with anxiety on safe routes of maximum difficulty).

It is a fallacy to presume that bolt protected mixed climbing is free from its share of psychological stress. When fear of failing is the issue rather than fear of falling an entirely different series of psychological strategies can be utilised to help you get the best from your game.

Feeling the pressure

The climbers who are prone to suffering from 'redpoint stress' or 'onsight anxiety' are always the ones who fail to draw upon any type of mental preparation rituals. The climbers who cope with pressure best are the ones who not only have a specific preparation sequence, but they also practise it during training rather than hauling it out of the closet once or twice a year and expecting it not to be dusty. For most climbers, a lack of belief in the value of mental training lies at the root of the problem, yet even those who are more open-minded often lack the discipline to see their mental training routines through to the conclusion.

When preparing for a climb that we desperately want to do, the brain creates a less familiar emotional climate, compared to the training environment, which causes functioning to be sabotaged. The tendency is to dwell on the significance of negative performance-related factors (such as not feeling strong or recovered) and to focus on difficulties as opposed to possibilities. The more time we spend casting our mind forward to the outcome that we desire and then back to these negative distracting factors, the less head-space is left for concentrating on crucial present issues during the ascent. Put simply, if you find that you want to 'have done' the route rather than to do it then you are too aroused to be at peak effectiveness.

Starting Out

Equipment

Mountain Safety

Ice : Style·Ethics

Ice : Techniques

Mixed : Style·Ethics

Mixed : Techniques

The Mind

Training

Destinations

Mark Garthwaite staying focused on an M7 in Bear Spirit Cave, Canada. Photo Neil Gresham.

Starting Out

Equipment

Mountain Safety

Ice · Style·Ethics

Ice · Techniques

Mixed · Style·Ethics

Mixed · Techniques

The Mind

Training

Destinations

'Clean housing' the brain

The best winter climbers usually draw upon a variety of different sources to develop and refine their game-plan for coping with anxiety. Some will use Eastern practices such as Zen, combined with conventional sports science techniques, and mixed in with a blend of practical tips that they have learned from their climbing partners and their own experience. They are trying to clear all the clutter out of their heads in order to make way for a calmer mind-state that enables spontaneous climbing to take place without distraction.

Books have been written on this subject, but to summarise it neatly, the best approach is to allow yourself a few moments of calm before the ascent, just to tune into your environment, then deal with your doubts methodically rather then haphazardly or worse still, sweeping them under the carpet, then visualise the route, give yourself a bit of a 'pep-talk' with a few positive commands and then prepare for battle by relying less on your conscious mind and more on the subconscious or 'auto-pilot'. And above all else, give yourself some feedback after the ascent - if you were successful then ask yourself why, and if you weren't then forget the excuses and focus on the practical steps that must be taken to settle the score. A more detailed plan is given below:

Mental preparation routine

Relax and focus - attune to your environment

Whilst sorting your gear or stretching at the base of the route, attempt to filter out distractions with a simple meditative exercise. Attempt to tap into your real state of 'consciousness' and genuine self

Neil clearing his head of clutter while gearing up at Vail, USA.

awareness which lies below all the chaotic thoughts on the surface.

Observe these thoughts first in order to nullify them, then note the presence of your ego and make an attempt to reduce its significance. In so doing, establish a sense of proportion and remember that doing the route might seem like the world to you but it means remarkably little to others! Now clear your thoughts in order to 'centre' your attention. While doing all this, breathe deeply and steadily, exhaling harder than normal and then breathing in through your entire chest rather than just using your mouth.

Starting Out

Equipment

Mountain Safety

Ice : Style-Ethics

Ice : Techniques

Mixed : Style-Ethics

Mixed : Techniques

The Mind

Training

Destinations

Nick Bullock in mentally challenging conditions on *Riptide*, WI6, Canada.

Dealing with doubts and distractions: black box technique

This is a useful technique for detecting potential distractions (or 'attention leaks' as they are sometimes known). However, it requires a great deal of practice in order for it to be effective. The idea is to go through literally everything that is worrying you, no matter how trivial, and for each problem to attempt to come up with a practical solution. Go slowly, one problem at a time so that you don't overload, and speak to yourself deliberately rather than chattering randomly. An example problem would be: 'my arms feel poorly recovered', a solution would be 'I've warmed up thoroughly and I also remember a time when I climbed well in a similar state'.

Deal with objective information face on and accept that you can never hope to fully quantify the subjective! Drip-feed each worry and solution from your conscious mind into your subconscious, by posting them into a metaphorical 'black box'. By doing this in a semi-conscious 'trance-like' state, it can, (with much practice) have the effect of destroying your worries for long enough, to stop them surfacing and causing a distraction during the ascent.

The crucial point is to go back to the black box after the ascent in order to realise just how few of your worries actually proved to be significant. By doing this, you will come to understand just how much we over-inflate the negative and underplay the positive and you will believe in the process more next time.

Visualisation

Almost every climber finds themselves rehearsing the moves of a redpoint project in their head at some point in their career. However, visualisation is a technique that has never-ending scope to be developed. The more detailed and authentic your visualised image, the more powerfully it will assist your performance. Try to imagine yourself actually climbing as opposed to watching yourself on a TV screen. Incorporate as many different senses as you can (imagine the tension in your muscles and how each axe or crampon placement feels).

Don't imagine it to be too easy or you will disappoint yourself! Imagine it to be hard but visualise your self coping well. Use key words to prepare you for certain parts of the climb (a technique known as emotional gearing) - for example 'power' for the crux or 'relax' for the rests. A close attention to the small details will make all the difference. Visualisation can also be used effectively for onsight climbing too, by imagining yourself climbing well on the route, but in a more general fashion. Be very wary of engraining the wrong sequence when you read the route first and keep your options open.

Starting Out | Equipment | Mountain Safety | Ice : Style-Ethics | Ice : Techniques | Mixed : Style-Ethics | Mixed : Techniques | The Mind | Training | Destinations

Transition - 'the calm moment'

A final mental check list that you've done all your preparation:

> I'm calm and focused because I've done my attunement exercise.

> I won't be distracted because I've done my Black Box.

> I know the sequence because I've done my visualisation.

And then finally some positive self talking such as: 'Fear of failure - there is none'; 'difficulty - you thrive on it'; 'pump - you can manage it.'

Accept responsibility for your performance and be prepared to give to it rather than asking what you might receive if you 'succeed'. This will help you focus on the immediate quality of every action. Go forward with full being. Remember that there is no good or bad outcome - it is all learning. Prepare for transition to a more subconscious mind state. Prepare to react!

Action

While climbing, intuition and reaction are the guiding processes as you act out a high stress situation.

The sensation of climbing is key to helping you stay on course and not get distracted. The conscious mind is now on the 'back burner' as a checking mechanism to prevent the subconscious from making an error.

One experiment is to use the metaphor of being more 'robotic' but beware taking away the 'effort' or emotion away from your performance. Another is to repeat your key words as you climb. Above all else, remember never to give up! It may sound obvious, but in the heat of the moment it can be so easy to convince yourself that you may as well let go because you wouldn't have made the next move anyway, but with an onsight a good rest may just be round the corner, and with a redpoint you might just surprise yourself! The next hook can always be the one that gets you to the top.

Summary

Tenets of the 'Mixed Warrior's approach'

> Our subconscious limits our performance.

> Learning via problem solving outside the comfort zone causes improvement.

> Rational fear is useful, illusory fear is a hindrance.

Starting Out

Equipment

Mountain Safety

Ice : Style-Ethics

Ice : Techniques

Mixed : Style-Ethics

Mixed : Techniques

The Mind

Training

Destinations

The Fang, 6, Vail. The grade can vary from 5 to 6+ depending on conditions and number of ascents. Here in bad condition, due to the fragility of the ice, a few days later the icicle was on the ground. Photo by Laurence Gouault Haston.

Starting Out

Equipment

Mountain Safety

Ice · Style-Ethics

Ice Techniques

Mixed Style-Ethics

Mixed Techniques

The Mind

Training

Destinations

Starting Out

Equipment

Mountain Safety

Ice : Style · Ethics

Ice : Techniques

Mixed : Style · Ethics

Mixed : Techniques

The Mind

Training

Destinations

Neil Gresham and Tim Emmett improvising
a little roadside training in Quebec.

Training

There is the potential to make training for ice and mixed climbing an incredibly complex topic, but the intention of this chapter is to keep things as user-friendly as possible.

If you're keen to take-on steeper ice pitches but are worried about getting the dreaded 'jelly-arm' at the end of a run-out, or if you're getting in to sport mixed but feel like you need to improve your body tension and lock-off strength then this chapter is for you. If however, you want to win the Ice World Cup or do the world's first M15, then you may need to research the subject more thoroughly.

Training requirements

The first step is to determine whether you're training for ice, trad mixed, sport mixed, or a combination of the three and then to look at their respective training requirements.

Energy systems breakdown

Strength and power

Maximum strength or power will be required for 1 to approximately 10 axe moves (of the highest possible difficulty for an individual) or 1 to 45 seconds of maximum climbing effort. Strength refers to controlled movements or static 'lock-offs' whereas power refers to fast, dynamic movements. Strength and power will frequently be required for hard cruxes on mixed routes but are rarely needed on ice routes.

Power endurance

Power endurance will be required for sustained sequences of approximately 15 to 30 axe moves (where the moves are at 60-80% of an individual's strength limit). This will equate to approximately 2 minutes and 45 seconds of all-out effort. By definition, it will not be possible to stop and rest for too long on a section of climbing that requires power endurance. This is the main fitness for sport mixed, although it may also be tested on hard

sections within trad mixed routes or short steps on ice routes.

Stamina

Stamina is the type of fitness required for anything in excess of 40 axe moves that are at 30-50% of an individual's strength limit. On stamina climbs you will need to shake-out regularly in order to de-pump. Stamina is the main fitness requirement for ice and trad mixed, but it will also be required for longer sport mixed routes.

Stevie Haston thankful for the hours he's put in training on the steep ice finish to *The Empire Strikes Back*, M11. Photo by Laurence Gouault Haston.

	Explosive Power	Arm Strength	Body Tension	Power Endurance	Stamina	Leg Fitness and CV
Ice	-	1	1	1	3	3
Trad Mixed	-	2	2	2	3	3
Sport Mixed	2	3	3	3	2	1

Training methods

These are given in approximate order of specificity to ice and mixed climbing.

Ice axe bouldering or circuits

Climbing around with ice axes on purpose-built winter woodies or disused outdoor stone walls, is by far the most effective form of training for ice or mixed climbing. For mixed training you can expand your tool repertoire whilst training the muscles in a more specific manner than is possible through rock climbing. Do short, hard boulder problems for strength and power, longer sequences of 15 - 30 moves for power endurance and random traverses for stamina. A helmet and a face guard are advisable.

The perfect training for steep modern mixed climbing; Matt Spencely on his woodie.

System training and pace training with axes

To increase the intensity or specificity of your ice axe boulder problems or circuits, try adding training rules such as: having to cut loose with your feet and replace them in control between each move or every other move. You could also have a rule of having to hold a lock-off for 5 seconds between each move. This will stop you from racing and get you climbing at a pace which is more similar to real mixed climbing.

Rock climbing (indoors or outdoors)

Indoor or outdoor rock climbing provides the most logical and practical form of training to keep you in general shape for ice and mixed.

The key to performing well at both summer and winter climbing is to tailor the style of rock climbing to complement your winter goals. For example, if you're going ice climbing then try to do long, pumpy trad or sport routes prior to your trip rather than short, fingery boulder problems. Similarly if you're going sport mixed climbing then your rock climbing should be as steep and juggy as possible and on small footholds to work body tension.

You can also try incorporating system training elements to your boulder problems or routes to make them more specific to mixed climbing, such as holding moves for longer or cutting your feet loose in between moves.

Bar exercises

The utility strength building exercises for mixed climbing are best performed on a standard pull-up bar. Make sure it is taped and has a really secure grip. If possible, hook your axes over it for an even more specific training effect.

For the pull-up and lock-off exercises use a knotted rope so you can have your arms at different heights in order to conform to the repetition targets. If the exercise feels to easy, and you manage too many reps, then move your arm lower down the knotted rope. If it feels too hard and you fail to do the required number of reps then simply move your hand higher up. The aim is always to fail or just about complete the last rep. Remember to repeat each set twice - once for each arm. If you can't make the targets even with your arms level then use a bungee stirrup or foothold for assistance. If you are a total monster then you may need a weight belt!

Rep and set guidelines

Take plenty of rest between sets but not so much that you loose momentum and cool down. The rep and set guidelines given below should only be attempted if you have done a more general strengthening program first (i.e. 2 to 4 weeks of general weights: 3 sets of 10 reps).

An inverted pyramid structure is recommended for pull-ups in order to obtain best results, but for all other exercises maximum and minimum values are given for reps and sets. These will vary according to your level and also according to your current stage within a phase of training. For example, a beginner should start a training phase by doing 2 sets of an exercise and build up to doing 3 or 4 sets

after a few weeks. Intermediates may start with 3 and work up to 4 or 5. Elite level climbers should start with 4 sets and then work up to doing 6 or 7.

Knotted-rope pull-ups

Arm exercises

Pull-ups (with 1 hand on a bar and the other hand lower on knotted rope)

x8, x6, x4, x2, x4, x6, x8

Do a minimum of 1 set per arm and a maximum of 3 with 2 - 3 mins rest between sets.

Lock-offs (with knotted rope)

At full lock, 90 degrees, and 120 degrees. Hold for 2 - 6 seconds, repeat 2 or 3 times.

'Power-pulls'

Use both arms at equal heights on the bar and pull-up as fast as you possibly can. Lower down in slow control and then repeat up to 5 times or until you feel a loss of speed. Do 2 to 4 sets

Typewriters

Use a fairly wide grip. Pull-up and 'travel' from side-to-side, touching your chin on each hand. Do 2 to 4 sets of 8 to 10 reps.

Abdominal exercises

Knee raises

Knee raises

Do a total of 3 or 4 sets of 8 - 20 reps. These can be made harder as you improve:
Stage 1: With legs bent and knees to chest
Stage 2: With legs straighter and out front
Stage 3: With legs straighter and out front and then alternating from side to side.

Front levers

Front levers

For maximum abdominal strength and body tension, the ultimate progression from knee raises is to attempt a front lever. Keep your arms straight and lift your entire body out in front of you so it is completely straight and horizontal. Bending one leg makes this slightly easier. Go for 3 or 4 attempts at 2 to 6 seconds.

Figure-of-four super-sets with axes on a bar

Super-sets

A method that is specific to the demands of steep sport mixed climbing, is linking some of the previous exercises together, either at random or in a pre-planned order. You can even include things like figure-of-fours and nines if you are training with your axes hooked over the bar. You can either do this for strength building (i.e. up to 12 reps or 45 seconds on the bar) or you can go for an endurance burn from 1 minute up to say, 5 minutes. To stay on for a meaningful length of time it may be worth having a foothold to return to! Try straight-arming your tools and shaking out before carrying on with the exercises.

Starting Out Equipment Mountain Safety Ice · Style · Ethics Ice · Techniques Mixed · Style · Ethics Mixed · Techniques The Mind Training Destinations

Anatagonist training

If your training is based on a combination of rock climbing, ice axe bouldering and bar-work then it will be heavily biased towards the pulling muscles in the upper body such as the back, the rear part of the shoulders, and the biceps. While these are the 'work-horse' muscles, ice and mixed climbing also require a great deal of endurance in the 'pushing' muscles which work in opposition (known as the antagonists). In particular the front part of the shoulders and triceps, will be tested on the ice when swinging your axe when fatigued.

Mixed climbing may also require strength in these muscles for stabilizing the body and making hard press moves. For this reason it is vital to do some training of the antagonist muscles. Those training for ice (or who are just looking for a minimum requirement for antagonist training) should simply do sets of press-ups - there is no beating them!

Mixed climbers who are keen to build strength should simply select the 'pushing exercises' given below for weight training (i.e. bench-press, military press and triceps press) and do pyramid sets for each (i.e. x8, x6, x4, x6, x8). Note that it may be worth combining extra abdominal training and cardio work with antagonist sessions to get maximum value from your training time.

> Avoid doing this type of training for prolonged periods (especially sets of 10 - 15 reps) as this may cause you to bulk-up and gain excessive muscle. **!**

Weights and multigym

The multigym is best used for a more general conditioning work-out in the early stages of a training phase. You can then move on to doing the specific bar-work exercises given above.

To implement the following exercises, simply do the following:

Week 1: 3 sets of 20 reps
Week 2: 3 sets of 15 reps
Week 3: 3 sets of 10 reps

Bench press (chest, shoulders triceps)

Lat pull-down (back, biceps)

Military press (shoulders, triceps)

Knee raises or sit-ups (abdominals)

Bicep curl

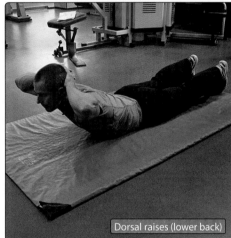

Dorsal raises (lower back)

Triceps extensions

Calf raises (go for higher reps, e.g. 30 - 40)

Starting Out | Equipment | Mountain Safety | Ice : Style-Ethics | Ice : Techniques | Mixed : Style-Ethics | Mixed : Techniques | The Mind | Training | Destinations

General circuit training

Ice and mixed climbing are renowned for giving full body pumps. In the early stages of a training program it is worth doing circuit training sessions to provide a base level of anaerobic conditioning to complement your cardio training. You can do these at home using floor exercises and moving from one to the other without resting. Prepare for the burn!

A sample circuit training program

> 1 minute fast run on spot
> 15 press-ups
> 1minute skip
> 15 sit-ups
> 15 pull-ups with a foot for assistance
> 20 squat thrusts

Rest 6 - 10 minutes then repeat x3 or x4

Leg conditioning and cardiovascular

If you are arriving at the base of the route in no fit state to climb then running, cycling or some off-season hill walking are a very good idea.

There's no need to be too scientific about this. During rest phases from climbing or general conditioning phases you may wish to go out up to 5 times a week. Cut this down to 3 when focusing on more specific climbing endurance and down to 1 or 2 during strength building phases.

Do 20 - 45 minutes of moderate to high intensity activity, subject to your fitness levels. If you cycle then try to spin fast in a low gear to avoid bulking up your leg muscles. It is unlikely that you will want or need to do weight training for your legs if you are doing cardio work. The only worthwhile supplementary leg exercises are calf raises which should be performed slowly and for endurance sets of up to 40 or 50 reps.

Tim Emmett getting another circuit in.

Starting Out

Equipment

Mountain Safety

Ice : Style-Ethics

Ice : Techniques

Mixed : Style-Ethics

Mixed : Techniques

The Mind

Training

Destinations

There's no use being able to do one-armers if you can't do the walk in. Freddie Wilkinson and John Varco, Scotland.

Starting Out

Equipment

Mountain Safety

Ice : Style·Ethics

Ice : Techniques

Mixed : Style·Ethics

Mixed : Techniques

The Mind

Training

Destinations

Planning a training program

The more you attempt to plan your training the more effective it will be. Before you switch off, this does not necessarily mean you have to follow a rigid plan, it simply means making a rough overview to help you to build-up to a peak so that you are fit for the winter season and then taper off without getting injured.

Basic training guidelines for intermediate level climbers

Beginners are advised to do slightly less and elites to do slightly more than the work prescribed.

✓ Do a minimum of two and a maximum of four 'climbing-specific' sessions per week.

✓ Do a minimum of two and a maximum of four cardio and stretching sessions a week.

✓ Do antagonist exercises a minimum of once and a maximum of twice a week.

✓ Build-up slowly over the first few weeks, doing mainly cardio and general conditioning and then moving on to specific endurance work.

✓ Do strength work in the middle of the overall programme.

✓ Start strength work with general exercises and then move on to specific exercises.

✓ If you train on two consecutive days then always do strength on day 1 and endurance on day 2

✓ Avoid doing strength and endurance in the same session.

✓ Use a combination of the above training methods and prioritise them towards your weaknesses or your goals, i.e. sport mixed, trad mixed or ice.

✓ Train for an overall period of 1 to 8 months and then 'taper-down' by reducing the workload and intensity gradually over a fortnight or so.

✓ With longer training plans of say 6 to 8 months, make sure you introduce 'active recovery' or full rest weeks every 6 weeks or so.

✓ During the climbing season do a reduced amount of training for 'maintenance' purposes and be sure to rest well before days on the hill.

✓ Take a fortnight off at least once a year.

If you follow all these guidelines, or even half of them then you will be doing a fair bit more towards planning your training than most climbers. But there is more you can do to make sure that your training is even more productive.

Audrey Seguy training on a conventional climbing wall with a pair of figure-of-fours - training tools designed to replicate mixed climbing without causing damage to the wall. Photo by Adrian Berry.

The advanced approach: periodised training

The principle of periodised training is to plan a series of mini training phases (microcycles) which are typically between 2 and 8 weeks in length and which run back-to-back as part of an overall cycle (macrocycle).

Each microcycle will have a given energy system (i.e. strength, power endurance, or stamina) as its overall theme or priority, but it will also make sure that the other energy systems are trained to a minimal extent in order to prevent losses. In other words you can focus on one aspect of fitness without losing the others.

The key to obtaining the most powerful results is to prioritise the overall macrocycle to the type of energy system that you wish to improve by tweaking the length and frequency of the microcycles.

Sample four week strength/power prioritised microcycle

	Mon	Tue	Wed	Thu	Fri	Sat	Sun
Week 1	R/CV	S/P	R	St	R/CV	S/P	R/CV
Week 2	R/CV	S/P	R	S/P	R/CV	S/P	PE
Week 3	CV	S/P	R	S/P	R	S/P	St
Week 4	R/CV	S/P	R	PE	R/CV	S/P	R/CV

Session split

Strength / Power (S/P): 10 sessions
Power Endurance (PE): 2 sessions
Stamina (St): 2 sessions
R = Rest
CV = Cardiovascular

This program has an overall bias towards strength / power sessions, but endurance work is still maintained. There is less workload in weeks 1 and 4 to allow for recovery between preceding and proceeding microcycles. You will notice that strength is always trained the day before endurance (unless a rest day divides them).

Sample 12 month power endurance prioritised macrocycle

April
End of winter season - rest month (light CV)

May
CV and general conditioning

June
Stamina priority

July and August
Power endurance priority

September
Strength / Power priority

October
Power endurance priority

November
Tapering - equal split of S/P, PE and St

December - March
Winter season - maintenance training only

Macrocycle split

Power Endurance: 3 months
Strength and Power: 1 month
Stamina: 1 month

Warming up

A thorough warm-up will not only reduce your chance of injury but it will assist your recovery and make you climb better too.

Few climbers realise that it can take up to 45 minutes from the start of a session before you can pull your hardest or climb at your best. If you jump straight on to hard stuff without building up then your body will simply shut down and fail to respond. So take your time and build up progressively, doing stints of light climbing interspersed with stretching.

The plan given below will work perfectly for training sessions such as ice axe bouldering or indoor rock climbing. It can also be adapted and used at the crag for sport mixed.

Pulse raiser (2-4 mins)

E.g. Jog on spot to warm you up and prepare your body for exercise.

General mobility (4 mins)

Shoulder circles (controlled) finger clenches, hip circles

1st 'climb-around' (2-3 mins)

Light, slow climbing movement on easy ground. Focus on technique, relax and trust tools, filter out distractions. Traverse at base of crag if outside.

Upper body stretches (6-8 mins)

Fingers, forearm, shoulders, neck, lats.

2nd 'climb-around' (2-4 mins)

On slightly harder ground, focus on accurate footwork and smooth, fluid movements.

Lower body stretches (3-5 mins)

On the floor or against a wall, or tree e.g. bridge / splits, frog (hip turn-out), high steps.

3rd 'climb-around' (2-4 mins)

On slightly harder ground - aim to get a light pump. Now focus on moving slightly faster whilst still maintaining form.

Rest 4 -5 mins

Progressive bouldering or endurance build-up (20-30 mins)

Complete a series of boulder problems or routes in ascending grade order, taking plenty of rest in between each one. Build up slowly over a period and try alternating between steep and less steep terrain.

A lat warm-up stretch

Nutrition

The bottom line

Ice and mixed climbing place great demands on strength, endurance and recovery, and clearly if you don't eat well you will limit your progress and risk injury.

Sports nutrition is a subject that is frequently blown out of all proportion. It is important to stick to a few basic principles rather than becoming obsessive or faddish. The following pages will cover nutritional support for training and tips to keep you fuelled up for days on the hill.

Es Tressider fuelling up with malt loaf after a long Scottish approach.

Balanced diet

Eat three meals a day with an overall balance of approximately 70% carbs, 20% protein and 10% fat. You will do this automatically if you generally eat meals like sandwiches for lunch and pasta, rice or potatoes with meat or fish and a selection of vegetables in the evening.

Healthy rather than empty calories

Avoid junk foods that provide calories without goodness. If you let things slip then try to boost up on fruit and veg which are high in vitamins and minerals. Alternatively take a supplement.

Low fat, not no fat

Fat is not evil. It provides great long term energy and maintains health if we eat the right types in small doses. Avoid highly processed vegetable oils and go for un-saturated olive oils. A small amount of fat also gives you the sensation that you are full, whereas zero fat foods will keep the hunger pangs raging.

Starting Out

Equipment

Mountain Safety

Ice : Style-Ethics

Ice : Techniques

Mixed : Style-Ethics

Mixed : Techniques

The Mind

Training

Destinations

Starting Out

Equipment

Mountain Safety

Ice : Style · Ethics

Ice : Techniques

Mixed : Style · Ethics

Mixed : Techniques

The Mind

Training

Destinations

Eating before training

Try to eat a minimum of one and a maximum of two hours before training so you are fully digested but not hungry.

Eating immediately before and during training

If you do arrive at the climbing wall or gym hungry or need a snack during training then go for a banana, energy bar or something that is quick to digest.

Hydrate during training

Isotonic drinks work well, although water is fine. Take small sips regularly, rather than downing a whole bottle and then drinking nothing for the rest of the session.

Go easy on caffeine

A quick boost in the morning or before training is fine as long as you make extra efforts to drink water on top of tea or coffee. Avoid drinking tea and coffee all day.

Eat straight after training

One of the most important principles of sports nutrition is to get carbohydrates and a moderate amount of protein into your system as soon as possible to assist glycogen replenishment and to promote fast recovery. Recovery drinks which have a protein and carbohydrate mix work very well for this purpose. Going straight to the pub on an empty stomach after climbing is quite possibly the worst thing you can do!

Composition adjustments

Try increasing your percentage carbohydrate intake during endurance phases and on hill days

Try increasing your protein intake before and during strength training phases, and especially after sport mixed climbing days. It is well worth taking protein shakes or amino acid capsules during strength training phases.

Reduce your overall calories slightly during longer rest periods and increase them freely during and immediately after ice and mixed climbing days.

Supplementation

Of the multitude of legal sports supplements that are designed to drain your bank balance, only a few may have a noticeable effect on boosting your performance. One of these is creatine which may have an effect on both strength and anaerobic performance. Read the instructions and don't expect miracles!

Dieting

Reduced calorie dieting may be a necessary evil for some climbers, either to get back down to normal weight or to attain 'fighting weight'. Either way, you should never work on a calorie deficit for prolonged periods. Remember you're likely to lose muscle (which is especially handy for sport mixed) and that it's vital to maintain protein supplementation. Reduce calories gradually rather than crash dieting and increase them gradually afterwards to give your metabolism time to adjust. You will pile the pounds back on if you binge eat.

Nutrition on the hill

Hill food is a personal thing and every climber has their own view. The basic problem is that what you should eat may not be what you want to eat; energy bars often freeze-up and chocolate somehow seems more appetizing. Try to nibble on rapidly absorbed foods rather than eating a huge packed lunch.

It's good to strike a balance between good nutrition and nice treats. Fruit 'n' nut mixes and cereal bars won't freeze and will provide good sustained-release energy. A good tip is to keep sports energy bars in the pocket of your thermal. If you can stand them, energy gels are great for a quick fix on a belay when your mouth is dry and they take up minimal room in your pockets.

Hydration

Dehydration will dramatically reduce your physical performance, so make yourself drink even though you may not feel like it. Monitor the colour of your urine to check you're not dehydrated: the darker it is the more dehydrated you've become. Isotonic sports drinks can be made with hot water to create a hill drink that won't dehydrate you like coffee or tea and will provide less of a sugar rush than hot squash.

Carb-loading

Some climbers may wish to experiment by slightly reducing carbohydrates a few days prior to a big day on the hill and then crash-loading them the night before. This technique used by endurance athletes can be quite effective.

Andy Kirkpatrick keeping going with a bagel.

Staying hydrated on the drive to the crag.
Photo by Neil Gresham.

Starting Out

Equipment

Mountain Safety

Ice - Style-Ethics

Ice - Techniques

Mixed - Style-Ethics

Mixed - Techniques

The Mind

Training

Destinations

Tim Emmett on *Critique de la Raison pure,* M9 with the French ice paradise of Tete de Gramusat in the background.

Destinations

The best way to improve your winter climbing is to get out there onto the real thing and have a go. Try to tackle as many different winter climbs as you can. The bigger the variety of terrain the bigger your experience and repertoire of skills will grow. From single pitch sport mixed through to multi-pitch ice routes, this chapter covers the most important and accessible winter venues around the world. It isn't an exhaustive list but the cliffs we've chosen would give most a life-time's worth of winter adventure.

Starting Out

Equipment

Mountain Safety

Ice · Style-Ethics

Ice · Techniques

Mixed · Style-Ethics

Mixed · Techniques

The Mind

Training

Destinations

Starting Out | Equipment | Mountain Safety | Ice : Style-Ethics | Ice : Techniques | Mixed : Style-Ethics | Mixed : Techniques | The Mind | Training | Destinations

Britain

While Britain lacks the high terrain of the European Alps and the Canadian Rockies its northerly latitude and at times ferocious maritime climate have made Britain's mountains a Mecca for winter climbing.

Scotland

The climate of Scotland, often derided as cold, wet and miserable, is precisely the reason why it has such unique climbing. When its damp maritime air collides with freezing polar winds, the snow begins to fall, the ice builds and more uniquely great hoar frost crystals build up on the rocks, blanketing the cliffs white.

With winter conditions possible from late October through to mid April, Scotland has one of the longest winter seasons of any climbing region. Add to this the variety of the terrain from single pitch snow covered rock buttresses through multi pitch pure ice climbs to six hundred metre long ridges, all usually ending the day with the possibility of a summit and it is easy to see why Scotland has a world wide reputation as **the** premier traditional winter climbing destination. With literally thousands of routes spread right across the highlands there is plenty to choose from.

Starting Out

Equipment

Mountain Safety

Ice · Style-Ethics

Ice · Techniques

Mixed · Style-Ethics

Mixed · Techniques

The Mind

Training

Destinations

Ian Hey enjoying full conditions on *Savage Slit*, V,6
Northern Corries, Cairngorms, Scotland.

Starting Out

Equipment

Mountain Safety

Ice · Style·Ethics

Ice · Techniques

Mixed · Style·Ethics

Mixed · Techniques

The Mind

Training

Destinations

The Arrochar Hills

Starting in the south, the **Arrochar Alps** lie less than forty miles north of Glasgow with the most popular climbing on the shapely mica schist cliffs of **The Cobbler**. The area is best known for its intense technical testpieces such as *North Wall Groove* (V,6) and *Deadman's Groove* (VII,7) although the traverse of the three Cobbler peaks gives a fine grade II.

Just north lie several relatively easily accessible crags (1 to 1 ½ hours walk); **Beinn an Dothaidh** and **Beinn Dorain** offer mostly steep mixed climbs (grade III-IX) including the hard classic *Messiah* (VII,7) although in icy conditions fun sport will be found on the icefall of *Fahrenheit 451* (IV,3). The nearby Beinn Udlaidh's mere hour's walk in and dozens of fine icefalls and gullies across the grades (II-VI) mean that during cold spells it is one of Scotland's most popular pure ice climbing venues.

Glen Coe

Heading northwards on the A82 one passes through the great valley of **Glen Coe**. The northern side is home to the four kilometre long *Aonach Eagach Ridge* (II/III) a superb alpine-style day out. The rest of the Coe's climbing is on its Southern flank. The distinctive 'perfect' peak of **Buachaille Etive Mor** guarding the eastern entrance hosts some of the Coe's strongest lines. *Raven's Gully* (V,6) and *Crowberry Gully* (IV,4) take huge deep icy clefts while right again *Curved Ridge* (II) is one of the best moderate winter routes in Scotland.

Andy Benson approaching Stob Coire nan Lochan, Glen Coe, Scotland.

The bulk of Glen Coe's climbing lies on the buttresses and corries of **Bidean Nam Bian**. The most reliable and hence most popular being **Stob Coire nan Lochan**. There are climbs here for everyone from many people's first taste of mixed climbing on *Dorsal Arete II*), through the steep classic gullies of *SC Gully* (III) and *Scabbard Chimney* (V,6) to some of Scotland's best hard buttresses such as *Central Grooves* (VII,7). In very cold conditions the west face of **Aonach Dubh** streams with numerous icefalls such as *The Screen* (IV,5) and *No.6 Gully* (IV,4).

Ben Nevis

Just over twenty miles away lies Scotland's highest mountain **Ben Nevis** whose north-east face is world famous for its winter routes. Known affectionately as 'the Ben', its biggest features are the four great ridges, *NE Buttress* (IV), *Observatory Ridge* (IV), *Tower Ridge* (IV) and *Castle Ridge* (III), each of which offer superb

mixed climbing that comes into condition quickly. In between these, the buttresses are cut with numerous full height gullies; the most famous of which *Point Five* (V) is the most coveted winter climb in Scotland. This tends to form from January onwards and it is normal to encounter three or four parties at any one time on the climb.

Later in the season after sustained freeze and thaw conditions the adjacent buttresses can build huge quantities of thin snow ice resulting in a unique collection of committing face climbs (usually in the grade V-VI range) with climbs such as *Indicator Wall* (V,4) often lasting until April. The Ben also has a series of superb pure icefalls although these are more fickle to build up. *The Curtain* (IV,5) is obvious from the corrie floor when in nick, while a little higher up *Mega Route X* (V,6) is highly sought after. Recently many of the buttresses have yielded high standard technical mixed routes such as *Darth Vader* (VII,8).

A momentary break in the cloud reveals Little Brenva Face on Ben Nevis in all its glory. Photo by Simon Hodges.

Starting Out

Equipment

Mountain Safety

Ice : Style·Ethics

Ice : Techniques

Mixed : Style·Ethics

Mixed : Techniques

The Mind

Training

Destinations

Starting Out | Equipment | Mountain Safety | Ice : Style-Ethics | Ice : Techniques | Mixed : Style-Ethics | Mixed : Techniques | The Mind | Training | Destinations

Aonach Mor and Creag Meagaidh

While dwarfed by the scale of its neighbour, **Aonach Mor**, just north of Ben Nevis, has proved popular as a high altitude, reliable early season destination. Accessed from the area's ski lift, an hour's walk leads to a wide selection of two to four pitch gullies and buttresses with a concentration in the intermediate grades (III-IV) plus occasional harder testpieces.

On a grander scale the great north-east facing corries of **Creag Meagaidh** offers climbs of a quality to rival those on the Ben. Under icy conditions Centre Post and Staghorn Gully both offer four-hundred metres of grade III ice climbing while experts will seek out the elusive *Fly* (VII,6) but it is at grade V that Meagaidh comes into its own. Almost a dozen big lines are available at the grade with perhaps the *Pumpkin* (V,4) the best, often forming great umbrellas of unusually shaped ice.

The Cairngorms

The **Cairngorm** range lies in the heart of Scotland and often benefits from colder harsher conditions than the west coast. On the **Aviemore** side the **Northern Corries**, sixty to ninety minutes walk from the Cairngorm ski area, are Scotland's busiest winter crags due to their ease of access and the fact that they are often the earliest and latest crags to be in winter condition. **Coire an t-Sneachda** is particularly attractive to novice and intermediate climbers with a wide selection of easy gullies (I-III) and moderate mixed lines (II-IV).

The steeper **Coire an Lochain** also has some fine moderate routes but is primarily known for its tough technical mixed climbing ranging from the Scottish classic *Savage Slit* (V,6) through to cutting edge testpieces such as *Happy Tyroleans* (IX, 9).

A mile or so across the summit plateau of Cairngorm lies the **Loch Avon** basin which is rimmed with several impressive larger cliffs. **Hells Lum** is the most visited with its collection of excellent 150m mid grade (III-V) ice routes.

Opposite **Carn Etchachan** offers some huge outings epitomised by Route Major a 280m grade IV. In between those two cliffs lies Loch Avon's flagship, the **Shelter Stone**. It is one of the toughest winter venues in Scotland with its major easier route *Sticil Face* a classic grade V. The harder lines are difficult to get in winter condition but when in nick *Citadel* (VII,8) and the *Needle* (VIII, 8) are amongst the best mixed routes in Scotland.

The east Cairngorms are accessed from **Braemar**. The standout mountain here is **Lochnagar** with its 250m high northeastern cliffs home to some of Scotland's most famous winter routes. While the approach is relatively lengthy (two and a half hours) the cliff is in condition regularly from early to late season, although many of the hardest routes such as those on the **Tough Brown Face** require ice. The numerous gullies splitting the coire give fine outings ranging from the classic *Black Spout* (I) up to the steep ice of *Polyphemus Gully* (V,5). The mixed climbing here is almost all tough with the classic being *Eagle Ridge* (VI,6).

North-west Scotland

The final area of note is the north-west of Scotland. Close to the coast and with most of its cliffs low lying, conditions here are harder to come by. Couple that with the longer drive for most and the area is much less visited in winter. For those who dare, the genuine wilderness, remoteness and the quality of many of the climbs add up to one of the most unique experiences Scotland has to offer.

A good starter are the twin mountains of **Liathach** and **Beinn Eighe**. Liathach is home to some of the most impressive pure ice lines in the country with *Poachers Fall* (V,5) and *Salmon Leap* (VI,6) the most coveted. A technically easier but equally memorable route is the traverse of Liathach main ridge, a huge and dramatic grade II. Beinn Eighe in contrast is a mixed climbing venue that, not being reliant on turf, comes in surprisingly quickly following snowfall and frost. **Coire Mhic Fhearchair** or 'the Triple Buttress' on the north side is one of the most impressive around. The 250m *East Buttress* is the easiest at grade IV and the *Central Buttress* the most sought after at grade VI while the *West Buttress Direct* is a superb grade VII. The walls in between are home to many of Scotland's steepest and most outrageous mixed routes (grade VI-VIII).

Skye

The final major tick to mention is on the **Isle of Skye** where the traverse of the great Black Cullin represents Scotland's most impressive ridge climb. More of a big alpine route than a traditional Scottish winter one, although no more technical than grade IV the ridge is a long and arduous journey.

Approaching Coire an Lochain, The Northern Corries, Scotland.

Starting Out

Equipment

Mountain Safety

Ice : Style : Ethics

Ice : Techniques

Mixed : Style : Ethics

Mixed : Techniques

The Mind

Training

Destinations

Wales

In past years, Wales was often a rival venue to Scotland, however recent mild winters have meant that it is now an elusive jewel in the crown of UK ice climbing.

The most likely to be in condition are the superb selection of moderate routes on **Clogwyn y Garnedd** such as the *Trinty Gullies* (I/II to III) which finish on the summit of Snowdon, or the *Snowdon Horseshoe* (I/II) a magnificent but lengthy and serious expedition in winter. At its best Wales has arguably a finer collection of pure ice climbs than Scotland. The Devil's Kitchen in **Cwm Idwal** dribbles with quality classic icelines such as *The Screen* (III) and *South Gully* (IV), as well as the spectacular *Devil's Appendix* (VI), which together with the fierce verticality of **Craig y Rhaeadr's** grade VIs offer the area's hard classics.

There is also plentiful mixed climbing with a smattering of tough and infrequently formed lines on **Cloggy** and a wider selection of equally testing routes on **Lliwedd** including a recent mammoth twenty pitch girdle. The best however is found in the Carneddau at **Ysgolion Duon** also known as the **Black Ladders**. When a low freezing level combines with a heavy snowfall the 300m classic *Central Gully* (III) and the tougher challenges of *Western Gully* (V) and *The Somme* (VI) will set the pulses racing of every winter climber.

Moving south **Cadair Idris** holds several long quality lines with the *Great Gully of Cwm Cau* (III) and *Trojan* (V) on **Cyfrwy** both truly outstanding, but unfortunately even more fickle than their northern cousins.

Tim Emmett on *The Devil's Appendix*, VI,6. At the Devil's Kitchen, Twll Du, arguably the most famous ice climb south of the Scottish border. Photo by Colin Wells.

Lake District

The Cumbrian fells in the north-west of England are home to hundreds of fine winter routes. Like Wales however, getting your route in condition can be the real crux and in even a good winter, very early starts and a lot of patience are required.

The most popular and reliable venues are **Great End** with its superb selection of moderate gullies (grade II-IV) that quickly come into condition once freezing levels drop and **Helvellyn** with its plethora of beginner to moderate gullies (grade I-III) that offer many English climbers their first winter routes. Helvellyn's great *Striding Edge* and *Sharp Edge* on **Blencathra** also give superb winter outings (grade I-II) under heavy snow, which although not on the scale of Skye's Cullin Ridge, still have an 'alpine' ambience to them. At the other end of the technical scale **Gable Crag** has established itself as the modern testing ground with *Snicker Snack*, a summer E3, current pick of the crop at VIII, 9, and again Gable is often in winter nick.

Andrew Woods on the final pitch of *Central Gully Left-Hand*, III,3, Great End, Lake District. *Central Gully* is one of the best and most reliable grade III gullies in England and on a clear day provides panoramic views north towards Derwent water, Skiddaw and the northern Lakes, inducing a remarkable sense of exposure for a gully climb.
Photo by Colin Wells.

Starting Out · Equipment · Mountain Safety · Ice · Style·Ethics · Ice · Techniques · Mixed · Style·Ethics · Mixed · Techniques · The Mind · Training · Destinations

Tim Emmett on *Critique de la Raison* pure M9 Freissinieres, France.

France

There are dozens of French winter climbing sites with some of the best found in the valleys of **Fournel** and **Freissinieres** surrounding the town of Argentière le Besse near Briançon in the Écrins. Fournel is the most reliable with more than one-hundred and twenty ice routes including many in the more moderate grades (WI3-5). Freissinieres has even more routes including some of the hardest ice climbs in Europe (Several WI7s) up to 550m long on the Tete de Gramusat. Conditions are best January to February with a wide range of skiing and other alpine resort amenities available.

Rivalling Freissinieres as France's most dramatic ice venue are the cirques of **Gavarnie** in the Pyrenees and **Sixt Fer a Cheval** east of Cluses near Chamonix. The latter was the home of France's two first WI7s and Gavarnie hosts routes up

to 500m high, needless to say both areas will suit top level climbers only. For more amenable fare the small ski town of **La Grave** in the Écrins has many grade WI3 to 5s within 15 minutes walking distance. These form very reliably and can be combined in a week with the ice climbs accessed by the ski lifts at Alp d'Huez.

The other Argentière adjacent to Chamonix in the shadow of Mont Blanc has several areas which are very popular once in nick. The most extensive selection of icefalls rim the basin below the Argentière Glacier icefall and are accessed in thirty minutes from the mid station cable car. Grades here range from WI4 up to the WI6 technicalities of the superb three pitch pillar of **Shiva Lingam**. Closer to the town of Argentière the numerous low angle falls (WI2-3) of the **Crèmerie** offer a perfect venue for first time ice leaders, that is if you can get a space in the queue for routes.

Italy

Just over the border from France in the shadows of Mont Blanc lies the village of Cogne which has established itself as Italy's ice and mixed climbing centre. The majority of the climbs are found in the parallel valleys of **Valnontey** and **Valeille** (the latter accessed from the village of Lillaz). Both valleys offer dozens of reliable routes usually two or three pitches in length accessed along cross country ski tracks, with walk ins from twenty minutes to two hours. Almost every grade of ice climb is on offer here from the classic WI3 *Cascade de Lillaz* through the very popular Patri routes (WI4-5) to the sustained 200m grade WI6 *Repentance Super* (see page 129). The Valeille valley also hosts some of the World's most famous mixed routes with *The X Files* (M10) and the multi-pitch *Empire Strikes Back* (M11). A wider range of shorter more accessible bolted mixed routes (M5-11) can be found in the **Haston Cave** in the neighbouring Valsavaranche valley.

Patri Right, WI4+, Cogne, Italy.

Starting Out

Equipment

Mountain Safety

Ice : Style-Ethics

Ice : Techniques

Mixed : Style-Ethics

Mixed : Techniques

The Mind

Training

Destinations

Switzerland

Kandersteg is Switzerland's and indeed one of Europe's best ice venues. A huge range of grades (although there are no beginners' routes: grades range from WI4 to WI7+) and styles are catered for with most routes within twenty minutes walking of the town. For the expert the nearby Breitwangflue has eight-pitch routes to rival anything in Canada with the easiest route being the world classic *Crack Baby* (WI6). An hour's cross country skiing up the valley accesses a very different experience at the 45˚ overhanging wall of **Ueschenen** home to dozens of hard mixed routes (M8-M12) with the classic being *Pink Panther* (M9+).

A much smaller venue **Isenfluh** known as 'Little Vail' is worth checking out if only for the novelty of the approach; by wooden sledge from the top of the cable car. The dozen or so climbs contrast from short ice routes (WI3-5) to a clutch of bolted roof routes (M8-M10+).

Neil at the lip of *Pink Panther*, M9+, Ueschenen, Switzerland.

Norway

Home to some of the longest ice climbs around, until recently Norwegian ice climbing has remained something of myth and legend, but new developments have begun to open this fantastic ice destination to visiting climbers.

The area of **Rjukan** two hours drive north of Oslo has become very popular particularly with British climbers following the publication of the Rockfax guidebook. With very reliable conditions (December to March), grades from WI2-7 and a huge variety of climbs from single pitch through to huge multi pitchers, all rising from the river gorge cutting through the town, Rjukan is an ideal place to spend a week's holiday.

The **Krokan** area is an ideal place for novices or those tuning technique as top ropes can be set up on many of the routes with ice possibilities from WI1 through to WI5. Moving down the gorge the **Upper**

Gorge is home to many of Rjukan's finest lines such as *Rjukanfossen* (WI4) and the world classic *Lipton* (WI7). Most distinctive as one drives towards town is the huge line of *Gausta Marathon* with 17 pitches of WI3.

Another area that has grown in popularity is the small ski town of **Hemsedal** which although spread out has a good collection of multi-pitch routes from WI3 up to the stunning 4 pitch WI6 *Hyndenfossen*. A forty-five minute drive is needed to the area of **Gol** with many fine single pitch ice routes from WI3-5 as well as a growing group of bolted mixed routes. For those of a more adventurous nature Norway offers almost unlimited potential. The **Laerdal** region has some outrageous looking 300m lines such as *Vettifossen* (WI6) while Romsdal has one of the world's biggest ice falls.

The Rockfax guidebook to Rjukan in Norway

Starting Out

Equipment

Mountain Safety

Ice : Style-Ethics

Ice : Techniques

Mixed : Style-Ethics

Mixed : Techniques

The Mind

Training

Destinations

USA

While lacking the concentration of ice climbs found in Canada, the USA has many excellent venues spread out across the country. In the north-east, **Lake Willoughby** in Vermont is the most impressive ice venue with many routes up 120m high. Down in New Hampshire, **Cannon Cliff** is home to many 200m high classics such as *Black Dike*, while **Cathedral Ledge** includes the thin ice mixed classics *Repentance* and *Remission*.

Colorado is home to several hundred ice routes spread across the state. The small town of **Ouray** has developed in recent years into a mini ice climbing centre due to the superb selection of ice routes rimming **Uncompahgre Gorge**. These are assisted to form through a network of clifftop hoses and with their reliability, ease of access and possibility of top rope set ups, they offer an outstanding place for novices to try the sport, or more experienced climbers to hone their technique. Higher up the valley

lie bigger natural lines including the classic *Birdbrain Boulevard* (WI5, M6). More long ice routes can be found near the town of **Telluride** with *Bridalveil Falls* and *Ames Ice Hose* both WI5+ attracting climbers from around the world. The small amphitheatre at **Vail** was one of the birthplaces of modern mixed climbing and as well as the superb ice pillars of *Rigid Designator* (WI4+) and *The Fang* (WI6) there are a fine collection of bolted mixed lines (M5-M10).

The towns of **Cody** in Wyoming and **Bozeman** in Montana are two further centres of ice climbing. Within ten miles of Cody there are over three-hundred ice lines making this one of the highest concentrations of ice in the States. **Hyalite Canyon** near Bozeman has fewer routes but many highly characterful climbs often involving a mixture of ice and dry tooling on its strange cobbled rock. Both areas benefit from very long seasons but Hyalite in particular can require a four wheel drive vehicle to tackle the forest track approach.

Neil Gresham weaving through the complex ice of the Colorado classic *Bridalveil Falls*, WI5+.

Neil high on *Stone Free*, WI5+, Rifle, USA.

Canada

Without doubt Canada is the World's premier ice climbing destination. The **Canmore-Banff-Jasper** area is the real mecca for ice climbers with its very long season (late November to March), plentiful information and a wealth of accommodation and facilities. There are hundreds of routes to choose from across the grades. In fact making a selection could prove to be your crux. Highlights to look for include the World classic 300m WI3 *Cascade Falls* which overlooks the Trans-Canada Highway, although like many routes here avalanches can be a serious problem particularly in warm conditions. On the other side of the highway juts the distinctive bulk of Mount Rundle, home to *Sea of Vapours*, *The Replicant* and *The Terminator* (all WI6 or harder), some of the most famous and dramatic icefalls in Canada. Lower down on Mount Rundle, *Professor Falls* is a lovely WI4 with steep steps interrupted by easier angled bowls.

The next main area is off Highway 93 south west of Banff where two very different venues provide the attraction. **Haffner Creek** is the area's mixed climbing playground with many single pitch ice and dry tooling routes. This is a good place for first time 'M climbers' with closely spaced bolts and grades from M5 upwards all within fifteen minutes of the road. By contrast **Stanley Headwall** is for experts only with some of the best multi-pitch ice and mixed routes in the world, classics here include the 160m, all ice, *Nemesis* (WI6) and *Suffer Machine* a 200m M7 and WI5 testpiece.

Just north of Banff the small town of **Louise** hosts a fine collection of moderate icefalls surrounding the Lake, with *Louise Falls* the classic WI4 with a tough finishing pillar. The stretch of the **Icefields Parkway** from Louise to Jasper contains the most concentrated stretch of ice climbs in the area culminating in the awesome sweep of **Weeping Wall**. Only ten minutes from the road most of the routes here are 150-180m long, however linking a route on the lower and upper walls can give six or seven pitches of sustained climbing.

Hidden off the highway east of Banff towards Calagary lies a particularly special area. **The Ghost Valley** is the home of many of the areas most spectacular long ice routes such as the 200m+ *Sorcerer* (WI5) and the 300m *Valley of the Sun* (WI3). More recently several very tough multi-pitch mixed routes have been established such as the *Big Drip* (M7+, WI7) and the extraordinary *Cryophobia* (M8, WI5+). The Ghost however is a serious area due to the adventurous rough approach that needs a 4x4 vehicle. With its remote and wild location a rescue would be unlikely and many parties approach in two vehicles equipped with shovels, camping and other survival gear.

Chris Cubitt on *Upper Weeping Wall*, WI6, Jasper, Canada.

Starting Out

Equipment

Mountain Safety

Ice : Style-Ethics

Ice : Techniques

Mixed : Style-Ethics

Mixed : Techniques

The Mind

Training

Destinations

Chris Cubitt on *Cascade Falls*, WI3, Ice Fields Parkway, Canada.

Quebec

Formerly under the shadow of its big brother Canada, french speaking Quebec has emerged in recent years as an outstanding winter climbing destination.

There are literally hundreds of icefalls here, although finding information about them has proved difficult. Some of the better known include **Montmorency Falls** (WI 3-5) a 200m wide sweep of ice within the boundaries of Quebec City. Part of the huge waterfall rarely freezes completely and it is normal to climb ice next to roaring water. Another unique aspect is that the falls are floodlit at night allowing midnight ascents; a truly memorable experience.

The **Malbaie Valley** has become internationally renowned for the icefall **La Pomme d'Or**, a thousand foot grade 6 with golden ice. Malbaie offers even harder mixed lines as well as many more moderate classics, all involving a lengthy approach. The development of bolt protected mixed climbing areas such as **Pont Rouge** has further increased the winter appeal of Quebec.

The classic Montmorency Falls WI3-5 Quebec.

Festivals

Many areas hold annual Ice climbing festivals hosted by local guides and experts and often subsidised by the region's government to attract visitors. With local knowledge, coaching clinics, demonstrations from top climbers, competitions and parties these festivals offer a fun way to check out an area and pick up tips from the experts.

Bozeman, Montana, USA (November)
www.barrelmountaineering.com

Ouray, Colorado, USA (January)
www.ourayicefestival.com

Pont Rouge, Quebec (February)
www.festiglace.com

Canmore, Canada (December)
www.canmoreiceclimbingfestival.com

Argentière le Besse, France
www.ice-fall.com

Kandersteg, Switzerland
www.ready2climb.com

Have an Ice Day

Starting Out
Equipment
Mountain Safety
Ice : Style·Ethics
Ice : Techniques
Mixed : Style·Ethics
Mixed : Techniques
The Mind
Training
Destinations

Thanks are due the following people who have assisted in the publication of this book:

Editing

Adrian Berry, Jack Geldard, Alan James

Illustrations

Ray Eckermann

Additional photographers

Colin Wells, George McEwan, Ian Sherrington, Stevie Haston, Laurence Gouault Haston, Mark Salter, Toby Whitley, Scott Price, Al Powell, Nick Bullock, Alastair Lee, Dave Pickford, Brian Duthie, Dale Bloomer, John Trudgill, Simon Hodgson, Mick Ryan

Companies

Black Diamond, Mountain Hardwear, Climber Magazine, La Sportiva, UKClimbing.com, Arcteryx, Snow and Rock, CAMP

Other contributions

Simon Richardson, George McEwan

Award-winning Rockfax guidebooks

Rockfax have an established reputation for providing some of the clearest and most user-friendly guidebook information available. The guidebook titles above cover ice climbing, trad climbing, deep water soloing and sport climbing and there are many more titles available. Deep Water (2007) and Lofoten (2008) both won the international Banff Mountain Book Festival Exposition Award.

TradCLIMBING+

The trad climbing volume of the 'plus' series covers all aspects of traditional climbing. Many of the techniques described in **WinterCLIMBING+** link well with those used for trad climbing.

SportCLIMBING+

The first book in the 'plus' series covers all aspects of sport climbing. The approach focuses on the positive things people can do to improve their own performance.

Check - www.rockfax.com